D1349034

*This highly readable collection of case studies from the public sector has relevance for all marketers. By their nature, these campaigns need to go well beyond generating 'intent to purchase' into the domain of attitudinal and behavioural change. A challenging objective. Impressively met.*

Mike Hughes, Director General,
Incorporated Society of British Advertisers

*This book is an invaluable aid and shares 25 years of learning within public service advertising. I recommend it to anyone with an interest in this area.*

Andrew Harrison, Chief Executive Officer, RadioCentre

*Outstanding. Very well written by experienced practitioners, full of evidence, practical frameworks and advice, and illustrated with rock-solid real-world cases. This should be required reading not only for the few involved in public service advertising, but also the many involved in developing, influencing or commenting on public policy and execution.*

Patrick Barwise, Emeritus Professor of Management and Marketing,
London Business School

*This fascinating book demonstrates the capability of advertising to influence social attitudes and to change behaviour. It also illustrates the role of research in generating vital insights to guide decisions and monitor progress. The experience assembled in this book should make it essential reading for anyone involved in researching and developing public service campaigns.*

David Barr, Director General, Market Research Society

*As the leading US producer of public service advertisements, the Ad Council applauds this book for showing how advertising can bring lasting and positive social change.*

Peggy Conlon, President and Chief Executive Officer,
The Advertising Council

*I would recommend that everyone involved in the development of government campaigns – policy officials as much as marketers – reads this book.*

Howell James, Permanent Secretary, Government Communication

*This book is a fantastic analysis of best practice in achieving behavioural change through the positive power of advertising and communications.*

*Persuasion is a much more effective technique of changing behaviour than law. Indeed, laws won't work without persuasion. This book vividly shows that marketing communications is the most effective and thoughtful way of presenting commonsense ideas to people, to change their lives for the better.*

Baroness Peta Buscombe, Chief Executive,
Advertising Association

# How public service advertising works

**Edited by**

**Judie Lannon**

COI
Central Office of Information

WARC

IPA

First published 2008 by World Advertising Research Center
Farm Road, Henley-on-Thames, Oxfordshire RG9 1EJ, United Kingdom
Telephone: 01491 411000
Fax: 01491 418600
Email: enquiries@warc.com
www.warc.com

A CIP catalogue record for this book is available from the British Library.

ISBN: 978-1-84116-207-2

Typeset by Godiva Publishing Services Ltd, Coventry
Jacket design by Glen Tarr
Printed and bound in Great Britain by Biddles Ltd, King's Lynn

# Contents

# Foreword

## The changing world of communications

The Phillis Review – an independent review, published in January 2004 – undertook a radical look at UK government communications and was a catalyst for change.

Many new initiatives have flowed from that report: the launch of the Government Communications Network; the appointment of a Permanent Secretary for Government Communications; and the launch of Engage, an education and best-practice programme that makes our communications more effective by putting our audiences first. The Engage framework is supported by a knowledge bank and I hope this book will add significantly to our overall fund of knowledge. A significant increase in the number of communications channels used in IPA winning entries since 2004 also reflects the government's transformation agenda, embracing digital communications and new opportunities for dialogue with the citizen.

*How public service advertising works* is a unique publication. Nothing else like it exists, so I want to congratulate the COI for its vision in commissioning this work, and all the contributors for their dedication in making it a reality. The support of the Government Heads of Marketing Group has also been vital to its success.

This book is both an educational tool and a showcase for the very best examples of public service campaigns. I recommend it to anyone interested in communications, be they a communications professional working in the public sector or a student of marketing and advertising.

Sir Gus O'Donnell
Cabinet Secretary and Head of the Home Civil Service

# About this book

By Peter Buchanan

Central Office of Information

The idea of a book on public service advertising has been germinating for some time. Originally the idea was tabled at a Heads of Marketing meeting by Anne Nash and subsequently supported by Hamish Pringle at the IPA. One suggestion was that it should be part of the COI's 60th anniversary celebrations, but I was concerned that it might have too much of a self-congratulatory coffee-table feel to it. My ambition was to publish something that would be educational and a source of reference for all those involved with developing public service campaigns on complex and challenging social issues. Someone I spoke to early in the process summed it up by saying, 'twenty-five years of learning to help us plan the next twenty-five'.

It is perhaps worth emphasising that public-sector communications is a fascinating and dynamic sector, offering a unique set of challenges not usually encountered in the commercial world. Unlike much marketing, it aims to fundamentally change behaviour, often bringing about attitudinal and societal change for the benefit of all.

The IPA Effectiveness Awards are respected around the world and held up as the gold standard. The case study papers are heavily evidence based and rigorously tested by experts. I was encouraged to see that, since their inception, nearly 80 public-sector papers have been successfully submitted and many have gone on to win Gold, Silver or Bronze awards. (As I write this piece, I can see that the commitment from the public sector remains as strong as ever: out of 42 entries in 2007, 14 were submitted by public service organisations and six went on to win awards, including the Grand Prix.)

Considering this wealth of data and despite the fact that time has moved on, with new marketing tools available, I thought that there must be fresh learnings when looking across time, audiences and themes. Spanning nearly three decades, there is a huge body of data and supporting commentary. In addition to many submissions from the major Whitehall departments, there are campaigns from Scotland, Northern Ireland and a host of other highly respected public-sector bodies; some of these papers have really stretched our understanding of the sector.

At the start, we ran a couple of workshops with some of the UK's leading planners – all authors of, or contributors to, effectiveness papers. It was a bit like chairing a Brains Trust! By a process of differing opinion, debate and subsequent elimination, we forged broad themes that we thought would be relevant and of interest to public-sector marketers and students of advertising alike. Getting people to stop what they are doing, asking people to start something new and measuring the immeasurable were some of the topics we discussed in these early meetings. The strongest ideas made it through to the final text, as you will see.

The book that has resulted covers many topics and explores dozens of challenges across a wide spectrum of policy and social issues. We hope this book will become a standard work and generate awareness regarding the quality of planning and the effectiveness measures available for public-sector campaigns. Whether you read it from cover to cover, or dip in and out as a reference for a specific campaign need, I hope you will enjoy the voyage of discovery that our talented contributors have taken us on, from the wider social and political overview provided by the highly respected journalist Matthew Parris, to the observations about the creative process by Jeremy Bullmore, Britain's well-known advertising guru, and finally the psychological perspective from Professor Geoffrey Beattie, Head of Psychology at Manchester University.

# About the contributors

**Geoffrey Beattie**

Professor Geoffrey Beattie is Head of School and Dean of Psychological Sciences at the University of Manchester. He got his PhD from the University of Cambridge (Trinity College) and is a Fellow of the British Psychological Society (BPS). He was awarded the Spearman Medal by the BPS for 'published psychological research of outstanding merit'. In 2005–06 Geoffrey was President of the Psychology section of the British Association for the Advancement of Science. He has published 15 books, many of which have either won or been short-listed for major international prizes. Geoffrey has also been the resident psychologist on all eight Big Brother series.

**Peter Buchanan**

Peter's first major career break was joining Saatchi & Saatchi as a trainee in account management in 1974. He was appointed to the London board in 1983 and made Group Account Director in 1987. At the start of the 1990s Peter moved to the integrated marketing arm of the Publicis Group – Impact FCA – as Client Services Director until 1994 when he joined the COI as Director of Advertising. He joined the Senior Civil Service in 1998 and was appointed Deputy Chief Executive in 2001. He is a member of ISBA's Executive Committee, the Government Heads of Marketing Group, the Images of Disability Steering Group and the Defence Recruiting Planning Group.

**Jeremy Bullmore**

Jeremy Bullmore was head of the Creative Department of JWT London and Chairman of the agency from 1981 to 1987. He was a non-executive director of WPP until 2004 and is now on the WPP Advisory Board. During his career in advertising he has held many positions including Chairman of the

Advertising Association, President of NABS and President of the Market Research Society. He writes columns for *Campaign*, *Management Today*, *Market Leader* and the *Guardian*, and was awarded the CBE in 1985. He has published many books, the most recent being *Apples, Insights and Mad Inventors* (Wiley, 2006).

### Will Collin

Will is a founding partner of Naked Communications. After graduating from Keble College, Oxford, Will began his career at BMP DDB as a trainee account planner in 1989. In 1997 he moved to media specialist PHD as Communications Strategy Director, then in 2000 he founded Naked Communications with Jon Wilkins and John Harlow. He is a regular speaker and commentator on communications issues, for example with the Account Planning Group, the Marketing Society and the Advertising Association. He is a Fellow of the UK Institute of Practitioners in Advertising, and also sits on IPA Council and the IPA Value of Advertising Group.

### Neil Goodlad

Neil began his advertising career at Simons Palmer Denton Clemmow Johnson in 1996 as an account planner on Goldfish and Nike. He joined Rainey Kelly Campbell Roalfe in 1999 and rose to the role of Planning Partner. His work there included recruitment campaigns for the Royal Navy and Royal Marines. A *Campaign* Face to Watch in 1997, it named him one of London's 10 Hottest Planning Director's three years later. He moved to Clemmow Hornby Inge in March 2002 and in 2004 became Managing Partner. Over five years, he's helped to make CHI the UK's fastest-growing independent agency, working on successful pitches for British Gas, Argos and RBS, among others.

### Alex Harris

After stints at GGT, Euro RSCG Wnek Gosper and WCRS, Alex became VCCP's first employee in 2002. She worked on the launch of $O_2$ and co-authored the Grand Prix-winning IPA paper in 2004. Having worked on a breadth of VCCP's client list, she is currently combining her role at VCCP with studying for an MA in contemporary English literature.

**Alison Hoad**

On graduating from Birmingham University Alison cut her teeth as a brand manager in P&G's detergents division. Inspired by the planners she worked alongside, she moved into agency life in the early 1990s. Since then Alison has been Head of Planning at both Lowe and Wieden & Kennedy in London and joined RKCR/Y&R in 2005, subsequently working with the Home Office developing campaigns for Crime Prevention and Domestic Violence. Alison also oversees the agency's work for the BBC and works on Virgin Atlantic, BT and Accantia. She has had a long-standing involvement with the IPA Effectiveness scheme. She has entered and judged numerous papers and was the Convenor of Judges for the 2004 awards.

**Rebecca Morgan**

Rebecca started her career as a graduate at DMB&B, where clients included P&G. She moved to BBH in 1993, where she spent 11 years working on accounts such as Lynx, LEGO, Dockers, Club Med and Barclays. Rebecca was promoted to the BBH board in 1998 and to Planning Group Head in 2002. During this time she won an APG Creative Planning Award and 'Marketing Communications Excellence Partner of the Year' for her work on Barclays. In 2004 Rebecca moved to BT, taking up the role of Head of Marketing Communications for BT Group globally. She joined Lowe in July 2006 as Chief Strategy Officer.

**Rebecca Munds**

Rebecca started her working life applying a degree in psychology to researching the social behaviour of bottlenose dolphins in Australia. She then returned to the tamer shores of Brighton in 1992 as a graduate trainee with Unilever's Van den Bergh Foods. She started her career in planning at TBWA in 1994 and has since worked across a wide range of accounts at TBWA, Lowe Howard Spink, Chiat Day Los Angeles and M&C Saatchi, where she was Deputy Planning Director. She joined Clemmow Hornby Inge in August 2003, where she is a Partner and works on The Carphone Warehouse, TalkTalk, Toyota and Lexus.

**Andy Nairn**

Andy spent four years as a planner at AMV BBDO, before joining Rainey Kelly Campbell Roalfe in 1997 to work across its Virgin business. In 2000 he joined Goodby Silverstein and Partners in San Francisco, where he won both of America's top planning prizes as well as being named one of the top ten planners in the world, excluding the UK, by *Campaign* magazine. In 2002 he joined MCBD as Planning Director and was subsequently named one of the top ten planners in the UK by *Campaign*. Andy has won 14 IPA Effectiveness Awards, including the 2005 and 2007 Grand Prix, and three *Marketing Week* Effectiveness Awards.

### Matthew Parris

Matthew Parris is a renowned writer and broadcaster. He was Parliamentary Sketchwriter for *The Times* for nearly 14 years, and now writes a regular column for *The Times* and also for the *Spectator*, as well as occasionally for magazines. He has written many books and received a number of journalistic awards, including the British Press Awards Columnist of the Year for 1991, 1993 and 1995, and *What the Papers Say* Columnist of the Year for 1992, 2004 and 2006. He was winner of the George Orwell Prize for 2004. He is also a frequent radio and television broadcaster.

### John Poorta

After ten years of working as an account man, John became a strategic planner in 1990. He was appointed Planning Director of D'Arcy in 2000 and became the Executive Planning Director of Leo Burnett when D'Arcy was merged into Leo Burnett in 2002. He is now Vice Chairman of Leo Burnett, London. John has had over 15 years' experience of working on public sector and COI campaigns, ranging from Drink Drive, Disability Rights, NHS Recruitment, Child Road Safety and Teacher Training Recruitment, to Benefit Fraud, Road Tax, Education Maintenance Allowances and the Home Information Pack. Most recently he has been working on the LSC's skills campaign, 'Our Future. It's in our Hands'.

### Charlie Snow

Charlie's first job in advertising was in the Planning Department at DMB&B/D'Arcy in the mid-1990s. He worked on a number of the agency's accounts including their COI/Government business, notably for the Department for Education and Skills. He joined DLKW as Head of Planning in September 2000. He heads up planning responsibilities on the agency's COI accounts, including Sexual Health (DH), Teenage Pregnancy (DCSF), Student Finance (DIUS), the National Blood Service and the RAF. Charlie has won numerous planning awards during his career, including two Gold APG Awards (one for his thinking on the Sexual Health campaign), and the APG Grand Prix and a Gold IPA Effectiveness award for the Child Literacy campaign.

**Richard Storey**

Richard is Chief Strategy Officer at M&C Saatchi and also runs its upstream strategy consultancy, The Refinery. Graduating from St Catharine's College, Cambridge, Richard learned his trade at BMP DDB London. After ten years he joined M&C Saatchi as a start-up. Leading its 'Brutal Simplicity' approach to planning, he helped M&C Saatchi grow into a UK top five agency with unprecedented speed. Richard has worked on a number of high-profile government initiatives, including Police recruitment, anti-social behaviour, tax credits and the Census. He has won five IPA Effectiveness Awards for clients such as British Airways, the Home Office and Scottish Amicable.

**Charles Vallance**

Having graduated from Nottingham University in 1986, Charles has worked as an account planner for various agencies, including RSCG and BBH. In 2002 he decided he'd start working for himself and, along with his three partners, set up VCCP. Their founding client was $O_2$, to whom they are eternally grateful. During the last two decades, Charles has worked on, and in some cases helped launch, a diverse range of iconic brands including $O_2$, ING Direct, Orange, Sony, BMW, Land Rover, Diet Coke, Coke Zero, Heineken and Dyson.

# Acknowledgements

This has been a fascinating journey of discovery. From imagining what a book containing so much wisdom and experience could possibly look like to actually completing it has been very rewarding. I am particularly grateful to Peter Buchanan who, supported by Anne Nash, Chair of the Government Heads of Marketing Group, originated the project, and to the contributors who went at the task with great energy, enthusiasm and seriousness to produce a work of lasting value and importance. Also, of course, my thanks to our outside contributors, Matthew Parris, Geoffrey Beattie and Jeremy Bullmore, who have enriched the book considerably by their observations and ideas. Finally, I would like to thank Hamish Pringle at the IPA for his support and advice, and Roger Ingham, also at the IPA, for his help with the Effectiveness Awards papers; Matthew Coombs, James Aitchison and Sophie Petrou at WARC for their advice and skills in producing the book; and to Janet Dixon at the COI for help with the meetings and manuscripts.

Judie Lannon<br>
Editor

I would like to acknowledge that without the financial support of a number of government departments, many of whom have also contributed Effectiveness papers, the whole project would not have been feasible.

The following departments have been generous contributors: Home Office, HMRC, Cabinet Office, GCN, NS&I, Department of Health, DWP, Food Standards Agency, Army Recruitment Group, RAF Recruitment and Selection, Department for Transport, Scottish Executive and DEFRA.

Peter Buchanan<br>
Deputy Chief Executive, COI

# About the IPA Effectiveness Awards

The case studies in this book are summarised versions of entries to the IPA (Institute of Practitioners in Advertising) Effectiveness Awards. A total of 39 cases are described which constitute about 50% of the total public service case submissions. The majority of these cases had won awards: gold, silver, bronze or commendation.

The IPA Effectiveness Awards were established in the UK in 1980 to investigate the science behind the magic of marketing communications. The aims of the competition are relatively straightforward – simple in words but enormous in scope:

- To prove that marketing communications work
- To show how marketing communications work and
- To measure their effects in hard financial terms.

Since their inception in 1980, 16 national competitions have been held along with a number of Regional and Scottish competitions. Over 25 years the IPA Effectiveness Awards have grown in scale and stature and have become the international gold standard of advertising case material.

## Access to the full case studies

The full versions of the case studies included in this book, each of which are up to 4,000 words in length, are held in the IPA's dataBANK (www.ipa.co.uk). The case studies can also be accessed via the publisher's online service at www.warc.com or may be read in the relevant volume of *Advertising Works* – see the Appendix at the back of the book for full references.

# Overview

# From a political and social perspective

 By Matthew Parris

Government is the third largest UK advertiser behind consolidated P&G and Unilever, say John Poorta and Rebecca Morgan in their key chapter on measuring advertising success. If these two estimable businesses will forgive crude product categorisation, I can rephrase that: only soap is marketed more vigorously than the government's messages.

So how it's done, and with what success, matters tremendously, and it's perhaps surprising that the attempt to assemble evidence and experience in a systematic and in-depth way has never been undertaken before.

You will read in the following chapters a lively, informative and undoctrinaire collection of papers. Plain-speaking and direct, the book is intended not so much as a textbook as a symposium. It takes stock at a time when official advice and information is growing in volume, ambition and reach. The role and cost of public service advertising has become a hot media topic, and its practitioners know that, to a degree that would surprise their more staid and less imaginative predecessors, the profession today is being watched with intelligent interest: often sympathetic, sometimes critical.

This book compares experiences. It asks as many questions as it answers. We amateurs from the world of the media and politics are at least aware of some of these questions.

The book is structured, of course, and case studies and conclusions are described with care and rigour; but there is no attempt to corral contributions and arguments within a single methodology. In fact as one proceeds it becomes ever clearer that experiences and contexts differ mightily, that there is no single 'public service' methodology of advertising, and that any attempt to frame one would quickly founder. Times, models, messages and audiences are changing fast.

Reading *How public service advertising works* as an outsider with some experience in politics and media commentary, I found the variations in experience as striking as the similarities. Several unifying themes do emerge, but not every case study points the same way, and in what follows I shall cast my net in search both of consensus and of disagreement.

## An expanding range of messages

On one thing, consensus is repeatedly and powerfully indicated by contributor after contributor. All agree that – whatever the lay person's impression of public service advertising may be – its practitioners are being asked to do more and more: becoming involved (sometimes simultaneously) in putting across an expanding range of messages that differ not only in content but in type – some pulling in contrary directions.

Sometimes the intention is simply to inform: Charlie Snow (in Chapter 3) usefully sets out the difference between, on the one hand, 'whole new thing' advertising (explaining London's Congestion Charge) and 'new way of doing something' advertising (self-assessment of tax), and, on the other, compliance advertising of the sort that TV licensing requires. Here citizens know their obligations and know how to discharge them; they just need persuading that they want to – not least by informing them of the consequences of failure.

Sometimes, however (see, for instance, Andy Nairn's reference – in Chapter 5 – to the campaign against domestic violence in Scotland), the mission is to change basic moral perceptions in circumstances where information, either about means or consequences, is not really what the target audience lacks.

Sometimes public service advertising seeks to alter behaviour by urging individuals to act selfishly in their own best interests – many of the public health, safety and security messages described by Richard Storey (in Chapter 1) are of this kind, and may involve a mix of useful information (how to avoid or extinguish a chip pan fire; how to reduce risk of stroke or heart attack) with emotional exhortation (How would you feel if your house was burgled? How would you handle an unwanted pregnancy?).

By contrast, a campaign may sometimes seek to persuade its audience to consider their own desires less, and the interests of others more. Unbelted rear-seat passengers may kill those in the front seats; drink-drivers kill pedestrians. But whether we are urging citizens to act selfishly or altruistically, Richard Storey memorably describes the required techniques as involving 'a careful marriage of alarm and reassurance'.

Would that we in the media (and politicians too) would strike that balance with similar care. Instead we tend to swing wildly between berating public service messages as 'alarmist' or 'nannying' and berating public service advertisers for failing to warn or inform sufficiently ('Why weren't we told?', 'Why was no warning given?'). Frankly, depending on mood and demand, columnists like me can write either type of column with our eyes shut!

The truth is, as Storey points out, that 'the public don't like being told what to do'. Yet the public also expect ever-higher standards of advice, explanation and warning. Public servants may wring their hands at the contradiction, but it is worth asking whether public service advertising itself does more than react: it has become a dynamic force, both creating new resistance and generating new demand.

The more government advertises the costs, dangers and rewards of different types of behaviour, the more irritated many citizens become at the intrusion; but the more citizens will also come to depend upon official advice in their lives – from cooking to contraception – and feel that the state has failed them when no steer is offered and they end up in the ditch. To those politicians who must require (and those public servants who must frame) the message, perhaps no more useful advice can be offered than that you're damned if you do and damned if you don't. A cautious balance is in order. For those journalists who write about these things, maybe it's worth reminding ourselves, when writing a headline calling for less (or more) nannying, how easily in other circumstances we could have written the headline calling for more (or less).

## Accurate targeting vs a scatter-gun approach

I was struck by the emphasis many contributors (like Andy Nairn in Chapter 6) put on targeting audiences accurately. This is exactly the way things are going in the media, and in politics too. Mostly it's because we can. There's now such a multiplicity of channels, outlets and types of media through which we can reach our audience, and such accurate means by which we can research and define it, that we cease to think of 'the British public' as an amorphous mass; and indeed it is not.

It's so much more effective (and cost-effective) these days to segment, that the point is not worth labouring, though I return to it below. Here, though, may I sound a cautionary note? For all the audience segmentation it is now possible to achieve, there does remain something called the British public; there is still something that might be termed 'public opinion'; and when successfully and full-heartedly engaged it is a very powerful thing, capable of sweeping niche patterns of thought and behaviour aside.

I certainly become conscious of that from time to time as a *Times* journalist and as a broadcaster. Concern about the vulnerability of children, for example, has been swelling for some time, right across society; so has the tolerance of homosexuality; so has intolerance of smoking; and the idea – given huge impetus by public service advertising – that drinking and driving was socially unacceptable gained ground and grew into a national orthodoxy much faster than many politicians or commentators would have expected.

For all that there are often key sectors of society whom marketing logic would suggest it makes sense to target, the potential tsunami effect of the development of a near-universal cultural norm may still argue, just sometimes, for a big-budget, scatter-gun, shout-it-from-the-rooftops approach. Never mind that much of the seed may fall on initially stony ground; peer-group pressure is a powerful force – and I would argue (for instance) that despite its expense and clumsiness, the 1980s 'tombstone' campaign on HIV–AIDS, and all those millions of leaflets, most of them doubtless wasted, may have helped establish a critical momentum in public concern. Such things are hard to measure.

## Difficulties in advertising prohibition

There's fairly broad agreement in this book that (as Alison Hoad puts it in Chapter 2) public service advertising is unusual within the profession in being so often asked to 'demotivate' people rather than motivate them: that is, to stop people doing/buying/consuming things, rather than urge them to rush out and buy, try or do something. This of course is often true; and so it can also be true that all those positive human motivations to which commercial advertising can appeal because it is selling a dream, a hope, a greed or a lust, tend to be absent from the means of appeal at the disposal of a public service advertiser.

But not entirely. The public service picture is not all greys and blacks. Human kindness, compassion, hope, obligation – even nobility – are among the public service advertiser's available crayons. As Neil Goodlad and Rebecca Munds point out (in Chapter 4) on recruitment campaigns, public-sector advertising may be asked to glamorise (or at least decontaminate) the image of a job or calling, and may do so most effectively. Blood and organ donation may equally be promoted with positive messages, as may the standing of minority or excluded social groups. It isn't all about whom or what we should shun: public service has things to say about heroes and heroism too.

Yet, oddly enough, I suspect we would find more widespread public and media acceptance of government's role in telling us what we shouldn't do, want, hope or admire, than what we should. Alison Hoad rightly points out that 'Keep off the grass' does not fill people with joy as a message, but it's very well understood, and seldom questioned. There remains (and as an instinctive conservative I acknowledge it) a feeling that the advertising of prohibition is a core, if uncongenial, function of public-sector communications, whereas urging positive choices on us can be more problematic and, perversely, resented more because it may be considered inappropriate.

What every contributor seems to agree is that (as Alex Harris and Charles Vallance put it in Chapter 8), society has moved 'from deference to reference'. Offering information to the public in a spirit of helpfulness that appeals to their intelligence rather than their obedience goes down better than a message that seems to bark at us, and 'Keep off the grass' works as a message only when people can immediately see why. In other circumstances, explaining why is hugely effective. More than one contributor mentions the Department of Transport's outstanding Think! campaign (Chapter 7). New ways of looking at something, new facts, engage us.

### Facts vs fear

Any journalist would concur: we in the media like new facts, and politicians love them – true or dodgy. The 'Guess what?' and 'Hey, Mum!' factor is part of our job too. And when much of what I've read here blurs in the memory, I shall not forget that a dampened cloth is the way to put out a chip pan fire; that when I'm driving, an unsecured rear passenger could kill me in an accident; and that walking a mile uses up as many calories as running a mile. As traffic warden, the role of state-sponsored advertising may be grudgingly accepted; as nanny it is controversial; but as teacher it is (when conducted with flair) positively welcomed. Contributor after contributor in this book concurs that, from the public's point of view, 'Here's how you can ...' comes rightly and naturally from public service advertising; 'Here's why you should ...' needs to be handled with more care; and 'Never mind why: just do as you're told' must be consigned to advertising history.

And it is over public service advertising's role in exhorting, cajoling and chiding the citizen, that some interestingly contrasting – even contradictory – messages emerge from what I've read here.

I remarked earlier on our contributors' refrain that official persuasion can rarely (as commercial advertising can) sell a dream, or trade on an easy appeal to the acquisitive instinct. This is true. But we should not overlook one potent weapon in the public service advertiser's armoury: fear. Fear is a great persuader. Journalists like me know well that the public is very susceptible to being scared into or out of things, and fascinated by warnings about new dangers. Apart from the insurance industry, few commercial advertisers can trade on fear as reliably as government information (and print journalism, and politics) does.

But I would say of public service advertising, as I would of my own trade, that we need to be sparing in our recourse to this easiest of weapons. For two reasons. First is the law of diminishing returns. As campaigns for United Colors of Benetton found, shocking people works best the first time. It is always possible to create a sensation by going one notch further than anyone has done before, disgusting or terrifying your audience and attracting breathless media coverage. But by doing so unnecessarily you may debauch the currency of alarm, crying 'wolf' and making it harder for the next campaign to achieve the same impact. There is such a thing as shock fatigue, and it would be a pity if public service advertising becomes associated in citizens' minds with a relentless barrage of news about all the bad things that can happen to us, without any real sense of gradation of risk and penalty.

Richard Storey (in Chapter 1) speaks of the potency of the 'emotional worst consequence' in advertising dangers such as burglary, car theft or road accidents; but we should take care lest we scare people witless about the possibility of losing their in-car stereo, then find we've blunted their sensitivity to the possibility of losing their child in a car crash. Campaign architects who pride themselves on having sharply increased householders' fear of being burgled may find that for their next campaign they are charged with the job of combating that newly fashionable evil in politicians' minds: 'fear of crime'.

## The limits of tolerance

Caution is needed, too, in our approach to what Andy Nairn (in Chapter 5) calls, in his chapter title, 'Understanding subcultures'. This book chronicles huge advances in the perspective shifts that are necessary if an advertiser is to see the world as his target audience do. No case study is more often mentioned here than the 1998 HEA drugs campaign, which Will Collin describes (in Chapter 7). He rightly attributes the surprising counter-trend success of this campaign to its guiding principle of not trying to lecture young people, or scare them with bogey-man 'drug horror' stories of a kind they'd heard before and learned to discount in light of their own experience. Instead the campaign took it (implicitly) as read that many of its audience would use drugs, or had already; it offered them non-censorious, calm, 'insider' advice on sensible precautions.

I don't dispute this approach – indeed I've written columns recommending it – but we should not pretend that it is consistent with the 'Just Say No' or Zero Tolerance philosophy; and frank, practical advice may be seen (and is, by parts of the media and some morally conservative politicians) as conceding important ground at the outset, undermining attempts to recommend a moral rather than just a practical code. Those who devise these campaigns must be armed in advance with answers to the complaint that 'the government' is offering kids a users' guide to drug taking.

The same problems arise with government information on sexual health and contraception, especially when directed to the young. Official advertising campaigns are at the same time constrained (if they are to succeed) to embrace a matter-of-fact acceptance that people will and do break the law; yet constrained not to appear to condone criminality or immorality. Parts of the middle-market tabloid press are ever ready to pile in and condemn, fists flying, when this happens.

I cannot say how these two competing pressures are to be reconciled; it was a conflict that, when I served on the Broadcasting Standards Council, we often had to grapple with. But it's important, I think, for politicians (however nervous of another bad *Daily Mail* headline), for regulators (however nervous of the politicians) and commentators (however tempted by the easy cheer) to be robust in standing up for public servants who fashion advertising that makes a difference rather than simply takes a stand.

## Pistachio Nut Syndrome

I said I would return to the question of targeting. A fascinating cluster of questions is implicitly suggested, rather than explicitly identified, by contributions to this book. Suggestions are various and not always consistent. One is that 'censorious' public service advertising may have little impact, serving only to irritate or alienate those at whom the finger is wagged. 'Condemn the action not the audience,' says Alison Hoad (in Chapter 2), citing the need to identify tobacco, not the smoker, as the culprit. It is pointed out that most smokers already say they want to quit, so there's no point in shouting at them.

True – but why do they want to quit? In part because society is shouting at them. Their husbands/wives/mothers/children are shouting at them. Alison Hoad and others are right that, for the hard core of recalcitrants, moralising is pointless, even counterproductive. But one of the influences that may gradually diminish recalcitrance in that hard core is relentless peer group pressure. I'm afraid that moralising and censoriousness, however disagreeable, do play a part here. It may be perfectly pointless to shout 'Racist!' at members of the BNP (and indeed the logical conclusion of the 'get inside the heads of the subculture' approach might be to approach them in language that does not condemn their racism) but for every hard core member there will be ten waverers on whom cultural ostracism of the kind public service advertising can reinforce, may have some effect.

Shame, described in Chapter 2 as the key element in the Department of the Environment's successful anti-drink-driving campaign in Northern Ireland, does sometimes work. Shame is not a fashionable concept in public-sector discourse, but it is very potent.

Different and apparently inconsistent strands in the evidence cited by this book are perhaps best reconciled through an analogy I call the Pistachio Nut Syndrome. We are all familiar with the life cycle of the nut bowl as the drinks party progresses. Pre-party and at the outset there will be a full bowl, of which the overwhelming majority are crackable. By the time the last guests leave there is only a handful of nuts at the bottom of the bowl, the vast majority of which are uncrackable. Public service advertising targets various audiences, of which one is often the end-of-the-party pistachio bowl: the people who despite many official campaigns have still not been reached by anti-smoking, or anti-drink-driving campaigns, or exhortations to fit window locks to their houses.

It is quite right to say that it may be pointless megaphoning the 'stop it at once' message at these people, talking at them, or talking down to them. It may be equally pointless to furnish them with information they have heard before. We are talking here about a sub-culture that is really a kind of residue: people whom contributors to this book call the hard core. As John Poorta and Rebecca Morgan point out in Chapter 10, the tougher the nut a campaign is asked to crack, the more highly we should score what they call the 'quality of response'.

But public service advertising must also target wide new audiences that, if not positively virgin, are at least open to messages, ideas and new facts to which they may not yet be inured. These audiences haven't heard it all before. Typically, they haven't even thought about it. Shaming, arresting or 'think about it' messages may prove powerful here. Thus the pre-party nut bowl may be influenced by tones and messages that are wasted on the post-party residue.

The fact that the recalcitrant nuts are – at the same time – the audience most immediately in need of persuasion and the audience least susceptible to being persuaded, should not discourage official persuaders. Success rates with the residue may be disappointing, and some people's attitudes or behaviour will have to be allowed to die with them. But the only reason the residue is a residue is that all the rest have been successfully persuaded; and hammering home the message helps modify and reinforce an enveloping culture that will over time (and more slowly) bear down upon its recalcitrant minority. In this respect the advertising is indirect, but no less potent for insinuating itself only gradually into the mainstream culture, and thence into the uncracked nuts, in ways it is hard to quantify.

I doubt there's much left to say to people who still smoke, beyond 'here's how to stop when you decide to try', but that doesn't make the anti-smoking message redundant, for it has changed and is still changing our whole national attitude. I have never smoked and was never in any danger of starting, but am much less tolerant of the habit in others than when young. The whole of society is. We in turn influence the remaining smokers. Those health warnings on fag packets change attitudes among an audience at whom they are not ostensibly directed. In this regard, Poorta and Morgan's assessment of the hard-to-quantify element in a campaign's success – what they call the 'halo effect' – is especially worth study here.

## Accountability to an increasingly marketing-savvy audience

An entire chapter on accountability is a key contribution to this book. Politicians, the media and taxpayers themselves are becoming more exacting (even belligerent) in their insistence that public spending should be accounted for and its effects evaluated. Conceptual and practical tools for monitoring and quantifying the value of advertising campaigns will be an increasingly important part of a public service advertiser's toolbox in the decades ahead. Accountability is key.

This leads me to make – if I may – the only criticism I have of this whole fascinating and useful exercise. If success in politics and public administration is to be celebrated, it is important that the flip side, failure, is acknowledged too. People are more likely to credit claims for success when failure is identified and analysed. There is not much within these covers about any public service advertising campaign, or element within a campaign, that failed, or indeed was less successful than another. However invidious, it is helpful to let mistakes as well as successes teach the lessons.

A word in conclusion about something I believe may become a matter of growing importance in all advertising, not just in the public sector. Charlie Snow remarks (in Chapter 3) that studies show that 'students hate being marketed to; clever advertising is annoying and clearly designed to hoodwink them into something; what they claimed to want was facts presented in a clear and "no frills" manner; not obscured by any clever executional device'.

The public are becoming increasingly wise to marketing. People do see where advertisers are coming from. Resistance, especially to concealed advertising, is growing. Marketing, in other words, may be bad marketing. Marketing professionals have been (in my view) rather slow to pick up on this, and it's my observation both in politics and in business that individuals who make a point of not being too slick about their message may steal a march on apparently more professional rivals.

Public-sector advertising can take advantage of a cleaner image in this respect than that of its commercial counterpart. Official advice and information may sometimes have been a little dull in its presentation, but among its audience there has always been a measure of unconscious respect for its campaigns, which are widely recognised as being directed in good faith and not for profit, with the intention of helping people. In a society increasingly suspicious of the motives behind messages, this is a very great resource, and public service advertisers should not value it lightly, or squander it in campaigns that devalue the currency of something of which we should not be ashamed: honest propaganda.

# Part 1

## The aim of public service campaigns

# Chapter 1

# Initiating positive behaviour

By Richard Storey

M&C Saatchi

One of the particular challenges faced by public service campaigns is meeting challenging behavioural objectives.

A manufacturer may seek to increase market share by a few per cent, a retailer may look to stimulate footfall, or a service brand may aim to improve customer satisfaction by a point or two. However, the typical public service campaign is often required to produce dramatic transformations on pressing societal issues. Initiatives featured in this chapter have sought to reduce domestic burglaries, decrease the number of road fatalities, reduce injuries and deaths from domestic fires and cut coronary heart disease. No mean feat, particularly when the weapons available to achieve it are basically just words and pictures.

## Commercial campaigns vs public service campaigns

Commercial marketers find it easy to deal in commercial objectives, without specifying desired consumer behaviour. No one is going to criticise the marketing director for pursuing an objective of gaining share, boosting footfall or increasing price premium, even though it might be good practice to consider what particular consumer behaviour may be required to achieve these objectives. The public service marketer cannot realistically hide behind such broad commercial objectives. He or she must interrogate and specify as precisely as possible the behaviour to be investigated and how this could be prompted – a theme this chapter develops.

The difference doesn't end there, however. As many commercial marketing campaigns operate in a zero-sum game, their commercial objectives largely feature switched loyalty and substituted behaviour – for example, getting people to

13

buy one pasta sauce rather than another, incentivising people to try Pepsi rather than Coke, encouraging people to place a brand higher on their mental consideration list. While these are by no means simple challenges, they are focused on modifying existing behaviour rather than initiating it in the first instance.

The public service challenge is often one of creating entirely new behaviours. Rather than displacing the brand one usually buys, public service campaigns often face a 'competitor' in the form of 'doing nothing' or 'doing what I always do'. This has profound implications for the strategies deployed because the barriers that need to be overcome are based on attitudes that are ingrained, unconsidered or self-justified. Changing habits requires a strategy that confronts and challenges these entrenched attitudes, often using emotional discomfort as the trigger.

An intriguing consequence is that public service campaigns often seek to achieve objectives that are expressed in terms of a reduction – lowering crime, reducing fires, cutting down accidents, and so on – by encouraging the consumer to initiate behaviour, for example, take pre-emptive measures to prevent crime, check safety measures at home, wear seat belts. This requires a strategy that inspires positive behaviour on subjects that are negative, uncomfortable or distressing.

## Ten common themes

Analysis of a number of such cases reveals ten common themes that successful public service campaigns deploy in order to pull off this delicate balancing act.

### 1. What can communications realistically achieve?

> The strongest among the weak is the one who doesn't overlook his weaknesses.
>
> Danish proverb, unattributed

The starting point for many successful campaigns is a realistic appraisal of the influence communications can credibly have on their problem.

In *Advertising Works and How*,[1] Guy Murphy outlines eloquently the steps a marketer might take to positively influence the overall size of his market, rather than just increase his share of it.

This thinking, however, has its limitations when it comes to reducing problems such as fire, theft, accidents or disease. In many of these cases, communications are likely to have minimal influence over the overall cause of the problem. This is particularly true for situations that involve accidental behaviour, random occurrences or behaviour initiated by individuals intent on breaking the law – in other words, when the root cause of the problem is some means beyond the victim's immediate influence. Communications would have to work extremely hard, for example, to curtail the behaviour of a petty thief, eliminate a stray spark from a domestic plug or eradicate human error while driving.

Even if it is short-sighted to rule out communications ever having such an influence, in many cases it has proved more effective to look elsewhere for behaviour they can realistically influence. The following case is an excellent example of this.

## Case study: Home Office
### How advertising helps fight crime

### The problem

The author of this strategy considered the scale and cost of domestic burglaries (a conservative £100 million in 1982 in financial terms, not accounting for the human misery caused). Faced with a problem of this magnitude, he felt it 'advisable to consider how advertising can help solve or at least diminish it'.

However, he concluded: 'The short answer is that it cannot. It is judged unlikely that advertising could directly influence the behaviour of burglars and thereby bring about a reduction in crime.'

Instead, the team applied themselves to tackling the problem from the perspective of the potential victim, addressing the issue of how home owners could reduce the risk of themselves being burgled. This in turn led to a much more realistic behavioural objective of encouraging home owners to buy and fit window locks to deflect 'sneak thieves', who are relatively easily deterred.

### The solution

This piece of tangible action was dramatised by identifying the emotional worst consequence of domestic burglaries. Of the many anxieties associated with break-ins, qualitative research revealed that the most vivid was the sense of invasion and violation, a theme powerfully developed in the creative work, which featured magpies invading and ransacking a home.  ▶

## The effect

This approach worked because windows are the most common entry point for burglars and the fitting of window locks acts as both a physical and visual deterrent. As window locks are relatively inexpensive and easy to fit, the emotional distress the advertising dramatised could be simply and easily offset.

Indeed analysis of the effectiveness of the initiative centred on retail audits of window lock sales, showing that purchases grew substantially in regions that received the advertising (and, encouragingly, increased more than any associated rise in concern over burglary).

Source: *Home Protection – how advertising helps fight crime*. Boase Massimi Pollitt (1982) ·

Acknowledging the realistic influence of communications is a therefore a vital step in eliminating strategies that are unlikely to be effective and in redirecting the effort to those aspects of the problem that can realistically be influenced – in this case, window security.

This is invariably achieved in successful campaigns by interrogating the precise cause of the events or behaviour in question.

### 2. Identifying the precise cause

People are rarely called upon to explain their behaviour, particularly when it is habitual. Often when prompted to do so, they provide general responses that don't fully explain their actions: 'I've never thought about it', 'I don't have time', 'That's not something I worry about', and so on.

In order to affect behaviour, it is essential to look beyond these glib responses and understand in precise detail what lies behind people's action (or lack of it). The learning from successful IPA cases is that the more precision that can be applied at this stage to explain behaviour, the more accurately the strategic solution can be prescribed. There is a world of difference between the description of 'collisions between pedal cycles and cars' and 'an accident caused by a car driver misjudging the space required by a pedal cyclist moving over to turn right in heavy traffic'.

Sometimes it is the root of the problem that requires precise understanding, a good example being the causes of chip pan fires (1984 campaign). The team identified not only the main causes of such fires – namely overfilling and inattentiveness – but also the mechanics of the causes. Two scenarios were recognised: people underestimating the volume of chips, resulting in hot oil overflowing when the basket is lowered; and inattentiveness, caused by an unanticipated and unintentional domestic distraction such as answering the door or attending to a crying child. These precise scenarios were reflected in the resulting advertising, allowing it to appear both realistic and understanding.

However, precision can also be applied to a lack of activity. There is much to be gained from deep and insightful analysis of why people *don't* do certain things, as the following case illustrates.

## Case study: Health Education Board for Scotland
### How advertising increased physical activity

### The problem
The objective of this initiative was to reduce the incidence and impact of coronary heart disease and strokes in Scotland. Evidence showed that regular moderate activity could reduce their incidence by up to one-third and their mortality rate by 20%.

However, Scotland had the highest proportion of the population undertaking minimal physical activity (46% vs 31% in England). This was particularly prevalent among the 40+ age group, the very people most at risk of coronary heart disease (CHD) and strokes.

Qualitative research identified multiple barriers preventing older people taking physical exercise. Excuses typically centred around 'haven't enough ▶

time' and 'don't have the will power'. However, more profound reasons were eventually uncovered. Exercise was fundamentally associated with young people. It was felt to be of benefit only if vigorous and was associated with aerobics, 'running around with shorts on' and expensive gyms. In short, it demanded full-on commitment.

These perceptions effectively ruled out 'exercise' as the 40+ audience understood it. As far as they were concerned, there was little worthwhile they could do as they didn't have the time, money or inclination to keep up vigorous activity.

### The solution

Addressing these barriers led to the uncovering of a remarkable fact – walking a mile uses as many calories as running a mile. This led to a very tangible and accessible objective: get people aged 40+ to walk rather than take the bus or drive short distances.

This message was delivered by the then captain of the national rugby team, Gavin Hastings, a spokesperson who lent the proposition both credibility and accessibility among the 40+ age group.

Walking.
Take
exercise
in
your
stride.

### The effect

The campaign succeeded in shifting perceptions of walking as a good form of exercise, resulting in a significant increase in walking versus all other forms of activity.

Source: *'Gavin Hastings really does walk on water' – how HEBS used advertising to increase physical activity in Scotland.* The Bridge (1998)

In this case, it was a precise understanding of older people's reluctance to take vigorous exercise that yielded the 'walk a mile' solution.

This also illustrates an invaluable consequence of establishing the precise cause of existing behaviour: it helps identify what is perhaps the most significant factor in prompting social behaviour change – the tangible action.

### 3. Prescribing tangible action

In a scene in Monty Python's *Life of Brian*, Brian addresses a crowd amassed beneath his balcony that has mistakenly identified him as the Messiah. He preaches that they are all individuals of free will and should all 'work it out for themselves', go off and do their own thing.

'Yes, we are all individuals,' they reply in unison. 'Tell us what we should go off and do, Lord.'

As with much humour, this illustrates a fundamental truth about human nature and our need for leadership, namely that precise and directional instruction is far more likely to initiate a behavioural response than general proclamations.

This learning has direct applicability to public service initiatives. It is difficult for people to respond to general messages about health and safety. 'Think about how secure your home is against the threat of burglary' is unlikely to produce much by way of specific action, whereas 'Call your Crime Prevention Officer' or 'Fit window locks' is much more likely to trigger a response. As it happens, the response may not be limited to the action suggested. In the above example, some spill-over effect into the fitting of burglar alarms was anticipated, and indeed detected.

Public service campaigns in the IPA Effectiveness Awards are distinguished by such translations of the macro objective into smaller, more specific, more achievable 'tangible actions'. So much so that in many cases these become the central plank of the strategy.

Table 1 gives some examples to help illustrate this point.

The beauty of these examples is their utter clarity and obviousness. In fairness it should be pointed out that this simplicity is highly deceptive. Reading the cases, it is clear that each solution was arrived at only through great thought, analysis and research.

Anyone who cares to dispute this might consider, by way of example, what tangible action might be suggested to reduce the number of deaths from cancer, reduce so-called 'binge drinking' or curtail the use of mobile phones while driving. (Answers on a postcard to the relevant government department.)

| Table 1: Examples of macro objectives and their tangible actions | |
|---|---|
| **Macro objective** | **Tangible action** |
| Reduce domestic burglaries | Fit window locks |
| Reduce theft from cars | Remove valuables and display 'nothing to steal' sign |
| | Lock your car at petrol stations |
| Decrease deaths and serious injuries from road accidents | Drivers to give more room to cyclists passing parked cars or turning right |
| Decrease deaths from household fire | Check smoke alarm batteries every Monday |
| | Cover burning chip pans with damp tea towel (don't use water) |
| Increase child literacy | Read to your child throughout the day, not just at bedtime |
| Reduce unwanted pregnancy | Call the emergency contraception helpline rather than crossing your fingers |

In practice, the suitability of any tangible action depends on it being significant and straightforward in equal measure. Too challenging or stretching and it will be rejected as unrealistic. Too simplistic or familiar and it will be dismissed as nothing new.

The key to finding this balance lies in understanding the intransigence of the target audience.

### 4. Dealing with difficult audiences

The identification and prioritisation of the core target audience represents another major difference between public service and commercial initiatives.

Here a tough choice is frequently made between those audiences most likely to respond and those most in need of, or standing to benefit most from, changing their behaviour. On this point of principle, commercial and social practices are poles apart.

Commercial enterprises look for efficiencies and return on investment. Faced with the financial imperative, the natural inclination is to select audiences that are most likely to respond. Health-concerned mums are most likely to buy organic food, middle-aged people are more likely to take an interest in a pension proposition, young people buy more training shoes, and so on.

With public service cases, the frame for decision making is completely different. Social value is more important than efficiency. Return is measured in human terms – worth, benefit, quality of life – rather than necessarily in financial ones. (Although the IPA Effectiveness Awards do require entrants ultimately to establish a financial payback.)

This has a profound effect on audience selection. The public service strategist will prioritise the audience that stands to gain most from adopting certain behaviour, often because they are currently least likely to be doing it.

As a direct consequence, this audience is often the people least inclined to consider doing something about the issue. For example, research indicates that upmarket audiences living in comfortable areas are most likely to report anti-social behaviour, but downmarket audiences living in disadvantaged estates are targeted because they stand to benefit most, even though they are less disposed to 'dobbing in' their neighbours.

In the exercise example above, HEBS (Health Education Board for Scotland) identified an audience of older people who were negatively disposed to jogging and gym going, when commercial efficiency 'metrics' would have pointed to a younger audience. Likewise, campaigns aimed at enforcing the wearing of rear seat belts targeted 15–30 year olds who strongly felt it their right, their choice and their freedom not to belt up. Such emotional resistance demanded a highly emotive strategy, as we will see later.

This altruistic targeting decision does of course make life harder for the strategist. Aiming at the difficult audience demands harder-working strategies but is more likely to produce worthwhile changes.

Fortunately, the advertiser is not alone in attempting to get through to such difficult audiences.

## 5. Magnifying the effect through partnership

Think for a moment about the senseless use of plastic carrier bags, for example in supermarkets. A quick scan of newspapers and the internet reveals there are currently no fewer than 14 organisations attempting to influence consumers to reduce their carrier bag usage. Not all are united on the most appropriate tangible action, but all are aligned behind the cause – saving the planet.

Interestingly, in this case only one of the organisations is a public body.

Smart communications planners have worked out that, whatever the initiative, there are any number of organisations with agendas and objectives that are aligned, possibly even identical. It is therefore common practice to engage such organisations as partners and co-carriers of the message. It is often in the partners' interest to agree, as they too will have reached the same conclusion – that a problem shared is a message doubled.

Cooperation may take the form of joint funding, provision of advertising space and other messaging opportunities, or a general sharing of initiatives, campaign materials, teams, etc.

The Fire Authority for Northern Ireland secured private-sector sponsorship from a smoke alarm manufacturer to the tune of 50% of its TV production fees. Clearly the initiative worked in commercial terms as well as the altruistic interest.

The Home Office partnered with local councils and commercial car park operators to spread reminder messages on parking meters, pay-and-display tickets and car park barriers, encouraging people not to leave valuables on display. It was clearly in the interest of these partners to reduce the level of crime on and around their facilities.

Even back in 1982, the campaign to fit window locks was partnered with Crime Prevention Officers and commercial organisations concerned with domestic security, with a stated objective of creating a momentum that would aid their efforts.

While partnering with other influencers helps spread the reach of the message, coverage alone cannot guarantee an effective campaign. Advertisers must find ways to maximise the emotive power of their message. Here a number of cases highlight the power of harnessing the emotional worst consequence.

## 6. *Highlighting the emotional worst consequence*

Numerous studies have identified that emotional stimuli make far more effective prompts than purely rational arguments, when it comes to changing opinions and provoking a response.

Many public service cases take this one step further and maximise the impact and intensity of the problem from an emotional perspective. They identify and dramatise the 'emotional worst consequence' of their topic.

A key learning here is that this emotive prompt is rarely a straight and obvious deduction from the problem. Often a difficult audience's disinclination to take action reveals that they are immune to the direct consequences of that problem. This is typically rationalised with responses such as 'It won't happen to me', 'It only happens to stupid/careless/unfortunate people', 'You're just sensationalising the problem – it's not that serious' and the purely belligerent 'I know, but I'm not that bothered.'

For example, in tackling vehicle crime, the Home Office and RKCR/Y&R identified that theft from cars was simply regarded as an inevitability of life, 'something to be expected and tolerated, like bad weather'. Far from fearing this kind of crime, the audience were already primed and ready to dismiss it. The loss of items per se was not the worst aspect of the crime. People knew they could have them replaced courtesy of their insurer, so it was no more than a hassle.

To unlock this kind of resistance, it's often helpful to force consumers to imagine they have suffered the incident described, and force them to confront what their thoughts and feelings might be in that situation. This is typically done through projective research scenarios and techniques, or by the more direct method of interviewing people who have actually suffered the scenario being investigated. In either approach, the learning from effective cases is to look for the most emotionally resonant aspect of the situation.

The earlier domestic burglary case documented a similar phenomenon to car crime: the actual theft of items was less troubling than the thought of strangers invading one's home. 'Invasion' triggered many related emotions that were all powerfully distressing: violation, intrusion – for some women, even rape.

A summary of emotional worst consequences from other cases illustrates that people's worst fears are not always the most direct result of the problem but often an aspect related to it (see Table 2).

| Table 2: Summary of problems and their emotional worst consequences | |
| --- | --- |
| **Problem** | **Emotional worst consequence** |
| Domestic burglary | Violation<br>(Intrusion and degradation of personal space) |
| Theft from cars | Disregard<br>(For example, a £200 stereo stolen for just £10) |
| Not wearing rear seat belt | Guilt of killing driver/other passenger<br>(Rear passenger acts as lethal projectile) |
| Household fires | Guilt of negligence<br>(Responsible for the deaths of others who depend on you) |
| Unwanted pregnancies | Feeling alone<br>(Fear of judgement strangers might make if you reveal you had unprotected sex) |
| Blood donation | Other people's helplessness<br>(Families depending on you, waiting for your blood) |
| Anti-social noise | Isolation<br>(Despair, anger, interruption with no acceptable means of dealing with it) |

In the case of wearing rear seat belts, two different organisations working in different geographic areas arrived at very similar articulations of the emotional worst consequence and the most effective way of applying it.

# Case studies: GB and Northern Ireland
## How advertising saved lives

### The problem

Six years after it became law, less than half of rear passengers were wearing seat belts, a problem that was ultimately costing the country £210 million a year in deaths and injuries. ▶

Advertising was required to make what was a legal requirement become second nature, and make abuse of it morally unacceptable, the way it had for drink-driving.

The audience was a difficult one – young people aged 15–30 who not only travelled most frequently in the rear, but were least inclined to belt up.

They rationalised their complacency with a number of excuses. Wearing a seat belt was uncool and socially excluding. They felt uncomfortable, didn't feel vulnerable – they could adequately brace themselves and were only going a short distance – and didn't want to signal distrust of the driver. The paltry £20 fine for non-compliance was seen only to endorse their complacency.

However, research identified an even more deep-seated attitudinal cause. Young people felt not wearing a seat belt was a personal choice. It affected no one but themselves and was therefore a freedom to which they were morally entitled. As a consequence, the audience were immune to the suggestion that their behaviour could result in their own death. This was a risk they felt entitled to take (and besides, it wasn't going to happen to them).

## The solution

Based on this analysis of the problem, teams in Great Britain and Northern Ireland arrived at similar solutions. They sought to make not wearing rear seat belts morally unacceptable by dramatising the implications for other car occupants. It was identified that around 100 front-seat passengers a year were hit and killed by unrestrained rear passengers in collisions.

Dramatising this revealed the emotional worst consequence: the guilt of being responsible for someone else's death. This in turn reframed the non-wearing of seat belts from an act of personal freedom to one of moral irresponsibility.  ▶

## The effect

Analysis showed this provoked widespread reappraisal among young people, with dramatic changes in the perceived unacceptability of not belting up. This in turn caused a sudden and dramatic behavioural change, with a 23% uplift in observed wearing rates in the first year alone. Or, put another way, one life saved for every ten TVRs aired.

Sources: *Rear Seatbelts – Sudden impact: how can we measure the cost of a life?* Abbot Mead Vickers (2000); *'Damage': No seat belt – No excuse.* McCann-Erickson Northern Ireland (2002)

In this case it was obviously appropriate and effective to shock and confront. However, there are clearly subjects for which a more empowering tone is in order. The emotional worst consequence can still be leveraged, but rather as a means to be understanding, sympathetic and encouraging.

The key to success here lies in developing an appropriate tone of voice.

### 7. An empowering tone of voice

Marketers often talk about their relationship with their consumers as their most important asset. One pet food marketing director once remarked to me that 'Our business is not based on manufacturing and selling 300 million cans of cat food, but on sustaining relationships with five million loyal customers.'

It is fashionable at the moment to value the relationship with your consumers in terms of two-way interactive dialogue, with customers co-creating the brand's content. However, in the public service area, with its difficult subjects and difficult audiences, there is a more traditional benefit in the tone with which the advertiser engages his audience.

The simple truth here is that the public don't like being told what to do, particularly by government. The already difficult parent–child tone of voice becomes particularly problematic when coming from an authority. Many effective public service initiatives have therefore worked hard to establish a 'good' relationship with their audience, developing disarming ways of conversing and engaging, rather than simply talking at them.

In a campaign to reduce anti-social noise in Northern Ireland, the authors identified the 'victim' rather than the noise maker as the key audience. They identified the emotional worst consequence as the feeling of isolation caused by being subjected to the noise and the social pressures associated with it. They developed a tone of voice that reassured victims that their feelings of despair, anger and isolation were absolutely valid. Central to this was the key message that 'You're allowed to complain.' This empowering approach led to a 44% increase in calls reporting nuisance noise.

In an even more sensitive area, a similarly empowering approach was adopted by the Health Education Authority.

## Case study: Health Education Authority
### How advertising prevented unwanted pregnancies

### The problem
Assuming that advertising can have little influence over people's inclination to have sex, there are three realistic means of using it to prevent unwanted pregnancies. First, encouraging the take-up of family planning services; second, abortion (clearly an option of last resort); and third – the topic of the paper in question – emergency contraception.

In an emotive subject such as this, tone of approach was clearly critical.

In this instance the authors identified a series of rational misunderstandings about the products available, most graphically summarised by the unofficial name 'morning-after pill'. Facing widespread ignorance of the fact that it could actually be taken up to 72 hours after initial unprotected intercourse, there was clearly a role for rational communications. The product was rebranded under the name 'emergency contraception', which appropriately positioned it as a product of last resort (rather than as a method of course), that could be used up to three days after unprotected sex.

However, qualitative research revealed that there were other more complex emotional barriers limiting take-up. These centred on anxieties surrounding the process of obtaining the pill. Women were embarrassed about approaching people they vaguely knew, such as a doctor's receptionist, with an enquiry about emergency contraception. Having to admit to unprotected sex was a deterrent for seeking help as women were concerned about judgements others might make. This left them feeling alone and isolated, with no one they could trust to share their fears with. Faced with this, 'risking it' and doing nothing seemed the more palatable choice. (Besides, the chances were it wouldn't happen to them.) ▶

## The solution

Faced with these barriers, it was important that the solution was both perceptive and supportive. It deliberately and sensitively tackled the emotional worst consequence, reflecting the isolation felt by women at risk. Crucially, however, it did this in a way that was supportive and reassuring. A tone was selected that was deliberately matter of fact. It sought to normalise the subject, not skirt around it. It was couched in terms of an informed and helpful friend, offering calm reassurance and factual advice.

The message 'If your contraceptive let you down last night, you're not alone' carried all these values, as well as delicately repositioning the blame onto a failed condom, rather than uninhibited, irresponsible and unprotected enthusiasm.

A tangible action point flowed naturally from this: call our helpline rather than crossing your fingers.

## The effect

Analysis shows the campaign worked by virtue of this delicate balance between sympathetic tone and factual information. Misunderstandings about the timing of usage were corrected, propensity to use (if and when appropriate) increased and research among health professionals acknowledged the influence of the campaign in encouraging women to seek help.

Source: *Accidents will happen – making it possible to be wise after the event*. BMP DDB Needham (1996)

Developing an empowering tone is clearly one effective approach to getting the audiences 'on side' with your message.

Another challenge public service advertisers face is to represent their subject in a way that is both credibly realistic and personally relevant.

## 8. Overcoming denial: 'it's not me'

One of the most common causes of apathy or inaction among difficult audiences is their inbuilt denial instinct. It is easier to find ways to dismiss and deny a stimulus that doesn't conveniently fit with our beliefs, attitudes and desires, rather than accept it and change our perspective. The smallest discrepancy or ambiguity is enough to 'exempt' ourselves from any message we don't want to agree with.

Hence, people will argue that smoking kills, but it kills other people; speeding is something done by reckless people on motorways, not ordinary people in 30 mph zones; and heart attacks happen to people older than them.

Getting past this 'it won't happen to me' denial is a common challenge for public service advertisers, particularly in the area of personifying victims and at-risk audiences. Pre-testing research frequently reports the risk of portraying a victim that audiences are immediately able to argue is 'not me'. By definition, anyone that is cast as the victim is going to be different in some respect and audiences happily seize on that difference as an excuse to disassociate themselves.

The creative challenge is to find ways of depicting a scenario as entirely credible and realistic, without being so specific that audiences can excuse themselves.

In the case of vehicle crime, the agency found it more effective to represent and personify the criminal rather than to feature the victim. This allowed them to illustrate the emotional worst consequence of the crime in the most general sense, without having to specify who it happens to.

Domestic crime took this a stage further, by portraying the criminals as invading magpies (see pages 15–16) and suggesting the effect on the victim through the objects they disturb and violate. This was particularly powerful by dint of being both representative of the situation, but general in its metaphor.

A similar balance of reality and generalisation was achieved in the following case study on reducing the impact of fire.

# Case study: Fire Authority for Northern Ireland
## How advertising educated the public about fire safety

### The problem
Advertising can have some effect on the cause of some fires, for example by educating people not to smoke in bed or advising them to position candles safely. However, there is little it can do to prevent fires when the cause is outside human control (e.g. electrical). In these cases, it can however reduce death and injury by instilling fire-safe behaviour.

For this campaign in Northern Ireland, it was concluded that the principal message should concern smoke alarms, as these were the greatest determinant of safety once a fire had already started. As penetration of ▶

smoke alarms was high, but maintenance of them was low, the message was made very tangible – check your smoke alarm batteries every Monday.

This message was supplemented by four other specific pieces of advice: position candles safely, never fill the chip pan more than a third full, close doors at bedtime and have an escape plan.

However, the biggest issue was identified as 'life-threatening apathy'. People were adept at deflecting most messages with the excuse that 'it could never happen to me'.

This phenomenon was so strong that the team elected not to feature characters or protagonists in advertising. Research showed that the audience was quick to find reasons not to identify with the characters and therefore the scenario shown, even when the people and their circumstances were similar (if not identical) to the audience. Rather than creating engagement, featuring people created excuses to disengage.

## The solution

As credible realism became ever more important, the team got their breakthrough by visiting, studying and ultimately recreating real fire scenes. The image that captured this reality most was of human handprints in soot on the walls. The team used a similar device in the creative work, with finger-written messages scrawled in desperation in the soot.

This device allowed the campaign to look real, without showing the victim or target audience, thus removing the possibility of the viewer disengaging.

## The effect

The results show that this approach affected the widest possible audience, with 60% of them influenced to take some of the action prescribed. This led ultimately to a 14% reduction in household fires and a 12% reduction in fire injuries.

Source: *Fire Authority for Northern Ireland – writings on the wall*. Ardmore Advertising (2005)

This is an example of a creative representation of the problem that was both highly realistic and yet general enough to leave the audience no excuse to opt out.

An alternative approach is to reposition perceptions of the problem.

### 9. Repositioning the problem

Earlier we established that public service marketing must, almost by definition, seek out the most difficult audiences. In doing so, it must overcome apathy, denial, disassociation and many other barriers preventing that difficult audience from engaging with the problem.

Often the best way to do this is to change the way they perceive the problem.

In encouraging people to donate blood, the Scottish National Blood Transfusion Service faced a shortage of donors, compounded by the vCJD crisis. It found that depictions of the problem elicited sympathy but little action. It was all too easy for people to feel that others would come forward and donate. So it subtly reframed the problem away from a general shortage of donors and depicted instead particular patients waiting specifically for you to call and donate your blood. This repositioning from the general to the personal was shown to be four times more effective in recruiting new donors.[2]

A campaign to reduce pedal cycle casualties in 1982 repositioned the problem away from one affecting cyclists and instead placed the blame firmly on drivers. It showed that the problem was caused, not by the erratic behaviour of inexperienced cyclists, but by the arrogant behaviour of motorists not allowing cyclists adequate room in busy traffic.

A textbook example of engaging an audience by reframing perceptions of the cause of a problem is the following for vehicle crime.

## Case study: Home Office
### How advertising reduced theft from vehicles

### The problem

Research showed that the public had come to accept vehicle crime as a fact of life. They were resigned to the cause being evil criminals and felt the responsibility lay entirely in the hands of the Criminal Justice System. Using ▶

advertising to suggest the public themselves play a role in fighting vehicle crime ran the risk of being dismissed as government side-stepping the problem.

## The solution

The solution lay in understanding the precise cause of vehicle crime and using this to reposition the criminal in the minds of the potential victim.

Analysis of crime statistics and interviews with the perpetrators of vehicle crime painted a vivid picture of acts of opportunism pulled off by disenfranchised 'chancers' – a 16 year old with little or no stake in society who sees loose change under the handbrake as an opportunity. In other words, the enemy was not a sinister 'criminal' to be feared but a casual opportunist to be outwitted.  ▶

|  | NOW | FUTURE | EVALUATION |
|---|---|---|---|
| ATTITUDE | Vehicle crime is predatory<br><br>Vehicle crime is inevitable | Vehicle crime is opportunistic<br><br>Vehicle crime is avoidable | 'Most vehicle crime is opportunist'<br><br>'There are things you can do to reduce risks'<br>Increase in perception of ease of avoidance<br><br>(TNS Tracking) |
| RESPONSE | Block it out and hope for the best<br><br>– 'not my responsibility'<br><br>'RESIGNATION' | Vehicle thief is someone to outwit<br><br>– shared responsibility<br><br>'INDIGNATION' | 'People have responsibility to prevent vehicle crime'<br><br>Shift from 'police' to 'public/individual' responsibility<br><br>(TNS Tracking) |
| BEHAVIOUR | Do nothing | Take preventative action | Claimed and actual behaviour<br><br>(TNS Tracking and Crime Statistics) |

Replaying this personification to potential victims elicited a powerful emotional response. Their anger was not over the loss of valuable possessions, but the lack of remorse the criminals showed for their actions. They were incensed by the idea of personal possessions discarded without a thought, a £200 car stereo sold for just £10 or a car window broken just to grab a bag that contained nothing of value.

The agency was able to harness this indignation into a determination to stop the casual thief from getting away with it. Advertising showed vehicle crimes from the point of view of the thief, which had the effect of 'humanising' the criminal and increasing the audience's desire to outsmart him.

## The effect

The campaign was effective in preventing vehicle crime through creating a sense of shared responsibility (without overtly stating as much which would have been widely criticised). Perceptions of personal responsibility rose, as did awareness of how easy it was to prevent such crimes. Altogether, this led to a 37% reduction in crime over a five-year period, surpassing the 30% target, yielding a saving of £590 million in the costs of dealing with vehicle crime.

Source: *Vehicle crime prevention. Crime doesn't pay, but advertising to stop it does.* RKCR/Y&R (2006)

This campaign, like many others, achieved its effectiveness by successfully balancing negative and positive motivations, the final theme in this chapter.

### *10. Balancing alarm and reassurance*

Clearly, there is no set formula for effective public service advertising. However, when attempting to instigate new behaviour, communications have to deploy a balance of motivations, both positive and negative. Here, one consistent pattern does emerge: the careful marriage of alarm and reassurance.

The combination of the negative (often in the form of the emotional worst consequence) and the positive (often in the form of an empowering tone of voice and a relatively easy tangible action) is deployed in most of the examples referenced in this chapter.

Often, the emphasis of each approach is on the negative, as befits the subject matter and the entrenched attitudes of the target audience. But alarm is always offset with a positive and achievable tangible action.

Often it is the contrast between the intensity of the emotional alarm and simplicity of the solution that provides the motivation to act, by making the problem look worse and the solution appear achievable (see Table 3).

The last example in Table 3 illustrates a particularly creative use of the balance between negative consequences and positive behaviour. This is described in more detail in the following case study.

| Table 3: Resolving difficult problems by simple solutions | | |
|---|---|---|
| **Problem** | **Emotional worst consequence** | **Tangible action** |
| Domestic burglary | Violation | Fit window locks |
| Theft from cars | Disregard | Lock your car at petrol stations |
| Household fires | Guilt of negligence | Check smoke alarm batteries every Monday |
| Unwanted pregnancies | Being alone | Call our helpline rather than cross your fingers |
| Blood donation | Other people waiting helplessly | Call now rather than some time in the future |
| Anti-social noise | Isolation | You are allowed to complain |
| Pedal cycle accidents | Selfishness – failure to anticipate | Drivers to give cyclists more room passing parked cars |
| Organ donation | Leaving someone to die | Register and save a life |

# Case study: Scottish Executive
## How advertising ensured life after death

### The problem
Of all the competing good causes offering to improve or save lives, there is one that doesn't ask you to donate your spare change. It asks you to donate your organs.

Unfortunately, to become an organ donor, you have to die.                    ▶

The ghoulish prospect of considering your own death and being 'cut up on the slab' meant that while 91% of the population are 'in favour' of organ donation, only 23% had bothered to sign up. Even more significantly, refusal rates from next of kin ran at over 40%. Research showed that if more people joined the register and put their wishes on file, those refusal rates would drop.

## The solution

The Scottish Executive and The Union tackled this problem by dramatically contrasting the worst and best emotional consequences of organ donation. Critically, given the 91% vs 23% statistics, their approach focused ruthlessly on provoking action, not just intention to act.

They dramatised the consequence of inaction in a way that was real, personal and highly emotive: the death of a stranger staring innocently out of the page at you.

By contrast, they expressed the tangible action – register as an organ donor – as the direct opposite, namely the gift of life.

The campaign used the contrast between these two possible outcomes as the source of its drama. Public relations (PR) and advertising worked together, with each presenting the opposite extremes of the argument, simultaneously where possible.

This approach was particularly effective because it compelled the audience to choose an outcome. Not making a decision was not an option. This ▶

positioned the natural desire to procrastinate as effectively a decision to let someone die. It also channelled the natural desire of not wanting to see an innocent stranger killed, into the call to action.

## The effect

As a result, Scotland recorded a 33% increase in registrations vs a control of 6.5% in England where the campaign didn't run.

Source: *Organ Donor Recruitment. Life after death – the difficult business of signing people up to organ donation.* The Union (2007)

## What we have learned

Public service advertising often faces the challenge of prompting people to do something they aren't already doing but should be. The themes discussed in this chapter yield ten questions you might care to ask if you are hoping to solve a similar challenge.

1. What aspects of the problem can't communications realistically hope to influence?
2. Why, precisely, does the problem occur?
3. Which audience stands to gain most from doing something about the problem?
4. What for them is the 'emotional worst consequence' of the problem?
5. What simple and achievable 'tangible action' do you want them to take?
6. What tone of voice is most likely to empower the audience?
7. How can you depict the problem in a way that's both realistic and general?
8. How can you reposition the problem to make it less easy to ignore?
9. Which partners might you enlist to share your communications?
10. How will your approach balance alarm and reassurance?

## Notes

1. Green, L. (2005) *Advertising Works and How*. Henley-on-Thames: World Advertising Research Center.
2. Source: Blood Donation – new strategy, new blood. The Bridge, 2005.

# Chapter 2

# Reducing negative behaviour

 By Alison Hoad
RKCR/Y&R

The government is the only advertiser in the UK that aims to get people to stop, as well as to start or continue, doing something.

Every other media pound in Britain is spent on *motivating* people to do something, whether that be eating M&S melt-in-the-middle chocolate puddings, drinking Stella Artois or taking out health insurance with BUPA. A lot of government money is also spent on motivating people, be it to join the Army, to learn to read or to pay for a TV licence. The exceptional ability of advertising to motivate people to do these exact things (and many more besides) is detailed in a wealth of IPA cases.[1]

The cases discussed in this chapter are special because they aim to demotivate people from doing things – be that smoking, drink-driving or using illegal minicabs at the end of a night out.

## What's in it for me?

For people who were motivated by one of the campaigns mentioned above, there was clearly something in it for them. The M&S food campaign promises sheer indulgence, the Stella Artois campaign conjures up the provenance of Provence to reassure the drinker that they have made a discriminating choice, and the army recruitment campaign motivates people to join by explaining that its training opportunities equip people for careers beyond the army (see Figure 1).

In stark contrast, public health and safety campaigns have to encourage people to change their behaviour when often there doesn't appear to be much 'in it' for them – nothing immediate or concrete, that is, because the benefit is somewhat invisible. It is the avoidance of harm, not even actual harm, but potential harm. So even when people do stop their risky behaviour, they don't actively experience the benefit. They'll never know *if* they would have got cancer from smoking, got raped *had* they taken an illegal minicab home or caused an accident *if* they had driven under the influence of alcohol.

## Motivational vs demotivational ads

What makes the *demotivational* task even tougher is that not only is the benefit 'invisible' but in many cases so is the danger. People often don't believe the behaviour is risky or, alternatively, don't think the danger will befall them. We all know of relatives who have lived to be a hundred and smoked several packs every day of their life, or friends who have regularly had unprotected sex and never even caught a cold. The danger often isn't seen to be a clear and present one.

Another challenge is that often what constitutes risky behaviour in the clear light of day feels less so when people are in a less rational state – after a few drinks, at the end of a night out or in the heat of a passionate moment.

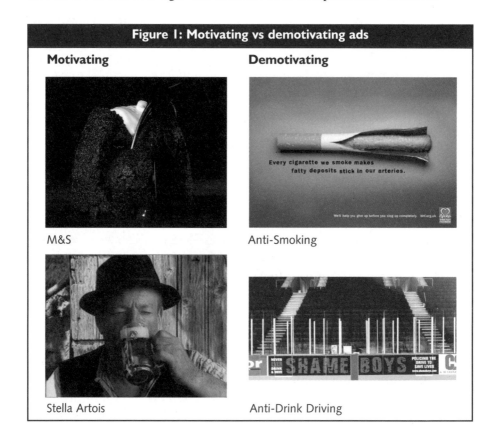

**Figure 1: Motivating vs demotivating ads**

| Motivating | Demotivating |
| --- | --- |
| M&S | Anti-Smoking |
| Stella Artois | Anti-Drink Driving |

So for all sorts of reasons, getting people to stop doing something that is potentially harmful to them and/or others is a big ask.

There are many lessons from conventional – or what can be termed *motivational* – advertising that can be applied to *'demotivational'* advertising. However, there are also some general challenges and learnings that are unique to demotivational communications, and that is what this chapter covers. There are no 'one size fits all' answers and many campaigns play off one or two of these 'lessons', which are simply observations on what seems to have worked.

## 1. How to get people to listen to a 'don't do' message (without it being counterproductive)

Luckily we are not automatons. Just because we are asked not to do something it doesn't mean that we won't. In many cases, the very notion of being told not to do something can make people switch off. Or it can actually make them want to do it more. That is what can be called the paradox of keeping off the grass (Figure 2).

**Figure 2: Keeping off the grass paradox**

If you have ever observed young children you will know that when they are told not to do something they rarely concur in the first instance. If they did then the phrase 'How many times do I have to tell you?' would not be as well known as it is today. As children become aware that they are a distinct being, they push barriers and use naughty behaviour as a way of exerting their independence. This rebellious urge can be very contagious. Tell a toddler not to put his food dish on his head and chances are he, and any other children he is with, will all put their food dishes and cups on their heads. The rebel reflex only intensifies with age. Teenagers may actively flaunt their disobedience, playing truant or collecting an Anti-Social Behaviour Order (ASBO) as a mark of honour. Or they may go underground, telling parents they don't smoke or do drugs only to find ways to do so when authority figures are not there. If you think this response is limited purely to young children or rebellious teenagers, ask yourself how often you have wanted to disobey the signs shown in Figure 3 simply because they were there.

Figure 3: 'Don't' signs

So any communication that aims to stop people doing something needs to take account of the fact that unless it's tonally right it could fail at the first hurdle and be actively screened out and rejected. And when developing communications for younger people it is even more critical that it doesn't fall into the ASBO trap of creating the opposite effect, ending up as a subject of ridicule, only serving to make a group feel better about the behaviour they are engaged in.

The following sections offer some suggestions on how to overcome the paradox of keeping off the grass.

### Condemn the action not the audience

Child psychologists advise that when disciplining children it is important for their self-esteem and learning that you condemn the behaviour rather than the child. So Tom isn't a bad boy when he throws his plate of food but it is bad to throw food. Smoking and smokers are a relevant parallel here. As intolerance grows, smokers expect to be treated as outcasts and bombarded by threats and statistics.

# Case study: British Heart Foundation
**How advertising helped to get 'under the skin' of hardened smokers**

## The problem

The British Heart Foundation (BHF) needed to find a new way to reach the rump of hardened smokers who had become desensitised to previous campaigns. These were the 'multi-quitters' who had tried, but failed, to give up three times or more. They were more than open to cessation communication, but while they heard it, they didn't listen. This was, to a large extent, because they felt got at: treated as pariahs by lecturing and huge, scary statistics. They could spot an anti-smoking lecture a mile away and would easily zone it out.

## The solution

The BHF's next campaign warned smokers of the ever-present danger of breakaway blood clots. It had a scary statistic: that a blood clot kills another smoker every 35 minutes. But it eschewed the expected shock tactics or telling off. The advertising portrayed regular, seemingly healthy people in regular, everyday smoking scenarios … unaware of the sinister blood clot moving under their skin, getting ever closer to their heart. The cigarette, not the smoker, was the enemy. Smokers were lulled into a false sense of security by the feel-good popular song 'I've got you under my skin'. The BHF was presented as the smoker's friend – simply there to help, not to chastise.

## The effect

This less censorial approach meant the campaign's multi-quitter audience did not zone out. Some 83% were aware of the campaign and more than half saw three or more elements. A total of 63% strongly engaged with the TV, with one-third agreeing they were 'completely drawn to it'.

During the campaign, awareness of the BHF as a place to help increased by 50%. In total, 225,000 people contacted it for help (two and a half times more than during the earlier Fatty Cigarette campaign). Most importantly, however, 17% of the target audience who saw the campaign gave up smoking. In contrast, only 11% of the target audience who hadn't seen the campaign gave up. It is estimated that the campaign helped to save over 5,400 lives (which means that, in purely economic terms, the campaign paid for itself more than 600 times over).

Source: *British Heart Foundation – How advertising helped to get 'under the skin' of hardened smokers.* Lowe & Partners (2006)

The British Heart Foundation decided to make the cigarette the enemy, not the smoker. By adopting the tone of a helpful ally rather than a disdainful judge, it gave smokers hope.

Its campaign communicated the ever-present danger of breakaway blood clots that can cause a heart attack at any time. It had a scary statistic – that a blood clot kills another smoker every 35 minutes – at its core. However, because it eschewed traditional shock tactics in the way it delivered this statistic, before they even knew it smokers were engaged in the campaign.

It did not portray someone on their deathbed but instead just regular people, seemingly healthy (even beautiful) in regular everyday smoking scenarios. It is the cigarette that is vilified, as the smoker is seen to be unaware of the clot that moves under the skin, moving ever nearer to the heart and a heart attack.

It took a feel-good, popular song about love and longing and twisted it to refer to heart damage (Figure 4).

**Figure 4: British Heart Foundation –
'I've got you under my skin' campaign**

Voice-over music: *I've got you under my skin. I've got you deep in the heart of me. So deep in my heart that you're really a part of me … I'd sacrifice anything come what might … In spite of a warning voice that comes in the night and repeats, repeats in my ear. Don't you know, you fool, you never can win. Use your mentality, wake up to reality. But each time I do, just the thought of you. Makes me stop before I begin. 'cause I've got you under my skin.*

Not only did this campaign persuade people to stop smoking it also positioned BHF as the smoker's friend, increasing awareness of the BHF as a helpful organisation by 50%.

Tobacco control or tobacco education (the official terms for anti-smoking) is an area that requires more than one communications approach, given that 76% of smokers want to give up for more than one reason. The BHF campaign is only one of a number of campaigns that have successfully tackled smoking and more are discussed in Chapter 8. The National Health Service (NHS) campaign detailed there uses heart-wrenching testimonials from dying smokers to lay bare the terrible consequences of smoking; another from Cancer Research UK condemns the tobacco industry for using misleading descriptors, such as mild or light, when in effect these cigarettes are no less harmful. Yet whether these campaigns are employing surprise, empathy or contempt, the one strand that unites all of them and underlies their success is that none of them condemns the smoker.

## *Pick your moment*

I have discussed why it is imperative that any public health and safety warning overcomes the natural instinct to close down or counter a 'don't do' message. Media choices are crucial in ensuring people are in the right frame of mind to listen and, ideally, act.

At its simplest, just as a zoo wouldn't put a 'Please don't feed the animals' sign on its outside gates (choosing instead to place them by the animals' enclosures), there will be places that are particularly relevant for 'don't do' messages.

When Transport for London ran a campaign highlighting the dangers of using illegal minicabs it developed a 'Point of Prey' media strategy that ran

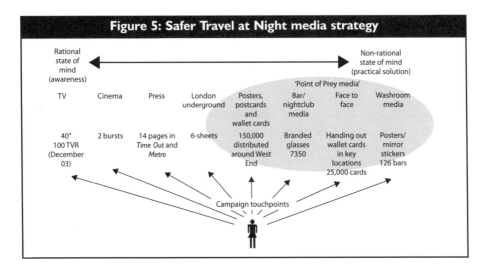

Figure 5: Safer Travel at Night media strategy

alongside broadcast media choices of TV and cinema plus posters. Broadcast media were designed to change attitudes towards touts. Point of Prey media were used in environments increasingly close to the decision-making point when women were more likely to make irrational choices (see Figure 5). It was designed to offer a practical solution to the problem since it gave information on safer ways of getting home.

## Case study: Transport for London
### How advertising was the catalyst for a sharp reduction in rape and sexual assaults by illegal minicab touts

### The problem
In the year leading up to October 2002, 212 women in London reported that they had been sexually abused by opportunistic, illegal minicab 'touts', using their minicab as an easy way to lure women into their car. Some 54 of these women were raped. Of course these are reported figures; the Home Office estimates that in reality more than 400 rapes took place.

Despite the introduction of a range of Safer Travel at Night initiatives (which expanded night bus and fully-licensed black cab availability, and introduced tighter regulation and policing of minicabs), there had been an increase in the number of minicab-related sexual offences (Home Office/BCS).

Research with the police and on the street indicated there were three main reasons why women continued to risk their safety in illegal minicabs:

1. lack of viable alternatives
2. ignorance – trusting that a minicab driver is legitimate, simply because he says he is
3. impaired judgement – a combination of alcohol and tiredness and the need to get home was causing women to take risks they wouldn't take under ordinary circumstances … 'It won't happen to me.'

### The solution
The solution lay in alarming women into realising that touts are not legitimate, regulated minicab drivers and that *anyone* could be behind the wheel: 'Know what you're getting into.'

▶

Broadcast media (TV, cinema) plus posters were used to change women's attitudes to touts when they were in a rational frame of mind. But to make the message stick at the moment of truth, when women were about to make the rash decision to use a minicab, it was crucial to employ 'Point of Prey' media that offered practical advice on safer ways to get home. Figure 5 explains this approach in detail.

## The effect

The number of women using illegal touts fell by 66%. The illegal minicab share of the night travel 'market' fell from 26% to just 10%.

Calls to Transport for London during late-night hours increased by 14% (in contrast to calls during daytime hours, which fell by 9%), suggesting women were looking for alternative means of transport home.

Most importantly, in the first year of the campaign, there were 85 fewer reported sexual assaults by illegal minicab drivers than during the previous year. There were 12 fewer reported rapes. By persuading women to find alternative ways of getting home, the campaign had given predatory touts less opportunity to attack.

This reduction in minicab-related sexual assaults occurred during a period when crime was on the increase and when more people were going out at night.

Reducing minicab-related sexual assaults involves seamless coordination between various organisations, all of which are crucial in making London a safer place in which to travel at night. But while other factors helped facilitate change, the paper shows that advertising was the crucial catalyst to changing women's attitudes to touts and encouraging them away from illegal minicabs and towards safer options.

The real 'cost' of a sexual assault is incalculable. Nevertheless, demonstrating financial accountability is essential to securing future funding for fighting this crime. Based on Home Office cost-of-crime statistics, it is estimated that the £820k investment behind the campaign paid for itself more than 13 times over.

Source: *Safer Travel at Night – 'Know what you're getting into'*. TBWA (2004)

Similarly the Health Education Authority (HEA) campaigns warning people of the dangers of sexually transmitted diseases have used 'Point of Shag' media alongside more broadscale media.

When picking your media moment it's worth considering whether it would be more powerful if the advertising were consumed by an individual, a couple or a group. HEA campaigns encouraging people to use condoms are interesting to look at, often successfully employing a media strategy that ensures couples see the campaign together.

This is an area that's worth a closer look and Chapter 7 looks solely at the successful deployment of innovative media thinking.

### *See the issue through their eyes*

Nearly all the cases you'll read about in this chapter look at behaviour (be that drink-driving, driving too fast or smoking) through the eyes of the target audience. Nowhere is the power of doing this writ larger than in the HEA drugs education campaign that ran in the late 1990s, which is discussed in greater detail in Chapter 5, with examples from the campaign. This campaign is an excellent illustration of how advertising was able to persuade young people to stop taking drugs precisely because it looked at drugs from young people's point of view.[2]

This allowed the HEA to understand that the problem wasn't what the outside world thought it was – a combination of evil drug pushers and a social pressure to conform. It was that when young people, by nature curious to try new things, weighed up the pros and cons of drug use they didn't really know much about the drawbacks so didn't perceive a risk. The role for advertising was simply to equip them with the facts and let them draw their own conclusions.

This empathy with the audience, the ability to understand that they made their own decisions, ensured the campaign didn't adopt a parent–child attitude that would have been counterproductive. Instead it treated the audience as equals, presenting a balanced overview of the pros[2] as well as the cons of drug usage, and wrapped up the idea with the line 'Know the score'.

### 2. Make the invincible feel vulnerable

*We see things they'll never see.*
*You and I we're gonna live for ever.*

So sang Oasis on their debut album *Definitely Maybe*. It's a truth that when it comes to public health and safety campaigns one of the biggest challenges is that people feel immune to the risks. Behavioural theory and indeed common sense tell us that, for people to change their behaviour, they must first and foremost *feel susceptible to the threat*.[3] Here are some strategies that have successfully made people feel susceptible.

## *Make the moment of invincibility the moment of vulnerability*

We have all heard of Pavlov's dogs but may be less familiar with his theory of the conditioned response. At its simplest, Pavlov's dogs would salivate when hearing a bell because Pavlov had rung the bell every time they ate so they *associated* food with the bell. By the end of the experiment the *association* was so strong that the dogs would salivate when they heard the bell even if food wasn't present.

There are a number of campaigns that seem to work in a similar way because they *associate* a very physical sense of danger or revulsion with the behaviour they are trying to stop.

First, let's return to the British Heart Foundation and to 'Fatty Cigarette', the predecessor to the 'Under my skin' blood clot campaign. Like 'Under my skin' it sets out to be anti-cigarette rather than anti-smoker but was much more shocking in its approach.

The campaign inextricably links cigarettes with the damage they cause to arteries, using the similarity in shape between the two to graphically portray the build-up of fatty deposits caused by smoking. The television ad used the iconic imagery of fat dripping from a cigarette (while the smoker nonchalantly

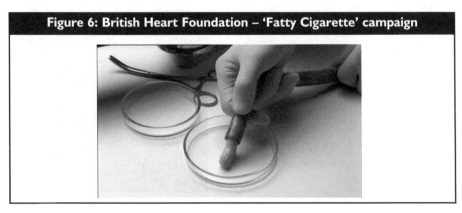

**Figure 6: British Heart Foundation – 'Fatty Cigarette' campaign**

With kind permission of Mike Parsons, photographer.

47

continued smoking unaware) to create a visceral response of revulsion among smokers. In doing so the campaign became 'portable' so that every time a smoker sees a cigarette they can't help but think of the fat collecting in their arteries, thus creating a Pavlovian response.

Second, let's revisit the Transport for London campaign, which aimed to stop women taking illegal minicabs home. The campaign had to persuade women to choose a less convenient form of transport, at a time when they were least likely to make a rational decision. The Point of Prey media strategy has already been discussed. It got the message as close as possible to that decisive moment where a woman might get into a tout's car – a moment when she feels invincible (believing it won't happen to her). In reality, however, this is her moment of vulnerability.

The creative idea dramatises this vulnerability by depicting the moment from the driver's point of view. It shows a harmless-looking guy who shockingly reveals that he is a convicted sex offender before innocently offering an unwitting woman a ride. It then informs the viewer that in the last year 200 women were sexually assaulted in illegal minicabs before finishing with the line 'Know what you're getting into'.

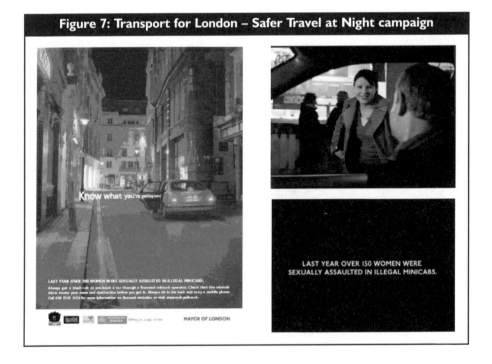

**Figure 7: Transport for London – Safer Travel at Night campaign**

This shocks the female viewer and that very real sense of danger is henceforth associated with the situation of a tout offering a ride. It dents your belief that it wouldn't happen to you and therefore makes it hard to accept a ride from a tout without feeling a shiver of fear.

Lastly, the recent alcohol-harm campaign from the Home Office also created a sense of physical fear that it associated with the invincible feeling of extreme courage you get when heavily under the influence.

The ad shows a typical city scene at closing time as the pubs empty. A drunken girl lets go of some balloons, which drift up to the top of a tall building. A rubber-clad Batmanesque superhero arrives on the scene and performs a series of physical feats, clambering up scaffolding to get to the top of the building. He then reaches for the balloon and, as he slips and falls, you see him as he really is, not as he (under the influence) sees himself. The reality is that he's a drunken young man hurtling towards the ground and sudden death. Cleverly the voiceover gets people to identify with the unavoidable truth that alcohol 'makes you feel invincible when you are at your most vulnerable' and it ends with the line 'Know your limits' (see Figure 8).

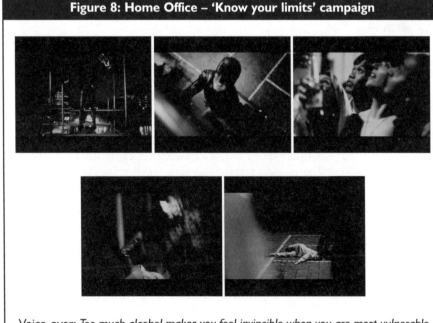

**Figure 8: Home Office – 'Know your limits' campaign**

Voice-over: *Too much alcohol makes you feel invincible when you are most vulnerable.*

With kind permission of Ian Kay, stunt performer.

*Make people feel responsible for the vulnerability of others*

When the Department of the Environment Northern Ireland was developing a campaign to combat drink-driving it identified that its target, namely young men were most pront to the 'invincibility syndrome'. In the main they were responsible and didn't plan to drink and drive, but on occasions did so when faced with the choice of ending their fun or not. They didn't see themselves as heavy drinkers, always believing that they could manage their drink. Consequently, they almost invariably under-estimated the amount they drank while over-estimating their ability to handle it.

Research showed that a key trigger for them was the death of a child. It was a much greater prompt to modify their behaviour and interrupt their invincibility syndrome than the suggestion that they could kill themselves, partly because of the guilt it would cause and partly because of the personal shame that would be heaped upon them by others.

## Case study: Northern Ireland
### How advertising helped to stop people drinking and driving

### The problem

Northern Ireland has the highest levels of road traffic fatalities and injuries in the UK. It's a problem that costs the economy around £450 million a year.

Between 1995 and 1999, driver alcohol was the second biggest killer on Northern Ireland's roads, accounting for 15% of all road deaths. Some 94% of alcohol-related road injuries were caused by men. More specifically, 17–24-year-old men were six times more likely to cause a fatality than the average driver. They were the core audience for the campaign.

These young male 'chancers' were driven by having a good time, believing they would live for ever. Perhaps surprisingly, they were pretty responsible in their pursuit of fun – never intending to drink and drive. They post-rationalised their behaviour on the basis that it was neither premeditated nor excessive, and that any risk was outweighed by their (alcohol-infused) confidence in their ability to handle a couple of drinks on one-off occasions. They weren't drunks. They were invincible. What could possibly go wrong?    ▶

## The solution

If they couldn't be made to feel responsible for themselves, then young male 'chancers' needed to be made to feel responsible for someone else who was more vulnerable. Research indicated that the death of a child was a much greater motivation to modify behaviour than the suggestion they might kill themselves, in large part because of the personal shame that would be heaped on them by others.

The advertising deliberately captured the confident yet seemingly moderate behaviour of the audience – but to devastating effect. A little boy is crushed to death by a car driven by a seemingly ordinary bloke who'd lost concentration after just one pint of post-football beer. It ends with the line 'Never drink and drive. Could you live with the shame?'

An 'intervention' media strategy intercepted potential drink-drivers at key seasonal periods – pre-Christmas and summer as well as key dates such as St Patrick's Day or high-profile football matches. Media were deliberately planned to interrupt the audience at their most vulnerable moments, either just before or while they were out having a good time. ▶

## The effect

There was near-universal awareness of the campaign. Just over a year after it launched, an astonishing 94% of 17–24-year-old male drivers were aware of it.

More importantly, it modified attitudes and behaviour. A year into the campaign, 52% of the audience agreed they could not drink any alcohol without their driving being affected – a 68% increase compared to pre-campaign statistics. The number of drivers who believed they could drink more than one unit of alcohol without it affecting their driving halved.

And, most importantly, fewer people died. Fatalities caused by driver/rider alcohol dropped from 43 to 24. The number of fatalities caused by 17–24-year-old men fell by 40%.

The paper shows how the 'Shame' campaign was by far the strongest factor in changing behaviour – stronger than the influence of the police, politicians, celebrities, journalists, press coverage, TV programmes, technical experts, doctors and even victims of road accidents.

Source: *Anti-drink driving – 'Shame' campaign.* Lyle Bailie International Limited (2002)

Many other campaigns have shown that making people feel responsible for other people's vulnerability can be a powerful trigger. People have been persuaded to wear seat belts in the back of the car, not because it will save their own life but the life of the person in front of them, and smokers have given up smoking because of concern for their families if they were to die from cancer.[4]

### *When ignorance is bliss, the truth acts as a wake-up call*

A number of the campaigns we've looked at use facts to wake the audience up from their presumed invincibility, be it the number of assaults committed in illegal minicabs, the dangers of drugs, or the likelihood of experiencing blood clots or fatty arteries as a smoker.

The more surprising the fact, the more powerful it will be. A compelling example of this was the Department for Transport campaign to stop people driving above 30 mph in areas where this was the speed limit. The issue here wasn't that people think they can be speed junkies and get away with it, they just didn't see driving above 30 mph as either speeding or reckless driving – that's reserved for lunatics who charge down the motorway at crazy speeds or drivers who have no concern for others. So for different reasons they too were immune to the risks posed by their behaviour.

The Department for Transport overturned this opinion and made people feel not just vulnerable but culpable, with a simple fact: if a child is hit by a car travelling at 40 mph they are much more likely to die, whereas if the car is moving at 30 mph the chances are they will live. The ad dramatised a child being hit by a car and killed and then coming back to life again, ending with the line 'It's 30 for a reason' (Figure 9). In doing so it makes the hitherto 'invisible' risk of driving above 30 and 'invisible' reward of obeying the speed limit readily apparent. And instead of a speed limit sign being just another law, just another thing we're told to do (like keeping off the grass), it becomes a reminder of the harm you can do if you drive above 30.

### Figure 9: Department for Transport – '40 can kill' campaign

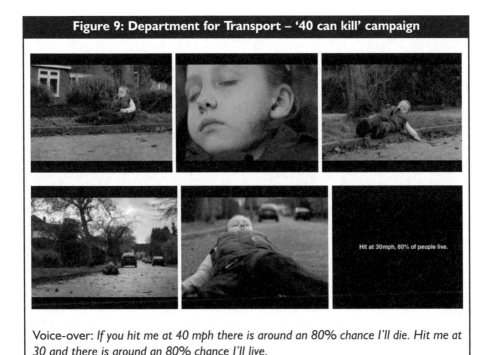

Hit at 30mph, 80% of people live.

Voice-over: *If you hit me at 40 mph there is around an 80% chance I'll die. Hit me at 30 and there is around an 80% chance I'll live.*

*Accept people feel invincible and move the debate to a place they don't*

There are always, however, different ways of skinning a cat. The insightful approach of the Home Office to making people feel vulnerable to the risks surrounding chip pan fires may still hold lessons for us today, over 25 years on.

## Case study: Home Office
### How advertising helped to reduce chip pan fires

### The problem

In 1981, 21 deaths and 1,372 injuries were caused by 15,000 chip pan fires. Chip pan fires were also the biggest cause of domestic fires and resulted in over £8 million of property damage and significant cost to the taxpayer, in the form of fire brigade and police resource and NHS support services. This was only the tip of the iceberg as 95% of chip pan fires went unreported.

The obvious solution seemed to be to prevent accidents happening in the first place. But this was easier said than done.

- Although deep frying was extremely common, most people had never experienced a chip pan fire. Most accidents were just that – an aberration from normal behaviour, probably caused by misjudgement (accidental overfilling) or distraction (being called away to answer the door, being in a hurry, etc.).
- People were unwilling to believe that accidents would happen to *them*: they knew chip pans were a potential hazard and believed they always took great care when using them. Accidents happened to 'other' people who were more 'careless' or 'stupid'.

### The solution

The solution lay in moving the debate to a place where people felt less confident.

There was a great deal of ignorance about what to do in the event of a fire and uncertainty about whether, in the heat of the moment, the individual would do the 'right' thing or simply panic. A containment strategy seemed to hold more potential. Moreover, demonstrating how to cope with a chip pan ▶

fire was a possible way to address the prevention issue. Instead of telling people 'don't do this because it might cause an accident' (which would be rejected for the reasons outlined above), the advertising could say 'Well, it's happened – unluckily – but here's what to do … putting it out isn't easy, so why not remember how it happens in the first place.' Rather than being accusatory, the advertising could offer advice that was unmistakably reasonable, helpful and positive.

The campaign line encapsulated the strategy: 'Fire: If you don't let it start, you won't have to stop it.' Two commercials were made that ran regionally from 1976 through to 1984. Both showed the cause of the fire and then the simple actions required to put it out.

1. Turn off the heat.
2. Cover the pan with a damp cloth.
3. Leave the pan to cool down.  ▶

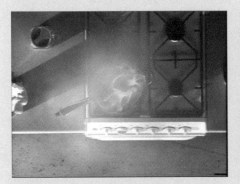

## The effect

Advertising awareness peaked at 90% in advertised regions.

There was no doubt that the advertising increased knowledge of the correct containment procedure: in advertised regions there was a significant increase in understanding of the actions required post the advertising, whereas in non-advertised regions there was no significant change. It also appeared that people were heeding the prevention advice.

1. In regions with advertising, reported chip pan fires were between 7% and 25% lower than in regions without advertising.
2. The number of reported chip pan fires was significantly lower during and immediately after the advertising aired – picking up as advertising memories became more distant.
3. The number of reported fires was higher in regions with lower advertising weights.

A 12% drop in chip pan fires represented an estimated saving of £1 million in property damage alone – excluding the more important benefit of fewer deaths and injuries, and the consequent savings in emergency service and hospital costs.

Source: *Chip pan fire prevention*. Boase Massimi Pollitt (1984)

Instead of telling householders how to prevent chip pan fires, the campaign told them what to do in the event of one. The audience felt pretty immune to the suggestion that they would cause a chip pan fire but felt a lot less vulnerable when it came to their ability to deal with one.

Young smokers can feel particularly invincible to the ills of smoking, believing as they do that they will live for ever. The social allure of smoking is also at its greatest for young and novice smokers, often using it as a crutch to look cool to their friends and the opposite sex. So to make them feel vulnerable the HEA needed to look at the problem differently.

Here's a campaign (Figure 10) that moves the tobacco debate away from health to beauty, which is of course an area where young girls do feel vulnerable.

**Figure 10: HEA anti-smoking campaign – targeting young girls**

And here's a more recent one (Figure 11) that informs people about the disappointing consequences that smoking can have on the male libido, again taking the issue to a place where the young (this time men) wouldn't feel quite so invincible. It's one of the few campaigns that aims to stop people doing something that uses humour.

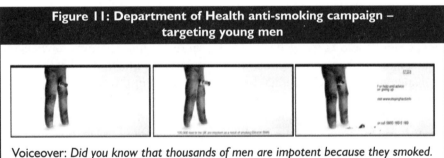

**Figure 11: Department of Health anti-smoking campaign – targeting young men**

Voiceover: *Did you know that thousands of men are impotent because they smoked. Probably not, because they don't like to talk about it. Every cigarette you smoke causes fatty deposits that restrict the flow of blood to your penis and this damage is happening right now. For help and advice on giving up visit stayinghard.info.*

The media strategy targeted occasions where both sexes would see it together, for example at the cinema. When the print ad in Figure 12 was placed in toilets in pubs and clubs, there was additional signage put up in the Gents, informing them that the ads were running in the Ladies too.

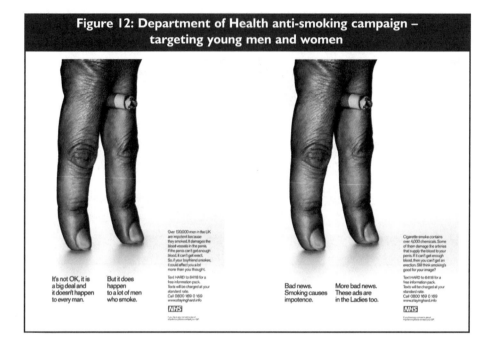

Figure 12: Department of Health anti-smoking campaign – targeting young men and women

### 3. Overcoming barriers to behaviour change

Making people feel vulnerable is however only the first step towards getting them to change their behaviour.

Even when people acknowledge the risks, there are huge barriers to changing their behaviour. Not only are we by nature creatures of habit but there can also be many physical and emotional barriers that stand in the way of people successfully changing their behaviour – for example, a physical addiction to drugs, alcohol and tobacco, the enjoyment factor[5] or an emotional need to conform to a social scene that judges safer behaviour such as condom usage to be uncool.

#### *Be a service provider, not just an information provider*

Many of the campaigns examined in this chapter harness people's good intentions and direct them to a place where they can find the help they need to stop doing whatever it is they want to stop doing. The smoking campaigns direct you to a helpline where people can find out more about the plethora of services the NHS now offers. The Transport for London campaign directed women to a telephone number from which they would be able to access the phone numbers of licensed minicab offices in their area as well as information on night bus routes.

Beyond this, many of the campaigns have acted as a spearhead for broader on-the-ground activities designed to make the desired behaviour change easier. For example, when Transport for London ran the 'touts' campaign it had already increased night bus routes and the number of available licensed taxis with the introduction of night tariffs.

## Reframe the normative beliefs

Many behavioural theorists believe that for behaviour change to occur it is necessary to change normative as well as personal beliefs. For example, some people who have unprotected sex are well aware of the danger but other emotional barriers stand in the way of them using condoms. It's what the Health Belief Model[3] describes as emotional and social costs – namely that people feel embarrassed, uncool or unmanly using them.

Today the embarrassment factor around condoms is a much smaller deal than when the HEA set out to tackle it head on in 1990 (although the need to normalise their usage still exits). The HEA campaign set out to normalise condom use by positioning them as normal everyday items. The first ad showed an everyday woman, Mrs Dawson, going about her everyday job, which just happened to be at a condom factory. Mrs Dawson's remarks imply that more people are using condoms and the ad finishes with the invitation to 'Keep Mrs Dawson busy. Wear a condom.'

A second commercial features a rather elderly Mr Brewster and a condom from his youth, which he affectionately calls Geronimo. We see him remarking upon how uncomfortable it was and musing on how much improved today's condoms are.

These helped to ensure that condoms entered everyday vocabulary, no longer in themselves constituted embarrassment and led to them becoming a more everyday purchase with ever more sales going through grocery stores.

The HEA 'Know the score' drugs campaign that was discussed earlier also changed normative beliefs. It caused young people who believed drugs were not dangerous to realise that there are potential risks. This change in normative belief was explained by the Theory of Reasoned Action (Figure 13).

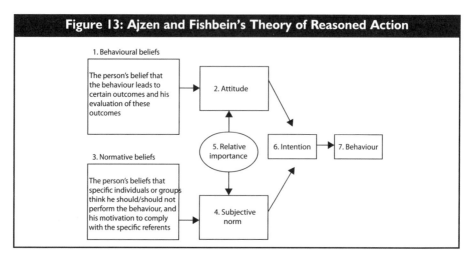

Figure 13: Ajzen and Fishbein's Theory of Reasoned Action

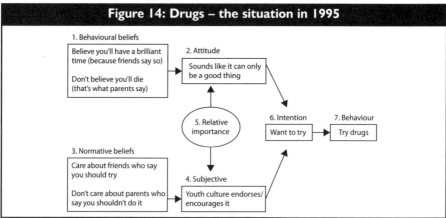

Figure 14: Drugs – the situation in 1995

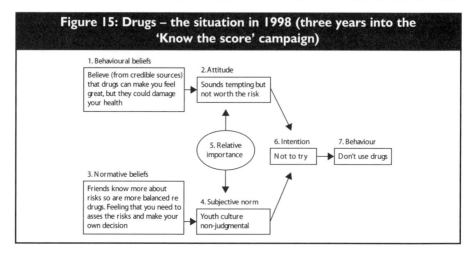

Figure 15: Drugs – the situation in 1998 (three years into the 'Know the score' campaign)

## What we have learned

Asking people to stop engaging in behaviours that could be harmful to them is a big ask. People don't like being lectured at and often don't see why they should stop doing what they do because they don't see the danger or feel immune to it. This chapter has reviewed those campaigns over the past 25 years that have successfully done so. It shows how advertising can demotivate people just as successfully as it can motivate them. It is hoped that, along the way, it has shone the light on some tried-and-tested strategies.

This chapter is by its nature backward looking. But many of its findings are as relevant today as they ever were – some even more so. We live in an increasingly individualistic culture and are more used to having power in our own hands. The 'keeping off the grass' paradox has never been more pertinent nor has the need to empathise with the audience in question. If we fail to see the behaviours through their eyes we fail. Period.

Some of the most pressing problems facing the nation today such as knife crime and anti-social behaviour are emanating from some of our most marginalised groups – how easily the term 'hoodie' has sprung up and how easily it has become a sub-group, set somehow apart from the rest of law-abiding society. If communication is to have an impact with the young disenfranchised it has to see these behaviours through their eyes.

This isn't easy when the media that surround us don't do this. Negative headlines concerning anti-social teenagers have increased sevenfold since 2000 and 70% of all media coverage of teenagers is negative. Look at any newspaper on any given day and you're most likely to read about ASBOs, teenage pregnancy, gang culture or disruptive behaviour.[6]

To look beyond this and to empathise will undoubtedly require innovative research methods and media choices. By looking at the world through our audience's eyes we may find new strategies. Who knows, maybe we'll discover that the best way to help reduce casualties arising from knife crime will be to focus on what to do in the event of one happening, just as the Home Office did with chip pan fires over 20 years ago.

## The search for new approaches

There are other changes afoot in our culture and in our media landscape that future campaigns might harness These are discussed in the following subsections.

### *Multiplying the impact of campaigns through the broader media fabric*

Traditional broadcast as a medium will always have its role in public health and safety campaigns but the web should be an ever more powerful tool. It leap-frogs the paradox of 'keeping off the grass' because it can both enable communication to act as a communal self-help group, and also invite any audience to take on an idea and make it their own.

However, it is possible that many more smart media choices won't even look like a media choice at all – for example, associations with content, brands and experiences that the youth audience trust. Or a campaign that is its own content: Channel 4's *Jamie's School Dinners*[7] persuaded people not to give kids junk food by dramatising the ills that lurked there.

### *Empowering people to change*

We live in a time when people who can motivate and galvanise swathes of the public are celebrated. In an era of personal freedom and empowerment it is politicians like Nelson Mandela, celebrities like Bono and Bob Geldolf, and even self-help gurus like Allen Carr[8] that are our high priests.

Hope and the power of positive thinking are proving persuasive and, accordingly, the dominant brands and their core philosophies are unashamedly can-do, from Honda's Power of Dreams, to Boots' quest for the British public to Change One Thing, to the campaign to Make Poverty History.

This feels emotionally out of step with many of the campaigns we have looked at thus far, which have mostly used negative triggers: the envisaged shame of killing a child, the visceral repulsion of fatty arteries, the shock of getting into a sex offender's car, the fear of falling to your death while under the influence. These are serious issues, and shock and fear are often successfully employed to wake people up to their vulnerability. But perhaps there could be a more constructive path every now and again?

We could learn from some of the self-help gurus, most of whom encourage people to think about what success looks like. Allen Carr's Easyway clinics encourage people to focus on the deeper reasons why they smoke rather than focusing on why they shouldn't. The clinics aim to channel the smoker's will against the cigarette rather than leaving them with a conflict of wills.

It seems Nicorette has successfully modelled its advertising on this approach.[9] It dramatises the battle in a way that makes the audience feel they can win the war on smoking one cigarette at a time. Its main trigger is the pride people feel in themselves for giving up, as opposed to the fear of the consequences if they should fail. It has a positive and confident tone.

### *Supporting people in their behaviour change*

Advertising is only the tip of the iceberg in bringing about behaviour change. Massive progress has already been made and all the recent campaigns examined here had broader elements to help people make the desired change to which the campaign directed them.

However, I suspect we have much to learn from the likes of Alcoholics Anonymous in terms of harnessing the strength of others who are trying to change the same behaviour. Certainly the digital world we live in and the extraordinary phenomenon of social networking should make this a viable option for future initiatives and campaigns.

We have seen a shift from information providers to service providers, and the next step may well be providing the forums and tools to enable people to help, support and mentor each other.

## Notes

1. The cases mentioned can be found in the IPA Awards 2004 and 2006.
2. It was the first campaign to acknowledge there were positive effects of drugs.
3. The Health Belief Model (Rosentock, Strecher and Becker) states that to change their behaviour individuals must have sufficient concern about health issues and believe that: they are susceptible to the illness and hence perceive a threat; illness could be avoided with appropriate behaviour change; and behaviour can be changed with an acceptable cost.
4. Figures 8–12 are from government campaigns but have not been submitted case studies and have not been published in the IPA Effectiveness Awards or on warc.com.
5. More than 40% of smokers agree that 'I don't think I could give up smoking because I'm addicted.' BMRB, 1999.
6. *Make Space*, Youth Review, 2007.
7. *Advertising Works 15*.
8. Allen Carr's *The Easy Way to Stop Smoking* has been a best seller since it was first published; it has been translated into 25 different languages and there are 40 Easyway clinics across the world.
9. *Advertising Works 15*.

# Chapter 3

# Encouraging law-abiding behaviour

 By Charlie Snow
DLKW

Government communications are often described as public service campaigns or public information campaigns. This chapter is very much about the latter: the governmental duty to inform the public about something they have to do because the law says so. The more formal description is communications to encourage 'compliance'.

There have been many compliance campaigns delivered through the UK's Central Office of Information over the years; recent examples would include telling people that they must get a Tax Disc for their car, must take part in the Census, must follow the new Disability and Age Discrimination Acts, must get an Energy Performance Certificate if they plan to sell their house, or that they must not smoke in public places any more, because they are legally prohibited from doing so.

Many law-abiding citizens are quite happy to go along with the law, and do what they are told. But most of us living in a free society find it hard being told what to do, however sensible it might be. Despite the fact that over three-quarters of the public supported the recent 'Smoke Free' legislation in England, some influential figures complained openly about the unfairness of it – David Hockney has given the law a right going over in the media; and some flout it quite openly – Keith Richards made his point by lighting up on stage at a recent Rolling Stones concert.

The word 'compliance' in itself can suggest a sense of weakness – beyond it being 'the act of complying with a wish, request, or demand' it is also a 'disposition or tendency to yield to the will of others'. Maybe that's why people can get so cross.

However, nothing seems to raise the hackles more than being told to pay up for something because the law says so, however justified that law might be. This chapter looks at the tough end of compliance: telling people that they have to pay for the Congestion Charge, that they have to pay tax, and that they have to pay for a TV licence.

What's interesting about these three successful IPA cases is that they focus on compliance at different stages of development:

1.  A whole new thing – Congestion Charge
2.  A new way of doing something – Tax Self-Assessment
3.  A long-term and ongoing issue – TV licence.

Despite being at different stages, there are, however, some similar themes that emerge from these cases that provide useful learning for anyone devising, creating and executing a compliance campaign.

There are also some similarities in the background context.

## The background context for communications: it's tough out there

There are five key contextual issues that these case studies share, along with many compliance campaigns, all of which have implications for communications.

1.  *Unpopularity.* They are unpopular to varying degrees; some, like the Congestion Charge – referred to by one newspaper as 'the work of Satan', face a barrage of antipathy, scepticism and resentment. The recent hoo-hah over Home Information Packs and Energy Performance Certificates is another good example of the type of hurdle these campaigns need to overcome. There tends to be political sensitivity and much media comment surrounding them.
2.  *Myth and misinformation.* Not only do they tend to receive negative comment from the media, they also suffer from misinformation and myth. On the Congestion Charge, the media were talking about 'buying a daily ticket' or 'toll booths'; with TV licences, apparently TV detector vans are few and far between.

3. *Complex subject matter.* All are dealing with complex subject matter. Often there are many messages that have to be deciphered and delivered. Even a Minister has admitted that he needs help with his tax form!

4. *Complex audiences.* All are dealing with complex audiences: both the broad audience and the specific audiences within it. So within the 8 million people that can self-assess their tax, there are the self-employed, higher-rate tax payers, partners, directors, landlords. And within the 6 million London drivers there are those who are exempt from the charge or who receive a discount, including Blue and Orange disabled badge holders, alternative-fuel vehicles, and fleets with 25-plus vehicles. The broad audience needs to be given the general information; the specific audiences need to be given their specific information.

5. *Tendency to play 'ostrich'.* The natural human reaction to having to face up to these issues is to play 'ostrich' – bury your head in the sand, procrastinate and just hope it all just somehow goes away.

All of which says that compliance campaigns need to be clear and calm, deliver accurate information, be simple, cover all audiences with relevant information, and get the information to people even if they don't want to receive it.

These themes will be discussed and expanded upon when exploring best practice for compliance campaigns. We need to answer the following questions:

- When to say something? Timing the campaign.
- What to say, and how to say it? The message, tone and approach to adopt.
- Where to say it? The media to use.

All these areas are important. Thinking about and applying some of the answers to these questions can help in devising successful compliance campaigns, and overcoming many of the difficulties outlined above.

## Three key recommended communication strategies

### *Get the advanced timing right*

Timing of communications campaigns in the private sector is always important – ensuring that what you are advertising is freely available to your consumers. Nothing can be more frustrating to a consumer than being stimulated to go and buy something only to find that it is not in stock. In the fmcg market, advertising campaigns are tightly focused on a time period just after the product has been launched into the trade.

Timing of compliance campaigns is also critical, but much of the energy and focus of communications needs to concentrate very much on the time before the product is launched – that is, *before* the legislation comes into force. Everybody who will be affected by a particular law needs to be aware of that law and have the relevant information fully understood and digested by the time that law comes into force so that they know precisely what to do.

Successful execution of compliance campaigns requires rigorous planning and unfurling of communications before critical dates. In fact, dates can play a key part, and feature prominently, in these campaigns: 17 February for the launch of the Congestion Charge; cut-off dates of 30 September and especially 31 January for tax self-assessment.

But while it's important to go early with communications, it's also important not to go too early, thus losing relevance and momentum.

A strong recent example of the successful timing and roll-out of communications is the 'Smoke Free' campaign in England, which was firmly structured around the key date of 1 July 2007, when the legislation would be enforced. The campaign launched on 12 May, 50 days before the enforcement date. On launch day, the Public Health Minister, Caroline Flint, said: 'With only 50 days to go until England goes smoke free, our aim is to ensure that everyone is aware of the new law, how it will affect them and what they need to do to prepare.' The information campaign gathered momentum so successfully that by the end of June 2007 data showed that 96% of businesses and 95% of the general public were aware of the law, with three-quarters supporting smoke-free legislation.

The Tax Self-Assessment campaign is structured around two key dates: 30 September, before which time HM Revenue & Customs – as the Inland Revenue is now known – will do calculations for you, and 31 January (the cut-off date). The end of January date is of utmost importance as the National Audit Office estimates that up to £300 million would be lost if 10% of self-assessment taxpayers did not file on time. Hence, like 'Smoke Free', the date plays a big part in the campaign, quite literally (see Figure 1).

The London Congestion Charge campaign is probably the finest example of the importance of successfully timing communications for a compliance campaign. Communication campaigns for privatisations proved to be a useful reference point for devising the plan. As with privatisations of public utilities, people had to undergo a steep learning curve, and there would be no second

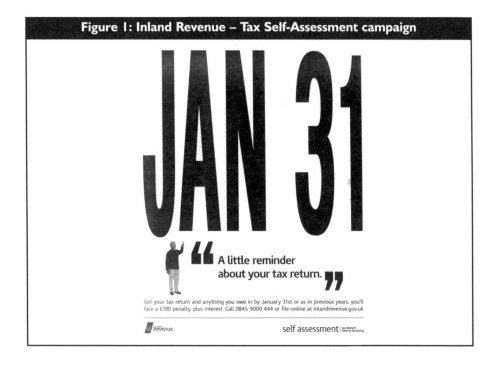

Figure 1: Inland Revenue – Tax Self-Assessment campaign

chance. The British Gas privatisation (well documented in the IPA dataBANK) was used as a model for the gradual unfurling of messages using a broad mix of channels.

The nightmare scenario was that on 17 February 2003 six million Londoners would wake up, read or hear the news reminding them that 'today is the day', phone to find out whether they were affected and thus cause system melt-down. This would have proven a complete disaster as the eyes of the world were on London to see if this unprecedented traffic management system could prove effective.

To ensure that this scenario did not happen, and that the system would work from day one, a rigorous communications programme was put in place. The programme started to unfurl a full three months before launch. It contained many elements that all helped people to self-identify, know whether they were affected, and explain what their options were, in order for them to act in a timely way. In this case, the stakes were upped: it was structurally and com-mercially imperative that people had time to digest the information and act accordingly in advance of the Congestion Charge being officially launched. Interestingly, the paper describes needing to encourage a peculiar combination of inaction (those not affected by the charge, knowing this, and not over-loading the system) and early action (those pre-registering or making other plans well in advance, help to manage the demand on the system).

The campaign encouraged people to follow a journey from Awareness to Understanding to Action or desired Inaction. By the time of the launch date there were 500,000 pre-registrations for payment channels, discounts and exemptions – much of which could be put down to the successful timing and momentum achieved by the communications campaign.

Here is a fuller summary of the Congestion Charge paper.

## Case study: Transport for London
### Making sure it worked on day one

### The problem
This was some challenge – the launch of the largest traffic management system in the world. The date for introduction was set to be 17 February 2003. Communications needed to inform people about what was or was not expected of them; the messages were complex and the targets fragmented. No one had come across this sort of charging system before, and very few people wanted it. The background commentary ranged from the sceptical to the inaccurate to the all-out aggressive.

Crucially, the Congestion Charge had to work from day one. London drivers needed to know exactly what to do, or what not to do, from the day the scheme was up and running or there would be system meltdown. It was as important to address the people who did not need to do anything – non-drivers, drivers outside the charge zone, or those exempt from any charge – as it was to talk to those who would be directly affected. The efficient management of the system was of the utmost importance; unnecessary calls needed to be kept to a minimum. A lot of money, credibility and pride was at stake. Communications were well and truly under the spotlight.

### The solution
A new model of advertising was developed, called the 'Action Briefing Model'. Communications needed to make people aware of the scheme, ▶

understand what was required of them, and then act accordingly.

With a duty to reach as close to 100% of Londoners as possible, a fully integrated communications campaign broke over four months before the February launch date. It delivered manageable bite-sized chunks of information in an accessible manner within a distinctive visual world dominated by the striking 'C' symbol.

## The effect

Two weeks before launch, research showed that awareness of the scheme was at saturation levels, at around 97% among Londoners. Over 85% of Londoners knew they were not directly affected by the scheme (non-drivers, and those exempted and discounted), and this meant they would be unlikely to jam the call centre on day one, thus avoiding system meltdown.

Knowledge of the key facts about the scheme was also strong, with most measures registering above the 80% mark: for example, £5 daily charge, penalty charge, methods of payment, exemptions.

The communications campaign was proven to play a central role in the successful and efficient launch of the Congestion Charge scheme. The campaign's two greatest contributions to making the scheme work from day one were:

1. Over 500,000 pre-registrations for payment channels, discounts and exemptions by launch day, entirely the result of the public information campaign.
2. Promoting widespread adoption of new payment channels; 25% of payments via the internet, 19% via SMS texting, pioneering its use as a transactional channel.

By September 2003 it was estimated that the Congestion Charge was generating net benefits of around £50 million (economic benefits are worth around £180 million, against total costs of around £130 million). This estimated £50 million net annual economic benefit compared with a one-off launch marketing communications investment of £12 million.

Source: *Central London Congestion Charge Scheme – making sure it worked from day one.* TBWA/Fishburn Hedges (2004)

## *Tell it as it is*

### 1. Message

There seems to be a set approach for delivering messages in compliance campaigns – tell it as it is. Public information campaigns are obliged to give the public key facts and dates, telling them what they need to do and when they need to do it. It is their legal duty to provide simple, accurate information clearly and unequivocally. This approach enables the campaigns to counter the myth and misinformation that can be spinning about in the outside world. The aim is to replace any sense of speculation with accurate information.

Those that devised the Congestion Charge strategy describe it as a whole new communications model. It is not the typical communications model of Salience, Persuasion, Involvement, Familiarity/Favourability or Sales; it is the 'Action Briefing Model' – a clear articulation of what people need to know in order to act correctly.

Because of this duty to inform, compliance campaigns tend to be quite straightforward with their creative ideas. There are few big, clever conceptual thoughts that cloud the immediate reading and understanding of the message. More often than not, it's about giving the facts straight, not creating a clever conceit in which facts are in danger of being buried.

This is how the creative approach is explained in the case of the Congestion Charge:

> *In communications terms an 'idea' is a means of capturing people's interest and imagination to sell a product, service or message. We quickly realised that the Congestion Charge itself was the 'idea', a big bold plan that everyone instinctively knew would have a major impact on life in London, getting an instant, often very emotional response, whether positive, negative or simply inquisitive ('How does it affect me?'). We didn't need to create interest or emotional engagement, the Congestion Charge itself did that. Rather we had to deliver a clear and timely briefing on what was involved and how to act.*

Indeed, in some cases it can seem somewhat inappropriate to have clever, conceptual creative ideas in compliance campaigns. The campaign for TV Licensing describes some research that was conducted among students. It suggested that students hate being marketed to; clever advertising is annoying and clearly designed to hoodwink them into something; what they claimed to want was facts presented in a clear and 'no frills' manner, not obscured by any clever executional device.

## 2. Design

In order to achieve cut-through, what these campaigns all share is very strong visual language, proving the value of good art direction and design. We all recognise their simple, uncluttered and distinctive worlds. Two examples are shown in Figure 2.

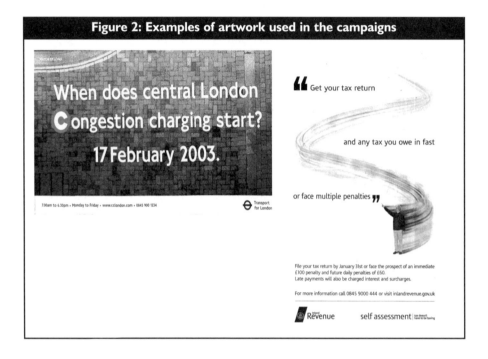

**Figure 2: Examples of artwork used in the campaigns**

We all know the familiar brand worlds, and how they have developed over time: the clean, simple, white world inhabited by Adam Hart-Davis for the Inland Revenue; the road background of the Congestion Charge replaced by the more recent illustrated world, with its strong use of blue. The striking 'C' symbol of the Congestion Charge, which in itself has come to symbolise the brand and the system – a truly simple piece of design that features on all pieces of communication (including the penalty charge!) and has infiltrated all our minds.

It is the design of the campaigns that achieves the branded cut-through and salience, within which relevant and important information is delivered.

It is a similar style of advertising to that adopted by many retailers (think Tesco, Sainsbury's, WHSmith), insurance companies (esure, Norwich Union, Sheila's Wheels) or utilities (British Gas, 118 118). All these examples use strong visual worlds or vehicles to deliver relevant information on their latest deals and product offers.

### 3. Tone

Above and beyond the factual information there are distinctive tones and approaches applied. There seems to be a split in the tone adopted for the well-established issues – for example, TV Licensing – and newer issues – for example, Congestion Charge and Tax Self-Assessment.

Tactics and tone for long-running campaigns tend to get harsher and more severe over time. The tone of all the TV Licensing campaigns is threatening and penalty-heavy, like recent campaigns for vehicle tax and benefit fraud. In all cases, the strategy is to use the improved efficiency of the anti-evasion system as the threat. The focus turns to the inevitability of being caught, and the consequences and penalties as a result. The famous 'Eyes' and 'Aerials' TV Licensing campaigns work to the proposition that 'the detection system is systematic not random'. While the creative strategy gives the appearance of being aimed at deliberate evaders, the approach is designed to frighten potential lapsers into renewal.

Newer campaigns are in a position to take a lighter tonal approach. The Congestion Charge campaign plays a deliberately straight-batted approach. With all the hysteria fizzing around in the media, the campaign aims to be a calming influence. It adopts an approachable, colloquial tone structured around questions – most people's natural response to the initiative: Will there be toll booths? How much is it? How can I pay? It then goes on to provide the clear answers.

There is an interesting journey of information across the four-month period of the campaign before launch. At the outset there are some light suggestions as to the reasons why the charge is being put in place (delivered by the comedian Bob Mills): 'London is not designed to cope with the current volume of traffic', 'Today, the average car travels at the same speed as cars did in 1904', 'The charge is designed to help reduce congestion to school holiday levels all year round'. As the actual launch date comes into being, information on penalties and fines is introduced calmly and clearly as part of the whole mix, although never as a threat. This appears to be a good structure for flighting the messaging: justification messages (within legal bounds) early on, being replaced by penalty messages near the cut-off date itself.

Probably the most interesting paper for tonal guidance is that for tax self-assessment. This was a campaign that underwent a radical shift in tone, all of which proved highly beneficial. Previous Inland Revenue advertising had featured a cartoon character called Hector who was perfectly charming but a bit dull; this was followed up by Mrs Doyle, who literally started to hector us to 'Go on, go on, go online!' – voted one of the most irritating ads of its time.

The brand started to grate and get on people's nerves, as if the whole subject of tax wasn't trying enough! The decision was then made to present the brand in a more supportive manner, recognising that tax forms are intimidating and complex for most ordinary people, who naturally shirk away from them and procrastinate from filling them in and submitting them. The brand has successfully shown itself to understand the human fears, and help overcome them; all of which is beautifully summed up in the campaign line: 'Tax doesn't have to be taxing'. Adam Hart-Davis is there to represent empathy with most people's concerns, and to help overcome them calmly. The humanity of the brand is helped along in the print material with the use of the inverted commas.

## Case study: Inland Revenue/HM Revenue & Customs
### Tax doesn't have to be taxing

### The problem

Many people get a bit sweaty at the very mention of the word tax: it's a short, but complicated word and one that causes considerable resentment. Tax Self-Assessment was introduced in 1997 as a means to make the collection of tax more efficient; in many ways, it makes the process more daunting for people. So, communicating information in this area is a tough business, with a sizable and diverse audience and complex subject matter.

From a business perspective, it becomes even more imperative that communications do their job, and that as many taxpayers as possible file on time, by 31 January and preferably online. The National Audit Office estimated that £30 million is lost for every percentage point of the total audience that does not file by 31 January. So every percentage point, or fraction of a percentage point, matters. In 2001 the number of people filing on time had declined. If that decline continued at the same level it was predicted that the overall percentage would fall to 88.4% by 2005. It was also important to encourage as ▶

many people as possible to file online: it was calculated that £3 would be saved for every return received online.

## The solution

In 2003 a big shift was made in the communications approach. Previous campaigns had been quite hectoring in tone, in danger of entrenching a negative attitude. The decision was taken to adopt a more supportive and reassuring tone – addressing taxpayers' concerns, providing support and hence prompting action.

Adam Hart-Davis was chosen as the enthusiastic face and voice of the campaign, telling people that 'tax doesn't have to be taxing' in a calm and colloquial manner, and providing people with clear information as to what they should do. The simple, clean, stripped-down visual world all helps with cut-through and ensures the messages get through.

The campaign was designed to run in the autumn and new year to coincide with the key filing dates.

## The effect

Data for the campaign (running across the tax years 2003–2005) demonstrated strong advertising awareness, and recognition of the more supportive tone being adopted. Almost half the target claimed that the advertising had directly prompted action, with a more marked effect among last-minute filers.

For the three years of the campaign (2003, 2004 and 2005) more returns were issued than ever before, with levels holding at 90.5%, above the forecasted decline, thus saving the Inland Revenue £159 million over three years.

Online filing increased significantly over the three years; by the end of January 2005 the Inland Revenue was receiving over 30,000 online returns every day. Based on estimates that every online return saves the Inland Revenue £3, the contribution was quantified at £26.1 million as a five-year saving.

So for a total campaign cost of £22.5 million over three years, a return of £8.22 was made for every £1 of investment.

Source: *Inland Revenue/HM Revenue & Customs – Tax Self-Assessment.* Miles Calcraft Briginshaw Duffy (2005)

### *Exploit multi-channel capabilities*

Compliance campaigns tend to adopt a strong multi-channel strategy. There are two key reasons why this is so.

First, because there is such an obligation to reach as many of the target audience as possible, and to maximise the opportunities for people to receive the information, it is critical that all avenues are used; this minimises the number of excuses that can be put forward by the target. Specific channels can of course be chosen to deliver relevant information to specific targets: for instance, direct mail to inform various groups of the discounts and exemptions on offer for the Congestion Charge.

Second, what the multi-channel approach allows is for the breaking up of complex messages into manageable bite-size chunks of information that can be readily absorbed by the audience. Because all the information is important news, there is a natural desire to get it all out there at once. However, this can lead to overload and confusion. All these papers are fine examples of splitting up the information into single headline messages that are easy to grasp and digest, building to a persuasive whole. They do not try to cram it all in together.

There are of course added strategic reasons for using different channels, and the TV Licensing campaigns (national campaign and student campaign) are both fine examples.

The big campaigns from the early 1980s were the first time that a concerted effort was made to coordinate all components of anti-evasion activity and to concentrate these at a localised level, across all media, in order to maximise their effect. The usual national message on BBC television was supplemented by a local campaign – posters, radio, PR in the local press, and the presence of detector vans in the area – to build a real sense of a 'continuous, nagging presence'. The campaign progressed in an area-by-area, month-by-month roll-out over a six-month period.

Equally, the student campaign demonstrates a very effective use of a multi-channel strategy, and a thorough way of measuring its effect. The campaign is aimed at ensuring that students on campus pay for a TV licence. It is designed to provide a sense of a 'blitz' on the ground, again to create the sense of an unnerving presence. Freshers' week was identified as a key opportunity moment, and especially drop-off day when the parents would be accompanying their children. Beyond posters and leaflets in halls of residence, there were application forms in student rooms and libraries, messages on aerial sockets, stands at freshers' week, targeted emails, texts and content on Student union websites. It proved to be a hard message to escape or ignore. An on-campus TV channel was even used to encourage students to create their own content and get the message across.

In evaluating the effect, a multiple 'brick analysis' was used that could split the effect of different channels, ranging from one brick (campuses where the minimum background messaging occurred) to four bricks (campuses that used all channels).

## Case study: TV licensing
### How advertising made a student TV licence 'the norm' over evasion

### The problem

There are approximately 317,000 on-campus student rooms in the UK. Some 45% of students take a television to university. With a TV licence costing £126.50 this means a maximum on-campus opportunity of around £18 million in licence fees. This money is at risk for a variety of reasons: many new students do not know they need a TV licence, many don't want to think about getting one (there are enough other excitements going on), and some simply think 'Sod it! I'm not getting one.'

### The solution

TV licence communications set out to: educate students about the need for a TV licence; to inform them of the consequences of not having one; to convince them of the reality that they will get caught if they evade. The approach is straight and direct. Over the years a multi-channel approach has been adopted, with the aim of high visibility, especially over students' first week at university. Examples of activity include posters and leaflets at drop-off day (when the parents are often in attendance too); messages on aerial sockets in students' rooms; a stand at freshers' week; student TV; and online activity.

Different levels of activity were used across different universities and the learning from each year's activity was applied to the following year's plan. ▶

## The effect

Taking a base level from 2003/4, there was a sales increase of 8% in 2004/5 and a further increase of 24% in 2005/6 with an ROI of 12:1 (10% up on the previous year). This was not due to an increase in the number of students in halls of residence or an increase in the number of students taking TVs into halls of residence. By 2005/6, 94% of students recalled the campaign.

The most interesting component of this paper was the innovative evaluation model applied to the campaign. This was known as the 'brick analysis'. It measured the varying levels of activity used across different universities. Four levels of activity were identified: from one brick – background-level broadcast activity (e.g. UCAS mailings, online ads, PR and trails on the BBC) – to four bricks – the full multi-channel programme.

Analysis of comparative purchase rates demonstrated that the four-brick activity was nearly twice as effective as the one-brick activity.

Source: *TV Licensing – 50 pints or a TV licence?* Proximity London (2006)

## What we have learned

### *Get the advanced timing right*

- Focus your energy on mapping out the delivery of the communications programme while being conscious of the legislative approval process.
- Construct your campaign around key dates.
- Maintain momentum right up to the launch date, and beyond.

### *Tell it as it is*

- Never lose sight of the duty to inform.
- Seek to find simple and distinctive visual worlds, vehicles and constructs to create cut-through, and use them to deliver information clearly and unequivocally. Don't get worked up about needing to create a clever creative concept to engage interest; there is a danger that this can cloud clear communications.
- With new laws and initiatives, aim for a calm, supportive tone; you can fall back on more threatening tones for longer-term compliance issues.

### *Exploit multi-channel capabilities*

- You have an obligation to explore all channels to get the message across to everyone, and to get specific messages to specific target groups.
- Use the multi-channel approach as an opportunity to break your messaging down into manageable, bite-size chunks that can easily be absorbed by the audience.
- As with any campaign, think how you can maximise the effect of communications by the channels you use.

## Conclusion

Compliance campaigns face their own particular challenges and restrictions. Many of them are deemed unpopular. But their duty is to provide people with the right information so that the target market knows exactly what they need to do when a law is enforced. As a result, communications need to be perfectly timed in advance of the enforcement date, they need to provide information clearly and unequivocally in a calm and authoritative manner, and they need to maximise the multi-channel capabilities.

# Part 2

## Identifying the target audience

# Chapter 4

# Recruiting for tough jobs

By Neil Goodlad and Rebecca Munds

Clemmow Hornby Inge

It's a tough job, recruiting for tough jobs. It's not enough for recruitment advertising to simply generate a large volume of responses, though that's frequently the first of many challenges. It must also deliver applicants to a recruitment pipeline, out of which some will emerge as actual employees. The candidates entering the pipeline must apply in the right numbers, they must be of the right quality and they must apply at the right time. Each of these is a Goldilocks amount: not too many, not too few; neither over-qualified nor under-qualified; applying at the right time and not just before or just after. This review explains how this was achieved in a variety of different ways and in greatly varying market conditions.

## Breaking through the barriers

The theme of our review is 'barriers'. All recruitment advertising must overcome the barriers standing between the desired target audience and the job. Frequently, the barriers are manifold. They can be practical, emotional, perceptual, informational and societal. Some perceived barriers are false and the task is to dispel the myth; others are real and must be addressed. Some barriers are practical; some are rooted in deep prejudice. Some audiences need to be informed, some need to be inspired, some need to be cajoled, some need to be reassured. In all cases there is something standing between the potential recruit and the job, which it is advertising's role to help remove or overcome.

We've drawn lessons from nine campaigns (summarised at the end of this chapter): two from the 1990s and seven from 2000 onwards, and we'll return to individual campaigns several times, as each tends to illustrate a wide range of challenges.

### Types of barrier: practical, emotional and advertising-related

Looking back over the long history of successful public service campaigns, a wide range of barriers to effective recruitment can be observed and they can be categorised under three broad headings: practical, emotional and advertising-related.

Practical barriers tend to be governed by the job itself, its requirements, qualifications and application process. The job may be new or drastically changed, or there may be a lack of knowledge about what the job requires day to day, what type of person and qualifications are needed and how one goes about applying. Here, we might say the role of recruitment advertising is, at its most prosaic, required only to announce 'we're recruiting; this is the job and this is the type of person we need', and yet, as we'll see, even such an apparently straightforward message can come with its own unique complexities.

Emotional barriers are the subjective views held by a potential recruit. The job may not be one valued highly by society or it may have low status among the applicant's immediate peer group, and thus not be aspirational. The candidate may perceive problems in themselves or the job that outweigh the advantages, or society may simply have changed and old messages no longer have any traction. This is where the advertising must say 'this is why this job is right for you and why you are right for this job'.

Advertising-related barriers arise where previous advertising has generated its own obstacles, or where a more sophisticated management of media selection, media strategy and response mechanisms is needed to ensure the greatest likelihood of further enquiry by the potential applicant. We're talking about

| Table 1: Types of barrier | |
| --- | --- |
| **Practical barriers** | **Emotional barriers** |
| • New role | • Role carries negative social |
| • Changed role | baggage |
| • Misconceptions about the role | • Peer pressure discourages |
| • Misunderstanding of the | application |
| required qualifications | • Downsides outweigh upsides |
| • Changed demographic and | |
| economic environment | |
| **Advertising barriers** | |
| • Different audiences require different mechanisms/strategy | |
| • Barriers created by previous advertising | |

more than just the functional delivery of messages here – use of media can augment the message, particularly where a new audience or radically new approach is required.

## Practical barriers

Fundamentally, any recruitment advertising has to communicate the existence of the role, its basic requirements and the desired type of applicant for the job, along with how to go about finding out more. The particular task may be to announce a completely new role, or to explain how much a role has changed, or to address a misunderstanding, or to communicate practical information about the application process and requirements. These requirements exist outside of any particular personal or societal attitudes to the role. There may also be practical limitations independent of the recruitment task, such as unfavourable demographics, poor economic conditions or social change.

### *The role may be entirely new and must be announced to potential candidates*

The recruitment advertising for the Police Service of Northern Ireland (PSNI) effectively doubled as launch advertising for one of the key steps in the peace process, namely the replacement of the old RUC, which had been over 90% Protestant and was widely seen as partisan. The 50:50 Catholic/Protestant recruitment target was itself a statement of intent, as the 2002 IPA Effectiveness Paper acknowledged:

> *The ensuing recruitment campaign … set about transforming Northern Ireland policing by encouraging inclusivity and participation in a manner free of sectarian taint.*

Although seeming to give the campaign dual objectives, in fact the positioning of the new force as a new beginning for the region was an essential prerequisite for persuading Catholics in particular to join. It had to be made clear that the organisation recruits would be joining was new in both function and spirit. The campaign was thus as much about demonstrating that the role had changed, as about persuading people of its merits as a career independent of the historical baggage.

Another part of the dramatic reform of Northern Ireland's legal system is the new role of Lay Magistrate. The need for this is described in the 2005 paper as follows:

*The divided nature of Northern Ireland society meant that there were many unique barriers to be overcome. … Lack of inclusion across … society … leads to poor understanding and therefore suspicion. … Thus it was vital that the courts be seen as neutral, independent and fair, made up of ordinary people interested in representing and serving their community.*

The campaign also had to address the assumption that criminal justice was complicated, time-consuming and required specialist knowledge, none of which was true of the lay magistrate role. As with the PSNI campaign, every element of the approach was heavily researched among the public and stake-holders, forestalling after-the-event criticism by inviting everyone to con-tribute while ensuring that every possible banana skin was spotted.

There were multiple barriers here and the advertising approach dealt with the two elements of the campaign separately. In stage 1, the lay magistracy posi-tion was announced, launched and explained while in stage 2 actual applica-tions were invited. The two-stage process was necessary because the position was wholly new, in contrast to the PSNI, for example, which was replacing something else, and where repositioning and recruitment were achieved in a single advertising burst.

### The role may have changed considerably, requiring a recalibration of perceptions by potential recruits

After the Cold War the armed forces faced something of an identity crisis. The need for an army and air force was obvious when facing a great military power, but following the collapse of the Soviet Bloc there were some who asked whether there was a need for armed forces at all. All services were sig-nificantly cut back and something of a crisis of confidence occurred, not least in the face of constant press criticism. The 1996 IPA Effectiveness paper for the Royal Air Force (RAF) notes that:

*… the crumbling of the Berlin Wall, the introduction of glasnost and the collapse of the Eastern Bloc created an absence of tangible military conflict and meant that the immediate rationale for well-resourced and expensive defence capabilities suddenly disappeared.*

The Army paper from 1998 notes that:

*… the ending of the Cold War raised questions about the role of the Army and led to calls for it to be more cost effective … not only did this affect the*

*morale of existing soldiers but also the widespread headlines about redundancies further damaged confidence in the Army as a secure employer.*

The effect of these changes in the political climate was to rob the armed services of the glamour and excitement that had previously served them well, reducing the effectiveness of appeal to patriotism and service, and severing the link with glorious military campaigns of the past. Ironically one of the tasks of the post-downsizing forces' recruitment became to weed out those who were too keen, whose passion for all things military may have been a boon in the past but did not fit well with the new, professional force required.

The Army's new campaign instead focused on excellence, on personal development and on the challenge offered by an Army career. The emphasis was not on what the individual can do for the Army or RAF (and by extension their country), but on what the Army or RAF can do for the individual, reversing JFK's famous Cold War appeal to American patriotism and self-sacrifice, and attracting a different type of candidate.

### There may be misconceptions or misunderstandings about what the role entails

In 1996, the RAF faced an outdated public perception partly due to a long-time exclusive focus on the glamour and excitement of flying aircraft:

> *... throughout the 70s and 80s ... the strategy for aircrew advertising [was] to highlight flying and aircraft, which [was] the main appeal of the RAF to our target group, and to reassure them about their ability to cope ... with the demanding nature of the job.*

This approach worked in the Cold War days but post-glasnost such glamour and self-sacrifice held much less appeal to a new generation concerned to gather career-building skills:

> *... these [potential recruits] had acute concerns about the RAF as a potential career, centred around a lack of understanding about what a career in the RAF would involve ... The key barrier is a lack of recognition of the number of valuable roles within the RAF beyond the stereotypes of pilots and mechanics. The RAF was not seen to offer a suitable career for people not interested in flying.*

The solution was a campaign that addressed these misconceptions head on. It dramatised the multitude of different roles available – from cooks and musicians to weapons mechanics and fighter controllers – and used them alongside more generic executions that communicated the evolving role of the RAF, to focus on the benefits to the individual, under the umbrella strategy of 'personal reward for personal responsibility'. Bespoke career-specific executions ran in relevant trade magazines, addressing the incorrect perception that the RAF is all about pilots, and emphasising the personal development potential of an RAF career.

The Army faced similar challenges, described in both the 1998 and 2004 papers. From 2004:

> ... there was a huge problem created by the relative invisibility of the Army in modern society and the attendant increase in ignorance among civilians. Their main source of knowledge appeared to be folk memories of WWII and the Falklands, as well as modern TV documentaries and Hollywood films ... Myths abounded: you couldn't see your family until you left, you weren't entitled to holidays, your chances of dying were fantastically high, you couldn't have a girlfriend. None of these is true.

The paper goes on to describe a miserable perception of Army life, pictured as arduous field exercises, while being shouted at by sergeant majors. These are described as 'getting in' fears. Equally damaging were 'getting out' fears, the imagined lack of professional qualifications and training and thus post-service employability. The solution described in the 2004 paper is similar to that arrived at by the RAF:

> The answer lay in the fact that skills were learnt in an Army context, probably the most testing environment in which to work. If you could do these things in the Army, you could do them anywhere. Hence the positioning of the Army as 'the ultimate skills provider'.

The creative solution focused on individual trades, but plied within an Army context, emphasising the role of specialists within a team and as part of a larger machine. The endline was 'not your basic training', a thought that encapsulated the personal-skills focus and the nature of the challenge.

On the subject of misconceptions, the Scottish Children's Panel system faced a different type of crisis, described in a paper from 2005. It had so few new applicants as to call into question the viability of the entire system. Research explored perceptions of the Panel system from scratch, seeking to redefine them in a way that could increase both the breadth and depth of its appeal (or, indeed, to conclude that it was beyond saving, had that been the case). This research covered existing Panel members and a wide range of others from all areas of society. The existing local organising committees were heavily involved.

The research uncovered huge misunderstandings about the type of work undertaken by the Panels and the demands made on Panel members, as well as problems in the way it had previously been positioned. The Panel was assumed to be confrontational, dealing with troublesome, challenging children, and to operate on a national basis. When the pastoral (rather than policing) role of the Panel was explained, its local nature emphasised and reassurance given as to time commitments, most of the concerns of potential applicants melted away. The work is not easy and can be traumatic, but the focus on helping children rather than policing them made this seem a worthwhile effort rather than a painful experience.

### *Potential recruits may have no idea, or a misunderstanding, of the required qualifications*

The Scottish Children's Panel not only had too few new applicants of any sort, but those who did get involved were almost exclusively older, middle-class, well-educated women. While not seeking to belittle such stalwart supporters of the scheme, it is essential that such a programme be reflective of the community it is serving. Dominance by one group tends to grow stronger if left unchecked as the group attracts more kindred members and begins to put others off – in essence it becomes homogeneous.

This was exactly what had happened with the Children's Panels, where misunderstanding of the nature of the work was combined with a perception that the role required qualifications, time and expertise likely to be found only in a particular type of person. This left many feeling under-qualified and concerned that their views would not be taken seriously by such an elitist body. Such a concern cannot be addressed entirely by counter-claim: it has to be demonstrated. An emphasis on localness was key to alleviating this: not only did most people not realise that the Panels are unique to Scotland, they did not know that they are locally based. Generation of national pride in Scotland's innovative system and local pride in the work of a local Panel, combined with practical information about the time demands, greatly reduced perceptions of being under-qualified or unsuitable.

### *The demographic and economic environment may have changed unfavourably*

Police, RAF and Army recruitment are all greatly affected by demographic shifts and socio-economic cycles. These bodies primarily draw their recruits from those in their late teens and early twenties, pre-career, pre-family. In times of economic boom, such people have little difficulty getting other jobs, whereas in times of high unemployment, applications to the police and armed forces rise considerably, albeit that such people may not be the most enthusiastic candidates.

The UK has now had a sustained period of economic stability and relatively (in historical terms) low unemployment. It is government policy that 50% of people should stay in education to a further or tertiary level. And there are fewer 18–24 year olds in this generation than ever before, as long-term demographic changes start to bite. These factors all make recruitment much harder for the police and armed forces, greatly reducing the potential pool of applicants, while making those remaining an in-demand target for employers of all sorts. The effect has been to focus on improving the quality of applicants, ensuring a higher conversion rate from applicant to employee, without necessarily increasing the actual number of applications.

All the armed forces offer multi-skills training for the individual as a key selling point, while the Army explicitly describes the acquisition of skills usable once the individual leaves the Army and goes back to civilian life. This helps in the recruitment of ambitious, determined individuals with a focused, self-improvement mindset. The national police campaign, described in the 2002 IPA Effectiveness paper, also sought to improve the quality of applicants through emphasising the demands of the job, in this case with particular attention to the 25% of people who consider a police career at some point and who are thus at least partly open to dialogue. Conversely, one effect of the Army concentrating on skills acquisition is a reduction in applications from those described as 'Army-barmy', whose enthusiasm for all things military does not necessarily chime with the requirements of a modern armed service.

### Emotional barriers

Those are just the practical issues. Persuading potential candidates to apply will also frequently require the removal of various emotional barriers, including the value of the job in society's mind, the perceived response of the recruit's immediate peer group, difficulties or challenges in the job itself and the matching of the role to the hopes and expectations of its potential recruits.

In some cases these are misconceptions relatively easily addressed by information; in others they are seen to be serious institutional flaws in the organisation, requiring a much more significant rebranding exercise, a public repositioning and an internal rallying cry.

### The role may be perceived to carry some societal baggage, such as being seen as low status

By 1998 recruitment of teachers was facing a crisis, as years of negative publicity had damaged the status of the role. Simultaneously, however, the government was calling for a dramatic increase in teacher numbers. Recruitment advertising set out to address the idea that teaching wasn't 'a proper job':

> *Teachers' pay and status have fallen out of kilter with other occupations. Their status is often derided and teaching is seen by many of the well-qualified middle classes as little better than a second-class occupation.*

The advertising went through several phases. First, the message 'no one forgets a good teacher' sought to remind how influential a good teacher can be. This was followed by a campaign demonstrating the difficulty and thus value of a career in teaching, with the line 'those who can, teach', directly confronting one of the more unpleasant anti-teaching sneers. These two phases were aimed at those described as 'born to teach', i.e. who had already considered or were open to teaching, and at improving the status of the job (by 2001 an IPPR survey ranked teaching as higher in status than law and banking). These were people already emotionally attuned to teaching but who were put off by poor societal perceptions. A later campaign phase targeting a wider audience, less ready to embrace teaching, is described below.

This campaign had to effect some major social attitude adjustment to achieve its goals. A perception built up over several decades across many parts of society had to be overturned before the recruitment task could be achieved. Advertising is well placed to address such concerns and the example of teacher recruitment suggests that directly confronting the prejudice can be the best approach.

Police recruitment faced a similar public crisis of confidence in that period. The Macpherson Report[1] into the murder of Stephen Lawrence represented a low point in public perceptions of, and trust in, the police, to the point where perceived lack of respect ranked third, above pay, as a factor likely to put applicants off applying at all.

The approach taken was similar to the repositioning of teaching as a valuable and respected role, in that the creative emphasis was placed on how difficult the job actually is. This had the effect of engendering respect for the role by reminding people just what is required, allowing those inspired by the message to apply with less fear of losing face.

The message was stark, using well-known figures to explicitly state that they did not think they would be up to the police officer's job, drawing attention to the difficult situations he or she will encounter and the impressive qualities required to deal with them. The objective was simple: 'to make 999 out of every 1,000 people realise they couldn't be a police officer, but respect like hell the one who could'. The creative went further, challenging viewers with the question 'could you?', inviting both introspection and a revised perception of those who could. Research indicated that it was the challenge that drove the increase in respect, particularly among those whose personal answer was 'no, I couldn't'.

### Peer pressure may discourage potential recruits from pursuing an interest in a role

The effect of low public confidence in a service is most acute when it goes beyond a perception that a job would not be enjoyable or rewarding and becomes a fear that taking the role would actually damage the way a person is received by their peers. By the late 1990s confidence in the police was so low that one twentysomething research respondent commented that if he joined the police 'my mates would think I've gone soft in the head'. The use of well-known figures being brutally honest acted in part to give that respondent and his/her family confidence that his choice would not be mocked.

A similar dilemma faced those considering becoming a teacher in the face of the middle-class view that teaching was 'not a proper job' and 'those who can do, those who can't teach', sneers directly addressed in the advertising. The campaign sought to address both sides of this perception, reducing it with reminders of the value of teaching and overwhelming it with an emphasis on its pleasures and rewards, to the point of gently mocking the relatively unstimulating 'real' world in the 'headless' TV execution.

We discussed earlier the acute difficulties faced by the Police Service of Northern Ireland (PSNI) in its aim of achieving a 50:50 Catholic/Protestant recruitment split for a service designed to replace the old Royal Ulster Constabulary (RUC), an outmoded institution that was 90% Protestant. Aside from many rejecting the police as an emblem of Britishness, many more would not join because of peer pressure:

*When respondents [to a 1999 survey] were asked what might deter Catholics from joining the police ... 70% said that they feared intimidation or attack on them or their relatives. The next most frequent reasons were pressure from other Catholics (54%) and fear that they couldn't maintain contact with their family and friends (48%).*

The solution required an inclusive message, deft positioning and careful sensitivity to objections:

*The ... campaign steered a steady course through the claims and counter-claims of those opposed to reform. Thoroughly researched and examined in minutiae for political sensitivities ... only after full consultation with key government advisors and RUC personnel did we decide on our creative direction.*

A particular challenge was that: 'Advertising had to have widespread community appeal and a particular focus on the Catholic community, without identifying them openly.'

Careful research as to the key characteristics of the new force ensured that:

*Decisions [were] not based on hunch tactics. The success of this campaign was much too important ... All concepts had to be founded on irrefutable fact.*

For a campaign so politically sensitive, it is essential not just to be balanced and all-inclusive in pinning down the ideal messages, but to be seen to be so.

### *The role may be seen to have downsides, which recruits see as outweighing the positives*

Teacher recruitment had to move into a second, more difficult stage, having first targeted those pre-disposed to teaching (especially new graduates). From 2003 it was necessary to target those still emotionally open to teaching but already embarked on a different career or with serious concerns about teaching as a profession:

*They were potentially interested in teaching, but needed to be convinced about the day-to-day enjoyment of the job ... Research suggested that appealing to their altruism and raising the status of teaching would not work. They knew that being a teacher was difficult and of value, but that didn't motivate them to become one.*

The approach to overcoming this barrier was to emphasise the pure joy of teaching (by showing, for the first time, children in the classroom) while not being afraid also to have a dig at the less stimulating work that potential recruits may instead have opted for. This was a complete change in tactics but was necessitated by the different concerns felt by a new target audience. There was no attempt to disguise the difficulty of the job, rather its delights were emphasised.

A similar strategy informed the national police recruitment campaign, based on the insight that 25% of people contemplate a career in the police at some point, but very few of them ever take the idea further. These were targeted first, a strategy described as getting 'people to consider more' rather than getting 'more people to consider':

> *Advertising needed to force them to consider the Police more actively and in more detail, ultimately making a decision one way or the other.*

This reversed the previous tendency in police advertising (which was all local until this campaign) to entice new applicants with promises of excitement – a strategy that actually oversells the job, leading to the wrong sort of applicant and too many disillusioned officers.

A particular local challenge was faced by Hertfordshire Police in the late 1990s. Proximity to London means that Herts is relatively well-off, with low unemployment, while competition from the better-paid Metropolitan Police also acted to dampen recruitment. It was not enough for Hertfordshire to adopt the national strategy of appealing to those predisposed to a police career; it was also necessary to reach people who had never considered a police career:

> *An important part of the strategy was to position the role as an alternative to office work for 'nine-to-fivers' who may not have considered policing as a career option.*

Research among Hertfordshire police officers and potential recruits revealed that the job was seen differently to the national picture:

> *… it was very different to policing in other areas. Herts did not represent that grim inner-city challenge presented by typical Police recruitment literature and media stereotypes. Rather, it offered the chance to be involved in a genuinely communitarian role with high job satisfaction.*

Research among serving and potential officers emphasised variety, unpredictability, helping the public and real responsibility as key motivators. These coalesced in the line 'no ordinary career' (later evolved to 'a life less predictable') on which the campaign was based. In contrast to the national campaign, 'the [creative work] aimed to create a personality for the force that was friendly, approachable and (where appropriate) light-hearted'. Media usage emphasised the community approach and the 'unexpected' theme (see below). The overall Hertfordshire campaign was significantly different to the national police recruitment campaign – the result of local conditions that required a different target audience.

The challenge for the PSNI was the perception of the police as likely targets for sectarian strife and the very real difficulties of policing the peace. A similar emphasis in the creative work, on PSNI officers in everyday situations, helping the elderly and lost children, rather than pursuing and fighting criminals, helped to position the service in a more positive and motivating light.

## Advertising barriers

Finally, we turn our attention to barriers that are specifically born of advertising. Here it's important to recognise that the successful delivery of a recruitment message depends on the response mechanisms and media strategy as much as the content of the advertising itself. Advertising a role too heavily can seem to pressure potential applicants into a decision that they may prefer to mull over, particularly where a major change or commitment is required. Conversely, too light a campaign may not carry the impact needed to break through deep-seated (mis)perceptions. The method of response must be thoughtfully attuned to the audience too, for example allowing tentative or anonymous initial enquiries.

Different response mechanisms and media strategies are suited to different audiences and approaches.

Hertfordshire Police sought to position themselves as a local, community-focused organisation and used media to emphasise this point as well as to convey creative messages. Local media were the focus, but this brief was interpreted laterally, with posters placed in community centres such as schools, libraries, GPs surgeries and football grounds. Small-sized press ads appeared in different sections of the newspaper to illustrate the claim about a career of variety and surprises. Radio was used to boost the campaign around open days. All material pointed to a bespoke website. Media was used here not only to carry the creative but to demonstrate the core claim.

Scottish Children's Panels sought to attract applicants from a wider spectrum of society than had been the case previously. An innovative campaign ran everywhere from a supplement in the *Scottish Sun* to a revamped welcome pack for new recruits, including case studies of previous panel members. Campaign guides were distributed to local authorities, including artwork and campaign materials that could be adapted for very local recruitment drives. Creative work was developed to run in the sports pages, seeking to reach men, a hitherto untapped audience.

Teacher recruitment went through two distinct phases, each targeting a different group, and media strategy changed accordingly. In phase 1, targeting students predisposed to teaching, 'repeated a single message aimed at the audience from the moment [they] woke up in the morning to the moment they [went to] the union bar toilets at the end of the night'. By way of contrast, phase 2 'used a more sophisticated model of integration that tailored communications along the "customer" journey'. Whereas phase 1 applicants were expected to have decided to go into teaching, phase 2 applicants were more likely initially to be looking for more information, intrigued but not yet persuaded. A phone line (Teaching Information Line) and website answered immediate queries, while events (supported by direct marketing and outbound telemarketing) gave practical help and an opportunity to speak to those already in the profession. Messages tailored to specific concerns – for example, mortgage, family – were also produced.

The renewal of the Army campaign in 2002 led to a revised media strategy, targeting the core 18–24 audience through C4, five and satellite. This allowed for a more sustained presence and higher frequency, rather than the broad coverage of stakeholders typical of the previous campaign. The audience for the 2002 campaign was less convinced as to the merits of the Army and thus more effectively persuaded by a constant drip of information without the perception of pressure and the need for an immediate decision. This also provided scope for the use of 10″ TV ads to run alongside the 30″s ('top and tailing' ad breaks) while easing pressure on call centres vs the previous burst strategy.

### *Historical advertising may have created barriers of its own*

As part of the research into the decline of Scottish Children's Panels, it was found that previous advertising had contributed to the problems identified. It had tended to use sombre black and white images, communicating depression and helplessness rather than caring and inspiration, while words such as 'trouble' and 'challenge' confirmed the perception of confrontation and strife rather than help and support. The advertising had perpetuated the misconceptions that now threatened the existence of the Panel system.

Historical RAF advertising created the perception that the service was all about pilots and that any other functions (of which only mechanic was vaguely understood) were secondary and of little importance. This was never the case and was a particularly inappropriate message post-Cold War when the personal development and lifelong skills aspects of serving in the armed forces became a much more important recruitment driver than service, self-sacrifice and Battle of Britain-redolent glamour.

The Army found that its own mid-1990s advertising ('Be The Best') was, by 2001, having the unwelcome negative effect of being too successful in its depiction of the Army as a challenging environment, leading many potential recruits to respond to the 'bet you can't do this' challenge by concluding that 'now you mention it, you're right'. To many the Army was an unforgiving environment where the wrong decision costs someone else their life. The focus on infantry rather than the broad range of posts exacerbated this by ignoring examples of important Army jobs that would counter the unforgiving perception. This insight led to the renewed campaign focusing on skills for life and showing the full range of available Army jobs. A further change was made in the regular references to 'training' to emphasise that recruits are not just dropped in it but are properly trained and developed, to a standard exceeding civilian equivalents.

Police recruitment had a similar effect in the late 1990s. Much of the local forces recruitment advertising (mostly locally produced) emphasised variety, excitement, action. This attracted those more interested in car chases and helicopters than community support and painstaking detective work. The revised campaign was thus paradoxically aimed in part at putting off the most enthusiastic (but inappropriately motivated) candidates.

## What we have learned

### Overcoming practical barriers
- The fact that a role is completely new can be a great advantage, despite giving the campaign dual objectives, particularly where distance from the past is essential to successful recruitment.

- The amount of explanation required when launching a wholly new idea may necessitate a two-stage campaign, with the launch immediately followed by recruitment.
- Where there is controversy or political or social tension, painstakingly detailed research and the involvement of every party at all stages of the process is essential.
- When the role and purpose of a public-sector service changes, it may need to present a very different face to potential recruits and may even need to attract a different type of applicant.
- When society and people change, recruitment advertising must adapt to reflect the values and aims of potential recruits, not expect them to respond to traditional messages, however compelling previously.
- The individual life ambitions and concerns of each potential recruit are likely to be as potent a call to action as reference to a higher purpose or moral duty.
- Where a serious recruitment crisis exists, drastic reappraisal of the positioning and the messaging of the body may be required before any recruitment campaign can take effect.
- Perceptions as to suitability and the 'type' of person sought are as important as practical qualifications and in some cases may be more so.
- Population and socio-economic changes greatly affect the pool of possible recruits, potentially greatly reducing it and requiring higher rates of response or better-quality candidates to reach the same goals.
- Ensuring the greatest possible proportion of those in some way predisposed to the role is essential when the overall pool of possible candidates is reduced.

### *Overcoming emotional barriers*

- Emphasising how difficult a job can be raises its status and profile, and attracts those for whom such a role is rewarding, while also improving the quality of applicant by putting off the more casual interest.
- A negative view of a profession or role puts off those who are otherwise keen; reassuring them can provide rapid recruitment growth since they may need little other persuasion.
- Major attitudinal shifts, bordering on social engineering, may be required to address barriers to recruitment goals, notably where societal attitudes cause otherwise keen applicants to reconsider.
- Relentlessly addressing concerns and doubts impartially and one at a time, through careful research and continual consultation, creates a sense of inclusivity.

- Changing tactics completely to appeal to a different audience via a different message may be required when new barriers are faced; all campaigns evolve.
- Particular local conditions can require a bespoke approach, different to that taken nationally or even contradicting it.
- Seeking to gloss over or play down the difficulties of a job does not attract high-quality candidates; playing up the positives instead reaches those who see a worthwhile challenge.

### *Overcoming advertising-related barriers*

- Innovative media use can demonstrate the campaign point being made, as well as delivering the core message to potential recruits as efficiently and effectively as possible
- As times change, advertising messaging and imagery may not only cease to be effective but may create barriers that themselves need to be addressed.

## Conclusion

Recruitment advertising for public services is one of the most challenging of advertising arenas. The combination of practical, emotional and advertising-related barriers, standing between the potential recruit and the job in question, is often complex and typically entrenched. It requires all the ingenuity of the advertiser to help the candidate negotiate them – whether by reducing the barriers themselves, metaphorically helping the individual up and over the barriers or simply making the 'prize' on the other side so compelling that the candidate will strive to overcome the barriers, no matter what.

Many instructive strategies have been devised as a result. The Army and the RAF repositioned their 'product' to focus on the breadth and transferability of skills on offer, in place of the challenge or glory traditionally espoused. The police and teaching professions underscored the sheer difficulty of what these jobs entailed, to restore pride among candidates and respect among their peers. The Scottish Children's Panels, the Police Service and the Lay Magistracy of Northern Ireland all undertook painstaking research to closely define the misconceptions and prejudices that held candidates back, before picking them off one by one. And the local police force of Hertfordshire recognised a very different challenge from the national one and devised a campaign that reflected this understanding in an emphasis on community and variety.

As is so often the case, it seems that the tougher the challenge that is set, the higher the barriers that are faced, the more innovative and insightful the solution that is found.

# Case studies covered

### RAF: Fighting for the few

A complex and difficult set of challenges faced RAF recruitment in 1995–96. Post Cold War, the role of the armed forces had been subject to several reviews, there were considerable cutbacks in personnel, and recruitment advertising all but stopped as natural recruits (those already predisposed to join) more than covered recruitment needs. At the same time societal change led to a less positive view of the armed forces, the media being particularly critical, while changes in the aspirations and outlook of young people (less idealistic, more individualistic, less optimistic) further eroded the appeal of a career in the RAF. Previous advertising focusing on the glamour and excitement of aircraft gave way to an approach based on personal satisfaction, development and potential. A wide range of different careers were recruited for, addressing the misperception of non-pilots as lesser citizens. *J Walter Thompson (1996)*

### Army: Putting the Army back in business

The successor to the famous 'Be The Best' campaign (1994–2001) had to build on the achievements of that campaign while addressing the concern that adequate numbers of new recruits were still not being delivered. The previous campaign was found to have increased awareness of the fact that the Army was recruiting, but for most it had not offered persuasive reasons to join. Indeed, the 'excellence' approach put off some, who felt they could never match up to the standard or that it looked like too much work. Demographic issues (fewer men of the right age) and economic changes (low unemployment, more young people in further/higher education) compounded the challenge. A new group – those who might never previously have considered an Army career – were targeted, among whom a plethora of misconceptions needed to be addressed regarding the practical realities of life in the Army and the rewards they could expect. *Saatchi & Saatchi (1998)*    ▶

## Police: How thinking negatively ended negative thinking

Police recruitment was at a low ebb in the late 1990s as the reputation of the force took a battering from repeated crises. The job was perceived as being thankless, even unpleasant, and of low esteem, yet the recruitment standards were kept high. This was despite evidence that 25% of people will consider a police career at some point – a group who represent a latent target audience in need of enthusing. Advertising the generic positives of the job seemed to maintain the latent interest while not addressing the reasons for not acting on it. The new campaign positioned the job as challenging, difficult and not something that most people could do. Respected figures were used to make the point, seeking to raise respect for the police force as a career while inspiring applicants of a particular type (others, less desirable, were actually put off, another successful aspect of the campaign). *M&C Saatchi (2002)*

## NI Police: PSNI recruitment

The Police Service of Northern Ireland (PSNI) arose from the Good Friday Agreement as an explicit attempt to create a non-sectarian provincial police force serving and containing members of both communities, the old Ulster Constabulary having been over 90% Protestant and widely seen as partisan. Opponents on both sides created antipathy and controversy through which the campaign had to navigate towards a 50:50 Catholic/Protestant recruitment mix. The new service had to be seen as a Northern Irish service, not a symbol of Britishness, and it had to serve all parts of the community and be seen to do so. The challenges went far beyond recruitment targets because the PSNI is intended to stand for a new Northern Ireland, not merely law and order. *AV Browne (2002)*

## Hertfordshire Police: Thinking locally

Police recruitment in the late 1990s was a national problem, but particularly acute in Hertfordshire, where local issues compounded the national difficulties. As well as low public confidence, county border changes made the recruitment target even more daunting, while the proximity of the better-paid Metropolitan Police was a real challenge and economic success meant low ▶

101

unemployment and high housing costs in the county. This required reaching people who had never considered a police career, while maintaining high applicant standards. The approach focused on the local nature of Hertfordshire policing, namely away from the grimy city centre and towards a communitarian role with high job satisfaction, variety and friendliness. Use of innovative media placement emphasised the distinctive nature of the local campaign. *Bernard Hodes (2004)*

## Army: Over the wall of fear

The challenges of armed forces recruitment are unique: there is a minimum three-year term; the risk of death or injury; long periods away; and, paradoxically, the fact that some of the most enthusiastic applicants are wholly unsuitable while many of the more desirable candidates never consider applying. In the early 1990s there were the additional complications of post-Cold War debate over the role and scale of the armed forces, a deteriorating public perception of their organisation, the negative attitudes of family and careers advisers, low unemployment and unfavourable demographics. The advertising not only had to invigorate a new generation of soldier but also the Army as an institution, challenging it to live up to its own claims. The focus was on quality of applicant, increasing both quality and efficiency of recruitment, with influencers such as friends, family and society being just as important an audience as potential recruits. *Publicis (2004)*

## Lay Magistrates: Reaching those who count

Reform of the judicial system in Northern Ireland over the past decade has been dramatic and far-reaching. Among the key initiatives has been the role ▶

of the Lay Magistrate, through which ordinary citizens play a role in the court service. The historical divisions in Northern Ireland inevitably created major problems with trust, the criminal justice system being seen by many as partisan, formal, intimidating and removed from ordinary people. It was further seen as too male, white, Protestant, middle-aged and middle-class. These suspicions became actual fear in some parts – fear of both the criminal justice system and of the likely response in their own communities to engagement with it. Further practical challenges existed in the need to explain a new role, reassure as to the lack of the need for legal qualifications, explain how to apply, and explain what sort of person is needed. *Anderson Spratt (2005)*

## Children's Panel: Scottish Panel membership

The Scottish Children's Panel system was in danger of collapse in the late 1990s, recruitment having all but dried up and morale among existing panellists very low. Not only was advertising tasked with addressing the personnel crisis, it was to improve the representation of all parts of the community on panels and to invigorate the system, all with no significant increase in budget. Research identified key triggers to revitalise interest – notably the uniquely Scottish nature of the panel system, the local aspect of the role, reassurance that the role is open to all and that the time demands are not prohibitive – and a need for a positive description of the opportunity. *Barkers Scotland (2005)* ▶

With kind permission of Ian Dickson, photographer

### Teachers: A class act

Describes how a teacher recruitment crisis in 1997 was reversed between 1998 and 2005, bringing an additional 67,000 graduates into the profession. The task was considerable as the numbers required and the societal barriers were daunting. The paper describes two phases: 'Born to Teach' running from 1998 to 2003, aiming at maximising the number of new graduates choosing teaching; and 'Change to Teach' running from 2003 to 2005, targeting those in other jobs who could be persuaded to switch. The initial challenge was to address perceptions that teaching was no longer 'a proper job', reversing negative societal attitudes to both the pay and prestige of the role. Advertising focused on both the potential applicants themselves and the raw experience of working with children, covering both the practical aspects of the job and the emotional reward. The later campaign, aimed at career-switchers, offered further reassurance as to the practicalities associated with such a shift. *DDB (2006)*

And you thought magnesium was reactive.

With kind permission of Adam Hinton, photographer

### Note

1. The Stephen Lawrence Report of an Inquiry by Sir William Macpherson of Cluny, February 1999.

# Chapter 5

# Understanding subcultures

By Andy Nairn
MCBD

Many of the case studies described in this book are public information campaigns in the literal sense. In other words, they have been deliberately aimed at the broad mass of the population, as the communications priority was to create attitudinal and behavioural change on a national level.

However, not all public-sector campaigns are designed to work in this way. In fact, as society becomes more fragmented, social challenges are more likely to be located within specific demographic groups. It then falls upon government to address these problems so that inequalities within society – whether health-related, educational or in terms of law and order – are not unduly exacerbated.

From the policy-maker's perspective, this imperative is both understandable and laudable. However, from a communications point of view, such an approach can throw up challenges as well as opportunities. This chapter will outline some of the issues involved in connecting with niche audiences, and show how problems can be overcome by following best practice.

## The benefits of a targeted approach

The most obvious benefit of a targeted marketing approach is that it brings a sense of focus to the strategic process. Research can be conducted among a tightly defined group of people; highly specific insights can be gleaned about this audience; sharper creative ideas can be developed based on these insights; media monies can be deployed very efficiently, measurement can be more accurate, and so on. Given that budgets are often tight within public-sector organisations, the opportunity to concentrate resources where they can make the most difference can be compelling.

## The public-sector dilemma

However, this model – tried and tested in the private sector – typically assumes that the niche in question represents 'the lowest hanging fruit' – that is, those people who are already best disposed to the brand or message, and who are therefore deserving of special attention.

The problem is that in the public sector, this 'easy option' is not always available. Indeed, very often policy dictates that communications must target the hardest-to-convince sections of the population, precisely because of their 'unusual' behaviour. This is particularly true of mature issues, where marketers are often left with a rump of hardcore 'offenders' who are still engaging in behaviour that has long been abandoned by the population at large. But it's also true of emerging issues, where an activity has been grasped enthusiastically by a subsection of society but has yet to become mainstream. Whatever the stage in the life cycle, this means that, in the public sector, a focused approach often implies extra complexity and degree of difficulty rather than less.

## Specific challenges in engaging hard-to-convince audiences

At their most extreme, hard-to-convince audiences often exist as virtual 'subcultures', beneath the radar of society as a whole. Perhaps they are drawn from a particular ethnic community, a specific social group or a tightly defined age range. As such, they may face deeply ingrained cultural barriers towards behavioural change, which do not apply to the rest of society. They may also have their own traditions, cultural reference points, media – even language. All of which can make them impenetrable to the outside observer and impervious to mainstream communications.

A related challenge is that subcultures often build up their own mythologies – irrational and often patently false beliefs that are taken as true within the community. For instance, teenage gang members may fantasise that guns will bring them riches, when, for the vast majority, the opposite is true. Likewise, heavy drinkers may use legendary tales of elderly, whisky-swigging aunts to 'disprove' the health risks of alcohol. Or pensioners might avoid the flu jab, because they have heard that it can actually be harmful rather than protective. Once these beliefs gain critical mass, they are passed round the community, embellished, reinforced and entrenched so that they become very difficult to dislodge. Again, the effect is to reinforce current behaviour and prevent change.

There is also a tendency within subcultures to reject 'outside' interference. Often, such interventions are seen as authoritarian and even discriminatory. For instance, teenagers are often suspicious of government messaging on the basis that it seeks to curtail their freedom, or doesn't reflect the reality of their lives. Similarly, gay men can be cynical about health education messages that appear to be more concerned with their sexuality than their well-being. If the subculture feels as if it is under attack, then the shutters will come down and the message will be screened out.

Finally, and perhaps paradoxically, there is the difficulty that minorities don't always see themselves as such. After all, if all your friends, family members and workmates indulge in the same behaviour as you – how abnormal can it be? And if behaviour is normal, then how harmful or immoral can it be? Many public-sector campaigns flounder because they don't take into account the power of peer pressure or community behaviour in reinforcing the status quo.

## Overcoming these challenges

Given the challenges outlined above, perhaps the most useful advice when seeking to engage a subculture is to employ a little humility. After all, the marketing practitioner will often come from a background very different from the target market in question. Like it or not, they will probably have a very different demographic; a different social circle; a different outlook on life from the people they are supposed to be talking to. It is crucial that these values are not imposed on the subculture, as they will almost certainly be rejected.

On the other hand, it's equally important that the marketer doesn't resort to some crude stereotyping or second-guessing of what the audience must be like. We have all seen examples of venerable public institutions trying to 'talk yoof' to teenagers, or affecting earthy tones when communicating with lower socio-economic groups – and we can be sure that these attempts to over-compensate don't work either.

### *Deep understanding through qualitative research*

No, the solution must usually be to use research upfront, to avoid either of these pitfalls. In practice, this will typically require qualitative research, designed to really get under the skin of the target audience. Conventionally, this might mean focus groups (ideal if there is a strong social dimension to the behaviour in question) and/or depth interviews (preferable if the subject matter is more sensitive personally).

## *Imaginative methodology required*

However, given that subcultures are often difficult to recruit to traditional research, more unusual techniques might also be required to bring the audience to life. For instance, a photojournalist might be employed to capture life and attitudes within the subculture, at a street level. Similarly, an analysis of the community's social networking websites might be useful, to gain an insight into their peer dynamics.

## *Consult experts*

Academics – such as psychologists, sociologists and semioticians – might be interviewed for a theoretical perspective on the audience. Or frontline workers – teachers, call centre operators, JobCentre staff, community leaders – could be contacted for a more grass-roots perspective.

Whatever the methodology, the purpose of the research must be not only to understand the audience but to do so from a non-judgemental perspective. This latter requirement isn't always easy; for instance, it might appear unfathomable to us why an unemployed mum would continue to smoke during pregnancy, why an elderly rural man might drink-drive, or why an African woman might wish to circumcise her daughter. However, just as an actor must learn to see the world from his character's viewpoint, so public-sector marketers must strive to empathise with (if not endorse) their audience, if they are to capture their hearts and minds.

## *Tackling a subculture's mythology*

Once the subculture is fully understood, the next step is to tackle any mythology that may be holding back change, and replace it with more accurate and socially acceptable information. Again, this easier said than done. For starters, legends are, by their nature, easily digestible stories that require no expert understanding, whereas the truth is often quite complex. In addition, folklore is often rich in emotion, whereas the truth can appear somewhat dull and rational in comparison. However, good communications practitioners can always find ways of simplifying the most complex propositions, and turning dry statistics into vivid messages.

The following case study from the Health Education Authority is a great example of this in practice. It tells how marketers set aside their own prejudices about a subculture, to uncover an audience's true motivations. And it tells how this audience's popular mythology was systematically challenged using a disarmingly honest approach.

# Case study: Health Education Authority
## How advertising turned the tide on drug use

### The problem

Drugs represent one of the greatest social problems of the modern era. In the UK alone, in the period covered by this case, the drugs market was worth an estimated £13 billion and the associated social costs ran up to £4 billion p.a.

The 1990s was a period of particularly pronounced growth for drugs in Britain, as 'recreational' drugs, such as ecstasy and speed, spread from the dance floor to become a major part of youth culture. Within five years, the proportion of 14–15 year olds using drugs had doubled.

The government realised that urgent action needed to be taken to stem this seemingly unstoppable tide. However, after decades of unsuccessful attempts, using everything from educational initiatives to law enforcement techniques, the government also realised that a fresh approach was necessary. Hence, in 1996 it began to explore whether communications could help 'reduce the demand for drugs'.

### *Understanding the mindset of the subculture*

Research revealed that, contrary to popular media prejudice, teenage drug users rarely saw themselves as the victims of evil pushers or wayward friends. Instead, they admitted to being willing participants, attracted by tales of the excitement drugs could offer.

Interestingly, these stories were not matched by an understanding of the health risks of drugs: millions knew of no such dangers whatsoever, while others cited hazards that were patently untrue ('Speed makes your teeth fall out', 'LSD burns a hole through your hand', etc.). In short, mythology was rampant, with teenagers relying on rumour and counter-rumour to guide their decisions to try drugs or not.

Based on this understanding, the marketing team realised that instead of treating young people like children (innocent, helpless, in need of protection, deserving of a lecture), communications needed to talk to them like adults (openly, honestly, arming them with the facts and allowing them to make up their own minds). This would mean warning them of the health risks of drug taking, but also accepting that some of the medical evidence was unclear, and even acknowledging some of the pleasurable aspects of drugs use – a radical departure from all other communications in this field. ▶

## The solution

A highly graphic campaign was developed featuring young people in drug-taking situations, with a biology textbook 'cutaway' revealing the effects of a particular drug on the body – both good and bad. Crucially, each execution dealt with a specific substance, since young people rejected the lumping together of different chemicals under one handy label ('drugs'). This determinedly adult approach was then signed off with the non-judgemental line 'Know the score' and ran in teen magazines, ambient environments (cafés, bars, clubs, etc.) and on radio.

## The effect

After years of seemingly inexorable increases, drug use among teenagers actually decreased in both 1996 and 1997. Moreover, consideration of drugs among 11–25 year olds went down by 14%, while the proportion of drug users claiming to have given up doubled.

There was strong evidence that it was the advertising that was responsible for this shift in behaviour. First, there was very high awareness of the campaign among teenagers – peaking at 90% in certain parts of the country. Second, there was a very positive reaction to the idea and an extremely high take-out ▶

of the specific health messages conveyed. But perhaps most tangibly, there was a marked increase in calls to the National Drugs Hotline, with spikes in volume closely correlated to campaign activity.

In contrast, other factors could largely be eliminated as influential in this success story. For instance, the price of drugs actually fell over the campaign period, and availability rose. Likewise, smoking prevalence among teenagers (often linked to a subsequent progression into drugs) decreased, while clubbing (another environmental factor associated with drug use) did not change significantly.

All in all, the campaign was a great success – not just in terms of social policy but also financially. For instance, it is estimated that: the £2.3 million advertising spend diverted £28 million that would have otherwise have been spent on drugs into legal areas of the economy; it saved British industry £11 million per year by reducing absences from work; and it saved £3 million by removing the need for local health professionals to create their own materials.

Source: *HEA Drugs Education Campaign – how advertising turned the tide*. Duckworth Finn Grubb Waters (1998)

## Avoiding rejection by the subculture

Tackling the mythology within a subculture can be a crucial first step to effecting behavioural change. However, it won't work unless the source of the information is credible. Indeed, as we have seen above, the subculture will actively reject any information that appears to be a lecture from outsiders.

The HEA managed to get round this problem by employing a very even-handed approach (i.e. acknowledging the pleasures of drugs as well as the dangers), structuring the campaign carefully (e.g. treating each substance separately rather than lumping everything together as 'drugs') and using the subculture's language appropriately ('Know the score'). In other words, empathy and credibility were designed into the campaign at a strategic level.

However, even the most carefully constructed strategy can unravel if the execution is lacking. The following case study from the Health Education Board of Scotland (HEBS) demonstrates the importance of carrying credibility through into casting, scripting and production too, if the message is to avoid rejection by the subculture.

## Case study: Health Education Board for Scotland
### How advertising helped reduce adult smoking in Scotland

### The problem

Smoking prevalence has been slowly declining across the UK since the 1970s. However, tobacco usage has retained an unusually strong foothold in Scotland, especially within the working-class culture of the Central Belt. With smoking identified as the largest single cause of preventable illness and death in Scotland, accounting for over 10,600 mortalities each year, the Health Education Board of Scotland set out to address this most hardened of audiences: C2DE smokers.

### *Understanding the mindset of the subculture*

Scottish C2DE smokers exhibited many of the aspects of a subculture, as described above. They used mythology to play down the health risks of their behaviour, commonly citing relatives who had smoked into their old age as 'proof' that the dangers of smoking had been exaggerated. They resented outside interference from government agencies, arguing that their habit was one of their few pleasures in life and that any attempt to restrict it was an attack on their freedom. They did not see their behaviour as abnormal since, in their social circles, almost everybody smoked. Even those who had lost family members to smoking-related illnesses felt either powerless or unmotivated to change their behaviour. Perhaps most tellingly, these audiences had proved immune to several decades of health education messages, whether of the 'carrot' or 'stick' variety. Often, this was because they felt that these messages had been designed by non-smokers, for non-smokers and indeed featuring non-smokers. The challenge was how to engage them with a new approach.

### The solution

The agency's solution to the problem was not to use either a 'carrot' or a 'stick' but to combine both approaches for the first time. Specifically, hard-hitting messages on the health risks of smoking were married to more positive messages about the help available if would-be quitters called the 'Smokeline'. Importantly, great care was taken to ensure that the actual executions were as credible and empathetic as possible. For instance, health risks were communicated via a highly realistic TV commercial, set in a hospital, where a ▶

mother pleads with her son never to take up smoking. Both protagonists were cast to reflect the C2DE audience and appear to be 'people like us'. Meanwhile, the supportive message was conveyed by a friendly counsellor, of the sort employed by the 'Smokeline'. Again, she was cast to look like an ex-smoker herself, and thus avoid rejection as a healthy do-gooder. The whole campaign – from scenarios through scripts to sets – was crafted carefully so that it appeared to have been developed from within the subculture, rather than from outside.

## The effect

Over 84,000 people called 'Smokeline' in its first year – around 6% of all adult Scottish smokers. This was far in excess of original estimates, based on the experiences of 'Quitline' in England. Indeed, despite the number of lines being doubled from the second week onwards, and extra counsellors being employed, over 110,000 additional calls were still unfortunately lost due to an inability to meet demand. Encouragingly, smokers from lower socio-economic groups were particularly likely to call for help. Equally positively, call volumes rose virtually threefold during the campaign, compared to non-advertised periods.

Of those who called 'Smokeline', around 85% went on to make a quit attempt, and 24% remained cigarette-free one year later. Only 12% reported no change in their smoking behaviour.

Among Scottish smokers as a whole, desire to quit also rose significantly, with 20% claiming to be 'desperate or very much wanting to quit' post campaign vs 17% prior to launch.

Based on these figures, HEBS estimates that there would have been a 1.4% reduction in adult smoking in Scotland, compared to a natural decay rate of around 0.8%. The difference between these two percentage points (0.6%) can thus serve as an approximation of the campaign's effect. In monetary terms, this apparently small decline in prevalence represents savings of around £333 million to the NHS and Scottish industry (in terms of health costs and working days lost).

Source: *Health Education Board for Scotland – smoking sticks and carrots*. Leith Edinburgh (1994)

## *Normalising behaviour within a subculture*

Even if a subculture's mythology can be tackled and its concerns about outside interference addressed, behavioural change will struggle to take effect if the activity in question is still seen as normal within the community. This is perhaps the biggest challenge of all, since the barriers here are social and deeply ingrained. However, smart planning can again overcome such difficulties.

The following case study from the Department for Education and Skills (DfES) is a great example of how communications helped to normalise a seemingly alien concept for hard-to-convince teenagers.

# Case study: DfES
## How communications persuaded teenagers to aim higher

### The problem

There is a political consensus that education is of crucial economic importance to the nation. Research shows that graduates earn, on average, 35% more than the national average and are 50% less likely to be unemployed. As such they contribute more in taxes and are less of a drain on public resources, in terms of claiming benefits. They are even less likely to take part in crime, or succumb to drugs or alcohol abuse. With this in mind, the government set a target that, by 2010, 50% of young people should have had the opportunity to benefit from higher education before they were 30. The problem was that, to meet this target, huge numbers of working-class (C2DE) teenagers would have to be tempted into higher education, and they currently rejected it as an alien concept for middle-class kids. The fact that they knew relatively few friends and family members who had progressed to higher education merely seemed to underline the abnormality of this behaviour.

### *Understanding the mindset of the subculture*

Research revealed many reasons why C2DE teenagers dismissed the thought of higher education as 'not for me'. For instance, a disproportionate number came from broken homes and either lacked parental support or felt uncomfortable asking their parents for financial assistance. Similarly, many were distracted from their studies by peer pressure to experiment with drugs, alcohol, petty crime and truancy. Perhaps most of all, many underprivileged kids had been seduced by the celebrity culture so pervasive today: feeling that their educational and career options were limited, they dreamed of achieving ▶

instant success via less conventional means. For younger (pre-GCSE) children, this success tended to be fame-related: 'I want to be a footballer/model/pop star.' Meanwhile, for older teenagers (post-GCSE), the focus was firmly on financial wealth: 'I want to win the lottery/marry a millionaire.' Both audiences needed to have their ambitions channelled in more realistic directions, based on an understanding that education was a more effective – and completely normal – route to success.

## The solution

A new brand was developed to motivate C2DE teenagers without being pretentious: 'Aimhigher'. Then two different creative approaches were constructed, based on this platform. A press campaign for younger kids used celebrities as a way to promote more realistic ambitions (e.g. famous footballers were featured promoting more everyday sports-related careers, while supermodels were used to suggest the possibilities of working in the fashion world). Meanwhile, a campaign for older teenagers used striking images of material possessions cut down by a third, to emphasise the facts of higher graduate earnings.

## The effect

Some 79% of teenagers recognised the campaign – helped by media coverage, estimated to be worth around £1 million. Of these, younger pupils took on ▶

board the message that 'Higher education can help you get a good job', while older students surmised that 'Higher education will help you earn more later.' Perhaps most encouraging of all, the campaign performed particularly well against C2DE students, in contrast to previous activity in this area, which had always worked more strongly among ABC1s.

A total of 23,000 pupils, from 194 schools, attended the Aimhigher roadshow, with 80% of these saying that the experience had made them 'more positive about going on to higher education' and 97% of teachers agreeing that the event was 'an effective way of promoting higher education'.

In all, 15,237 individuals visited the Aimhigher website, with a similar number (15,018) calling the fulfilment line. Taken together, this meant that actual response was 44% above target. Due to multiple requests for fulfilment material, over 240,000 information booklets were distributed among the target audience.

It has been calculated that if just 1 in 1,000 of the pupils exposed to Aimhigher went on to attend higher education, an extra £80 million would be generated for the UK economy – more than offsetting the modest campaign spend and any costs related to putting these pupils through higher education.

Source: *DfES. We don't need no higher education*. Duckworth Finn Grubb Waters (2002)

## What we have learned

By their very nature, campaigns aimed at subcultures will differ greatly from each other. However, there is a common thread running through all these case studies, namely the importance of research – formal or otherwise. While careful planning is important for any campaign, it assumes critical importance in cases like this; for with the right combination of insight and empathy, even the hardest audiences can be won over and their behaviour changed for the better. Specifically:

- it is crucial to understand the subculture mythology in depth and tackle it head on
- equally, it is critical that any messages used don't alienate the subculture, resulting in rejection; thus balance is critical
- aim, as far as realistically possible, to make the desired behaviour normal within the subculture.

# Chapter 6

# Addressing multiple audiences

By Andy Nairn
MCBD

In mainstream marketing, the wisdom of focusing on a single target market is universally accepted. However, many of the public-sector case studies described so far have referenced secondary audiences, tertiary audiences and a myriad of stakeholders as being critical to success.

This chapter will explore why this phenomenon is so common within public-sector marketing, what the resulting challenges are, and how any difficulties can be overcome in practice.

## Go forth and multiply

Perhaps the main reason why targeting is more complicated in the public sector is that the issues themselves are more complex. In particular, there is a paradox whereby many examples of highly personal behaviour actually have a surprisingly social dimension.

Take smoking, for example. At first this might appear to be a highly individual choice and thus deserving of a highly focused targeting strategy, aimed at existing smokers. However, on closer inspection, one can see that the partners of smokers might also be worth considering as an audience, as they exert a strong influence on the smoker's desire to give up, as well as on their eventual success in quitting. Likewise, smokers' children, friends and co-workers might be considered legitimate and influential audiences. Even ex-smokers might be worth talking to, since the fact that they have given up now might not mean that they will remain smoke-free in future. In short, there are often many more viable audiences than at first meet the eye.

Another reason why multiple audiences are so common in public-sector marketing is that there is often a political imperative to speak to the whole of society rather than a subsection. This isn't always the case (indeed the previous section discusses how public policy is equally liable to point to a focus on a particular subculture). However, it can be a powerful factor, especially when an issue is extremely sensitive (and thus liable to cause offence if a specific segment of the population is singled out for attention); when the information to be imparted is a matter of life or death (and thus there is effectively a duty to 'let everybody know', even if they are unlikely to be affected in practice); or where there is an erroneous belief that the problem affects only a certain section of society (a misconception that would be exacerbated by a niche marketing campaign).

To cite a famous example: the government's first HIV awareness campaign ('Don't die of ignorance') was deliberately targeted at a mass audience (and a myriad of sub-audiences within that), precisely because the issue met all three of the conditions outlined above.

The other main reason for a multi-layered approach to targeting is the importance of third-party stakeholders in the public sector. Put simply, the issues at stake are typically too deep-rooted to be tackled by advertising alone. Instead, communications must work in tandem with frontline workers, be they the police, community leaders, teachers, nurses or trades unions. Indeed, increasingly, the public sector is being encouraged to forge partnerships with commercial organisations too (the Scottish Domestic Abuse case study described later in this chapter includes an interesting example of this arrangement in practice). These stakeholders then need to be considered as crucial audiences in their own right – people to engage, canvass, nurture and enthuse, just like any consumer audience.

## Multiple audiences, multiple challenges

The most obvious difficulty associated with multiple audiences is that the different groups may well have widely opposing points of view on the issue at stake, very different behaviours and completely divergent experiences. For instance, when addressing the problem of under-age sex, there might be a very sensible argument for constructing a target audience composed of teenagers, parents, teachers, medics and youth workers. However, there will almost certainly be massive tensions between these groups, in terms of their motivations, frustrations, aspirations and concerns. How, then, can marketing communications possibly hope to engage such different constituencies?

Ironically, the tensions between stakeholders are no less than those between consumers – indeed often they are even more marked. For while individual organisations within a 'cause' may share the same ultimate objective, frequently they have very different beliefs about how change can best be achieved. Sometimes these beliefs are shaped by political ideals; for example, when dealing with crime, should funds be invested in punishment or prevention programmes?

Alternatively, prejudices may be formed out of experience; for instance, frontline workers at a drugs clinic may be vehemently against a hardline advertising stance, as they may have found that addicts respond better to encouragement than to criticism. Perhaps most often, agendas are shaped by funding considerations, with individual organisations jockeying to get as much control of limited budgets as they possibly can. Whatever the reason, the end result is that stakeholder coalitions can often be uneasy affairs, with advertising given the unenviable task of bringing diverse parties together.

On top of all this, there's often a branding challenge, in terms of who the message should be from. This throws up difficulties for both consumers and stakeholders. In the case of the former, the problem is that different segments often look to different organisations for leadership on an issue. In extreme cases, they may even reject outright the preferred choices of other segments. In this kind of situation, how can marketers brand the campaign effectively, without causing unwanted division?

Ideally, stakeholders would reach a practical solution here, but this is where the second problem kicks in. While most organisations can see the objective need for simple branding, they also have a subjective – and understandable – desire to have their own contribution to the campaign recognised. Thus conversations often start with the laudably consumer-focused desire to agree a single 'author', but all too often degenerate into horse-trading and end up with a raft of logos being represented.

Next, there's a media challenge: how to reach these multiple audiences effectively and efficiently. Often the different segments will use very different information channels; here, there's a real risk that funds will be spread too thinly and the campaign will not make an impact on anybody. Alternatively, the various audiences may be relatively homogeneous in their media use; here the problem might be exactly the opposite, namely that different messages to different targets cannot be 'quarantined' effectively. Either way, there's often a particular onus on media people to make sense of the targeting model and make it workable in practice.

Finally, there's an evaluation challenge. Measuring response to a campaign among several audiences will add significantly to research costs. Indeed, in the case of certain stakeholders, quantitative research may be so prohibitively expensive as to be impossible, and even qualitative research may be impractical (as anyone who has attempted to recruit a group of police officers will tell you). This means that it can be difficult to assess campaign performance properly, ascertain whether communications are working as intended, or plan for the future.

## Overcoming these challenges

Conventional marketing wisdom trains us to be divisive, arguing that success can come only from delivering a unique promise to a unique audience. Much time is spent teasing out differences between target audiences so as to create communications that reach out to them more effectively than do competitors.

The challenge is to switch tactics. Rather than searching for differences, it is important to find ways to overcome differences, and identify the beliefs and attitudes that unite different audiences.

The challenge in managing these agendas is to understand where they come from, respect them and strive to find a common goal to which they can all agree.

### *Look for ideals and insights*

Such complex challenges demand a shift in perspective. Rather than regarding them as exhausting or a hassle, they need to be seen as an opportunity; after all, the very nature of these campaigns is to make a positive contribution to everyday life, be it direct or indirect. And no doubt this is also what each of the different target audiences is looking for. So as marketers we should refocus our attention on discovering the ideals and insights that unite differing audiences.

Far from being a challenge, we need to recognise that multiple audiences offer us a goldmine of information at our fingertips. Spending time talking to and understanding the concerns of each of the different audiences will deliver a wealth of insights. The differing perspectives will give us a more rounded view of the situation.

Talking to multiple consumer audiences will help us understand the emotions at an individual level and gain insight into the pressures they face. If different consumer groups are involved it will help us understand the different perspectives on the same problem.

## *Talk to stakeholders but be wary of agendas*

Talking to stakeholders will provide a bigger picture of the issue and allow us to benefit from their experiences. However, when talking to stakeholders we also need to remain mindful of their agenda and tactfully seek to understand their relationship with other stakeholders. Insights can also be gained by bringing together groups of different stakeholders to discuss an issue. Working together to negotiate an advertising objective may in itself deliver new insights.

The other advantage of working directly with stakeholders is that they will feel their voice has been heard and their opinions taken into account. Keeping them involved throughout the process will not only provide useful direction that can prevent a campaign floundering but will also secure their support when the campaign is launched.

## *Understand the campaign's subsidiary needs*

Finally, it is important to understand the subsidiary needs that stakeholders may have for a campaign; for example, information leaflets or posters that will help them take the advertising message directly to consumers.

The following case study is an excellent example of how working with front-line stakeholders gave a greater understanding about how to tackle the problem of domestic abuse. Talking to stakeholders revealed the reasons why past advertising had failed to work and challenged assumptions about the most effective way of tackling the problem. This opened the door to a totally new approach to addressing the issue.

## Case study: Scottish Executive
### Working with stakeholders to tackle domestic abuse

### The problem

Domestic abuse is a major social blight in Scotland. In 1998 the Scottish Crime Survey estimated that one in five women could expect to experience it within their lifetime. It is equally prevalent across all age and social groups.

Despite a previous high-profile advertising campaign to highlight the subject, there was concern that the campaign had done little to advance public knowledge. Indeed there was significant anecdotal evidence it had reinforced public misconceptions that domestic abuse was predominantly a working-class ▶

problem, usually alcohol related and had to be expressed as physical violence before it could be acted upon. A change of strategy was needed.

### *Insights into the complexities of abuse*

This was an issue where multiple stakeholders were keen to contribute to reduction in domestic abuse so a first step was to canvass their views. Stakeholders included the police, the prison service, Scottish Women's Aid and Victim Support Scotland. All agreed that both victims and perpetrators of domestic abuse constantly failed to recognise themselves in the advertising stereotypes presented to them. With such consistent insight, it had to be questioned whether directly appealing to victims or perpetrators was worthwhile.

High levels of domestic abuse cannot fail to have an effect on a community, and research revealed that people recognised that abuse was widespread and abhorrent. Sadly, it was seen as a private matter and there was a reluctance among many to get involved or condemn what might be seen as other people's business. Only when a child was involved would people acknowledge that a relative or friend might have a role to play.

### The solution

With this in mind, a new campaign objective was created. Rather than targeting the abuser or victim, the new campaign would seek to convince the general public that domestic violence is wrong and can never be excused or tolerated.

The new campaign turned the conventions of Adland upside down. Starting with the premise that abuse happens in the most ordinary households, the advertising recreated the idealised advertising family, drawing viewers in with reassuring clichés before confronting them with the harsh reality of abuse. No violence is actually shown, and tight shots of the victim and perpetrator kept them anonymous and created a sense of claustrophobia. Observing the children, confused and powerless, conveyed the damage done to the household.

Before proceeding with production, the team sought approval from key stakeholders.

### *Engaging multiple audiences to maximise impact*

To maximise community exposure, a briefing summit was organised with Scotland's top editors and programming chiefs. This gained unprecedented ▶

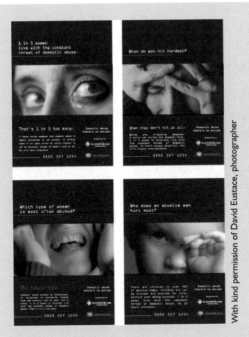

With kind permission of David Eustace, photographer

press and media coverage for the issue and subsequent radio phone-in discussions, and a storyline on STV's soap opera *High Road* helped bring the issue to the forefront of public life.

The private sector was also approached to secure technical expertise and financial support and, encouraged by the positive media reaction, Scottish Telecom agreed to sponsor a helpline.

Inclusion of a helpline required a delicate hand, as it would suggest that the advertising was aimed directly at victims. Initial executions featured either an introduction or caption for the phone number. Later executions featured the voiceover 'Whether it's you or someone you know', designed to keep ownership of the ad at its broadest.

## The effect

This campaign successfully garnered support from a range of audiences to challenge and change public beliefs. It achieved 78% unprompted awareness, the highest ever for the Scottish Executive. More importantly, it made a real difference to the attitudes of Scotland's public. Disagreement with the idea that 'abuse is a private matter' rose from 70% to 81%.    ▶

Scottish Women's Aid reported a rise of 200% in the number of calls it received – a rise it attributed to the success of the campaign rather than an actual increase in incidence.

Strathclyde Police (Scotland's largest police authority) reported a 75% rise in reported domestic violence incidents, again attributing this to a rise in reporting rather than incidence.

As the campaign did not directly target victims, calls to the helpline were down vs previous campaigns. But, tellingly, of the 1,400 calls received, some 400 were from men, whereas in the past callers had been overwhelmingly female.

Source: *Domestic abuse there's no excuse*. Barkers Edinburgh (2000)

While stakeholders can provide outstanding insight into how to address a problem, they can also form part of the problem themselves. The following case deals with the delicate subject of child literacy, and the roles that parents and teachers play in helping children reach desired literacy levels.

This is a case that illustrates the sensitivities of a key stakeholder group, namely teachers, and the need to avoid any implication that they were ineffective. Instead of branding teachers as an awkward problem, this child literacy campaign actively involved them in a programme to mobilise parents to become more involved in helping their children read. Not only did teachers feel acknowledged and appreciated, but they played a vital role in the success of the campaign.

## Case study: DfES
### Involving stakeholders in the problem

### The problem
Illiteracy is a significant problem among the nation's children and has stubbornly remained at similar levels since 1948. On average only 63% of children were achieving expected levels of reading by age 11. ▶

Achieving basic literacy levels is crucial to a child's chances of future success, so the government set itself the ambitious target of achieving 80% by 2002. Initiatives were set up to help schools meet the target. However, to achieve such a significant leap in literacy it would also be essential to mobilise parents.

Of particular importance were parents from lower socio-demographic groups, whose children typically performed 12% below average. They agreed that reading well was a necessary life skill for their children and that they had a role to play. However, many, having had bad experiences during their own childhood, lacked the confidence to get involved.

Time was another barrier. The government had spent the last decade advising parents that they should spend 20 minutes a day reading with their children, yet the realities of family life often made this difficult and left parents feeling frustrated.

Finally, the immediate association with children's reading was a book at bedtime. The combination of a lack of time and a lack of confidence turned this supposedly joyous, intimate time into a chore.

While primarily talking to parents, it was essential that the advertising should not alienate teachers. This presented a delicate situation. Many teachers consider education to be underfunded and themselves underpaid. Were they to be confronted by high-profile advertising they may be predisposed to view that money as better spent directly in schools. Equally important was to avoid the implicit suggestion that teachers were letting children down and therefore it was up to the parents to help. Any campaign to mobilise parents would have to tread carefully to avoid offence.

Reading didn't have to be just books at bedtime: it was anything, any time. It might be cereal boxes at breakfast, road signs in the car, sports programmes and so on. These natural reading opportunities occurred spontaneously in everyday life and freed parents from the bedtime book chore. Parents recognised these occasions but seemed uncertain as to whether that was proper reading.

## The solution

The advertising sought to validate these alternative reading moments and encourage parents to take advantage of them. Two commercials were ▶

created offsetting familiar book-at-bedtime moments with alternative reading moments. Drama was added using a nursery rhyme whose familiar refrain was broken by the vernacular of everyday situations. The campaign featured all ages within the target, and a sense of intimacy and naturalness was added by casting parents with their own children.

A phone number was included, allowing parents to request an information leaflet. It featured pictures of parents and children in everyday reading situations introduced tips on best practice, and offered answers to common questions.

## The effect

Tracking evidence indicated the advertising was noticed, engaged the target and persuaded the target to think they really could help with their children's reading. Further research showed a decline in agreement with the statement that 'children will only get better at reading if they read books'.

Calls requesting leaflets were triple the average COI television response and strongly correlated with times when advertising was on air.

A sample of parents who requested the leaflet were tracked and, after 15 months, nearly three-quarters were still actively using the information provided.

Nevertheless, the campaign could only be deemed successful if teachers were not alienated and antagonised. Far from antagonising them, however, the ►

advertising actually won the support of many and as a result galvanised a valuable distribution network. The order line received almost 7,000 calls from institutions requesting leaflets. Most got the number from the advertising. Postcode analysis of primary schools revealed that over a third were from more socially deprived areas.

Follow-up phone calls among teachers revealed a strong endorsement for the campaign. Over three-quarters saw it as very appropriate and half said it was very useful. Qualitative research revealed that teachers appreciated the sensitive approach, believing that it supported their work while championing the role of parents.

Most importantly, literacy levels improved. In the two years following the campaign, national literacy levels rose seven percentage points. In terms of leaflet requests from schools, many of which were in deprived areas, numbers rose by nine percentage points.

Source: *Reading and Literacy: how advertising mobilised parents to help improve their children's reading ability*. DMB&B (2000)

## What we have learned

Often there are a number of stakeholder groups  such  as family, friends, nurses, teachers, community workers  etc, who are relevant to influencing a particular issue.  So in many instances campaigns are aimed at multiple audiences.  Although individual problem behaviour is being targeted, this behaviour can have complex and deep-rooted social causes. Also it can be desirable to talk to society as a whole because of the need to mobilise other groups to tackle the issue together.

The key lessons here are:

- Search for unifying themes that are shared by these different audiences
- Look for the ideals and insights into the particular perspectives they have on the issue
- Talk to each of these stakeholder groups but keep in mind each will have its own particular agenda
- Understand the subsidiary needs of the campaign in order to help these different audiences augment the advertising effort in whatever way is appropriate.

# Part 3

# Engaging the target audience

# Chapter 7

# Innovative uses of media

 By Will Collin

Naked Communications

Government departments face the same challenge as brand owners seeking to influence their potential consumer: the need to gain the attention of an audience, and to deliver a message. However, the degree of difficulty rapidly escalates when the message in question is something people don't want to hear, or would rather ignore. Public service messages can be difficult to deliver successfully.

Because of this difficulty, government departments have by necessity been at the forefront of adopting innovative approaches to communications, long before this became seen as de rigueur. While integrated marketing communications and media neutral planning are now being embraced enthusiastically by brand marketers as a response to the fragmentation of consumers' media habits by digital technologies, government campaigns have been planned this way for ten years or more.

The essential change is to recognise that successful communication is not guaranteed by simply delivering the campaign to the audience as an 'opportunity to see'. People are not passive receivers, waiting to receive whatever messages are presented to them. Their attention is scarce and the sheer number of commercial messages directed at them is vast. Therefore they need to be engaged by, not just exposed to, a message if it is to be successfully communicated. This engagement could be achieved through entertainment, participation, intrigue, humour, shock or some other means.

Furthermore, their attentiveness varies hugely, dependent on the context and the subject matter. What is compelling in one situation can be irrelevant in another. Choosing the right moment to communicate can be as critical to success as choosing the right message.

This has meant moving away from a reliance on the traditional 'reach and frequency' approach to media planning where it is assumed that the main task is to present the message to as many people as possible, as often as possible. Instead the quality of exposure must be considered alongside the quantity. The aspects of 'quality' in this context are as follows.

- How much do the audience feel the chosen medium is part of their world?
- How relevant is the context (whether place or time) to the message that appears within it?
- Does the way in which the message is presented contribute to its impact?
- Do the audience find a consistent message each time they encounter different aspects of the issue (whether in advertising or elsewhere)?

There are numerous examples within the IPA Effectiveness dataBANK of government campaigns that have used media in an innovative way in order to achieve greater engagement and thereby better results. We will explore the ways in which innovative media usage was an essential component of success, using award-winning case studies as examples.

## Selective targeting of discrete audiences

It's commonly the case that a public service campaign will need to address multiple audiences rather than a single target. This reflects the fact that most government policies involve multiple stakeholders, typically including the public, the service provider responsible for delivering the policy, and influencers such as Citizens' Advice Bureaux, charities or community groups. And within the public audience there are often sub-segments defined by life stage, attitude or behaviour.

For this reason public service campaigns are rarely 'one size fits all', but are more likely to encompass a number of different messages addressing discrete segments within the overall audience. Therefore targeted media selection is often essential to ensure the right messages reach the intended audiences.

However, selective media targeting can achieve more than just an accurate delivery of the campaign. Many media are seen as favourite brands by their audience (sometimes expressed as 'my media'). People have stronger bonds to their favourite newspaper or TV show than they do to their choice of washing powder or toothpaste. Media brands can be the nucleus around which communities form (e.g. for devotees of *Big Brother*), providers of cherished 'me time' (e.g. women's glossy magazines) or signifiers of identity or tribal allegiance (e.g. football club fan websites or car customisation magazines).

Placing a campaign within such an environment achieves more than just efficient audience delivery: it signals a conscious decision to address that audience. From the audience's perspective, discovering a message carefully placed in their environment shows that the advertiser has clearly gone to the trouble of studying their lifestyle in order to track them down to that precise point. It reframes the campaign from being 'for anyone' into 'for me'. This increases the perceived relevance of the campaign and so enhances its persuasiveness.

Since many government campaigns need to address narrow subsets or interest groups within the population – from minority ethnic groups to disabled people, small business owners to new mothers – this self-recognition effect is highly valuable.

### *Communicating with the difficult-to-reach: infiltrating the youth 'fortress'*

Youth culture, and the adult culture of which the government is a part, could not be further apart. As the HEA Drugs Education campaign of 1998 says:

> *These two worlds were poles apart, living side by side but with no common ground. Young people dismissed parents and other authority figures as ignorant, out of touch and incapable of offering unbiased advice.*

The critical insight that shaped the campaign's strategy was to recognise that, contrary to the popular view, young people don't start taking drugs because they're pressured by wayward friends or targeted by evil pushers at the school gates. In reality it is a choice that young people make for themselves, based on what they know of the potential risks and likely enjoyment.

> *The fortress of youth culture was full of tales of the excitement drugs could offer, with young people as enthusiastic advocates of the drugs experience … when young people weighed up the pros and cons to make their active choice, the balance of evidence within their world was overwhelmingly in favour of drugs.*

The paper uses a memorable metaphor – a youth culture 'fortress' – to highlight the divide perceived by young people between their world and that of their parents, authority figures and the tabloid press (Figure 1).

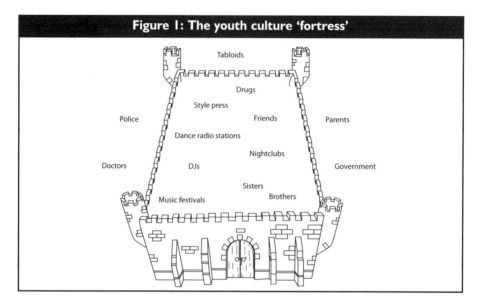

**Figure 1: The youth culture 'fortress'**

Tabloids

Drugs

Style press

Police · Friends · Parents

Dance radio stations

Nightclubs

Doctors · DJs · Government

Sisters

Music festivals · Brothers

Further research revealed that the one thing that had the power to change their minds was to provoke worries about the effect of drug taking on their health. The information they receive from youth culture fails to make clear the very real health risks associated with drug taking, and yet when these risks are appreciated, the balance of choice shifts significantly away from taking drugs. The problem was to find a way of communicating these health risks in a credible way.

The solution was to present health information in a candid, unbiased way, while acknowledging that drugs do have some positive effects. This story was told within media that infiltrated the youth culture fortress, such as youth magazines and dance radio stations, alongside the placement of campaign materials in youth venues such as nightclubs, record shops and music festivals. The paper highlights that this narrowly targeted media selection gave the twin benefits of increased persuasiveness and more efficient reach:

*These media are integral to youth culture – private, trusted sources of information, and environments where talk of drugs is appropriate. This media choice also enabled us to put our limited budget ... to great effect. Over three years our radio coverage was high and press coverage almost universal, both with high frequency.*

The result achieved by the campaign was that the previously growing incidence of drug use was reversed. Financially, the £2.3 million annual campaign budget has paid back across several fronts: £11 million has been saved from lost working days, and £28 million of consumer expenditure has been diverted out of the drugs economy and into legal markets such as food and clothing, not to mention the avoidance of the cost of dealing with future health problems associated with drug use.

## The benefits of mixed-media campaigns: the 'media multiplier'

The 'media multiplier' is a well-documented term that refers to the benefits of using multiple media channels for a given campaign budget. The two components to this multiplier effect are an increase in audience reach and an improvement in communications take-out.

The increase in reach is a direct result of the fact that there are newspaper readers who don't watch much TV, for instance, or radio listeners who don't read newspapers. Given the basic media principle that beyond a reasonable threshold of expenditure within any one medium, increasing the spend merely adds frequency of exposure rather than reaching new people, then it follows that spending the increase on introducing a second medium will broaden the overall reach.

To illustrate this, consider the overlap between the audiences for three media: commercial TV, national newspapers and commercial radio. Using research data from the IPA TouchPoints hub survey, Figure 2 (not to scale) shows the overlap between the number of people who watched any commercial TV channel, read any national newspaper or listened to any commercial radio station in the last seven days.

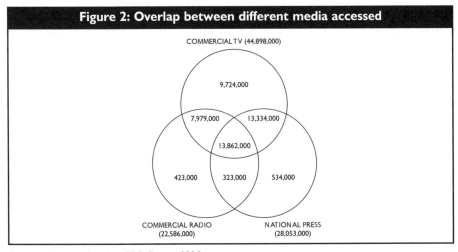

**Figure 2: Overlap between different media accessed**

COMMERCIAL TV (44,898,000)

9,724,000

7,979,000    13,334,000

13,862,000

423,000    323,000    534,000

COMMERCIAL RADIO
(22,586,000)

NATIONAL PRESS
(28,053,000)

Source: IPA Touch Points Hub Survey 2005.
Base: all adults 15+; sample size: 5,010.

The second benefit of the media multiplier is to improve the overall take-out from the campaign. This is because different media work in different ways, and fulfil complementary roles. For instance, while television advertising is well suited to evoking an emotional response to create positive imagery, newspapers are great at delivering product information. A mixed-media schedule can allow each channel to play to its strengths, maximising the overall effectiveness of the collective campaign.

### Advertising as providing a solution to the problem at point of sale

An example is the Home Protection case of 1984, illustrating how a previously successful regional test campaign to encourage householders to fit window locks was rolled out nationally. Rather than raising levels of concern about the risks of burglary in order to drive behaviour, the campaign exploited existing levels of concern and provided a positive, helpful and practical solution: fitting window locks.

In addition to traditional media (television and newspapers), the campaign also deployed grass-roots briefings for Crime Prevention Officers and point-of-sale merchandising in retailers stocking window locks.

Sales of window locks increased by 26% across the whole campaign area. However, since the TV advertising covered only certain regions, and while the newspapers were national, it was possible to identify a multiplier effect in those areas where both media were active.

| Table 1: The media multiplier effect | |
|---|---|
| | % change |
| Total campaign area | +26 |
| TV and press area | +43 |
| Press only | +2 |

Source: RAL

### Using a coalition of advertisers to increase the effect

Another approach is to integrate different advertisers in a coalition such as the Tobacco Control case of 2004. This is particularly effective with intractable public heath issues and can be used instead of a single 'blockbuster' campaign. This approach uses a coalition of different advertisers, each focusing on different aspects of the problem.

With three distinct and credible 'voices' (the NHS, Cancer Research UK and the British Heart Foundation), the campaign deployed a wide range of different communications channels. Television advertising, billboards and press were used alongside the web, various community-level channels such as posters in doctors' surgeries, and an extensive direct marketing programme. Non-traditional tactics included Second Hand Smoke messages on newborn babies' bibs. More broadly, the campaign encompasses the NHS Smoking Helpline and Stop Smoking Services.

The paper highlights the media multiplier effect as an important factor in its success:

*We can prove that the multiplier effect works harder than single campaign strands by looking at how smokers' attitudes are affected by advertising according to the number of strands they have seen ... Smokers who have seen more strands have significantly higher awareness of smoking-related diseases.*

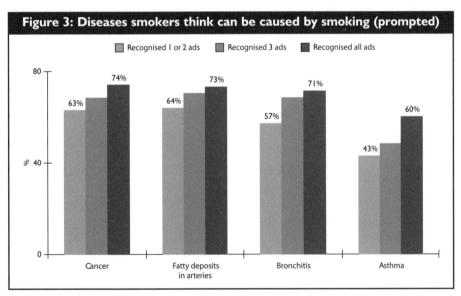

Figure 3: Diseases smokers think can be caused by smoking (prompted)

Base: smokers ($n = 1078$): seen one or two adverts ($n = 380$), seen three ($n = 289$), seen all ($n = 341$)
Source: BMRB Tobacco Education Campaign Tracking Study, February 2004

## *The power of an overarching 'brand' idea*

The Department for Transport case of 2006 is an integrated marketing tour de force, taking a plethora of road safety issues and audiences and combining them into a single, overarching campaign idea: Think!

The media mix was very broad, including TV, radio, cinema, internet and outdoor advertising; sponsorship; ambient media; partnership marketing; and even the road environment itself (e.g. road signs and parking bays). However, it avoided the risk of scattering its efforts too thinly across the many different media used by bringing all strands and messages together with a unifying creative idea. In this way each individual message contributes to the collective impact of the Think! campaign:

*Multi-media awareness of Think! creates an even stronger influence on attitudes and claimed road behaviour. Think! drives better integration which delivers a further boost to attitudes and behaviour.*

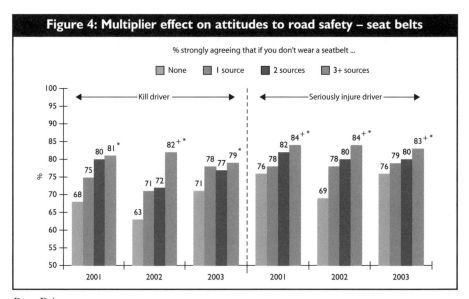

**Figure 4: Multiplier effect on attitudes to road safety – seat belts**

Base: Drivers
Source: TNS tracking study

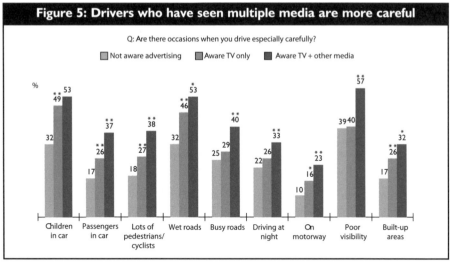

**Figure 5: Drivers who have seen multiple media are more careful**

Q: Are there occasions when you drive especially carefully?

☐ Not aware advertising   ☐ Aware TV only   ■ Aware TV + other media

Base: All drivers: not aware of advertising (*n* = 181); aware of TV only (*n* = 478); aware of TV and other media (*n* = 651)
Source: NOP segmentation study, 2006

## Waiting for the right moment: 'proximate media'

What is the ideal moment to influence someone? Common sense suggests that the context within which a message is encountered will have a significant effect on how it is received. It's the difference between the message being apt and being irrelevant – for the consumer on the receiving end, between a blank face and a spark of recognition. Given that the world is now saturated with brand messages in almost every venue, identifying those specific instants when the message aligns with its context is the key to being noticed, not ignored.

Furthermore, when the aim of a campaign is to stimulate people to change their behaviour, what better time to talk to them than at the point when they're about to undertake that very behaviour? If we have created a persuasive argument or influential stimulus that promotes or deters a specific action, it makes sense to deliver this as close as possible to the time and place where that action would occur. This could be termed 'proximate media'.

This is why increasing numbers of government campaigns are using 'ambient' media that place advertising messages into the fabric of everyday life. Not only can these achieve greater proximity between the advertising and the behaviour it's seeking to influence, they often also benefit from appearing unexpectedly in unusual places. This element of surprise can deliver greater impact and reward the audience with a sense of discovery.

### *Advertising as part of everyday life: Point of Prey*

The GLA Safer Travel at Night campaign of 2004 addresses the challenge of persuading people not to do something, namely get into an unlicensed mini-cab, despite it being late at night and there being no other convenient alternatives immediately available.

The planning process behind this campaign demonstrates how a close understanding of the audience's mindset around the time of the desired behaviour change is the key to identifying the right moments to communicate.

Recognising that conventional research would yield few accurate insights into the mindset of young women leaving a club after a boozy night out, the planners conducted observational research on the streets of Soho at 2 am. This was followed by interviews with the same women the next day:

> *We interviewed our research subjects the following day with two specific objectives. First, to develop an understanding of how people feel at the point they leave a club to go home. Second, to retrace the stages of the evening, with a view to identifying the 'touchpoints' for communicating our message in the relevant environment.*

This led to a media strategy that placed messages at the 'Point of Prey', i.e. the point at which the minicab driver or tout approaches the woman, and she makes the decision whether or not to get into the car. These messages were designed to offer a practical solution to the problem, such as the telephone number that would provide details of licensed minicab firms and information on night bus routes.

It should be noted that the campaign did not rely solely on these targeted ambient media. Alongside there was cinema and subsequently a TV campaign that sought to reach people in a rational, sober state of mind, in order to change attitudes to the touts. The target for this part of the campaign was not just the women themselves but also their boyfriends, friends and doormen, who might be in a position to stop them getting into an illegal minicab. More broadly it was to act as a rallying call for a wider range of stakeholders, such as the Public Carriage Office and Transport for London.

Proximate media are not a panacea, rather they are a way of maximising influence at the final stage of what will typically be a long sequence of influences

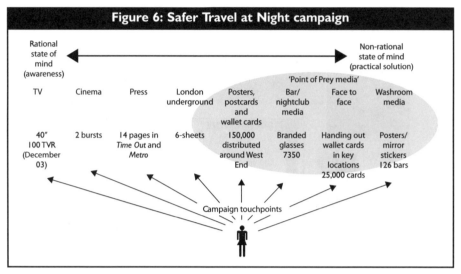

Figure 6: Safer Travel at Night campaign

Source: Transport for London

upon eventual behaviour. But as this case demonstrates, they can be a very effective way of bringing the message home at precisely the right moment.

*The total number of sexual assaults declined by 27% and rapes by 22% in the first 12 months of the campaign, as compared with the previous year. Overall this equates to 85 fewer attacks between October 2002 and March 2004.*

### Using proximate media under an umbrella theme: 'Think!'

As we have seen in the Department for Transport case of 2006 described earlier, the use of the integrated creative device – Think! – enabled the different strands of road safety communications to cohere into a single campaign.

Within a number of these individual strands there are examples of the use of proximate media. Examples include the targeting of 'drug-driving' (Figure 7), where the campaign was delivered in the vicinity of the dance music scene:

*Building on the link between music, dancing, drugs and driving we have connected with our target audience using fake cocaine wraps, car finder cards at festivals (Glastonbury and V), and a partnership with the Ministry of Sound online.*

**Figure 7: Department for Transport – 'Think' campaign, proximate media**

Another example is the use of roadside media that places the Think! message in the immediate context of driving (Figure 8).

**Figure 8: Department for Transport – 'Think' campaign, roadside media**

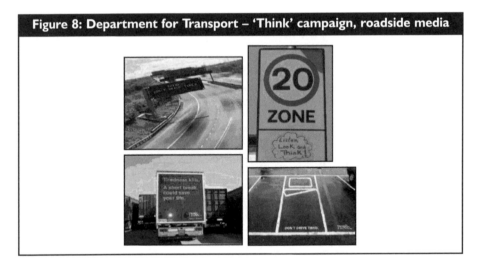

### A still unsolved problem: separating effects of proximate media

The issue that none of these case studies deals with is the ability to isolate the specific effect of the proximate media within the wider communications plan. Ambient and non-traditional media generally fail to be recorded by conventional advertising tracking studies, usually because this activity is highly localised and is therefore exposed to only a small proportion of the respondents in a (most probably national) sample survey.

It is of course possible to deploy specific research methods to capture the localised effects of proximate media – for example, targeted interviews in the immediate vicinity – but we have found no example of this within the IPA dataBANK of government campaigns. This remains a challenge for future award entrants.

## What we have learned

1. Increasingly, mass advertising is less effective for reaching discrete target groups – particularly when such groups don't want to hear the message. Using media that are part of the target group's world – specialist magazines for example – helps target more directly and personally.
2. The closer the message is to the behaviour to be changed or modified, the better. This requires detailed understanding of behaviour patterns to choose media that are part of that behaviour pattern.
3. A media strategy that co-ordinates different sponsoring organisations enhances the impact: different voices but with a similar message.
4. Whether using different sponsors or, more typically simply using different media, it is critical that there is a consistent overarching idea. The messages need not be identical but they should reflect a common theme.

# Chapter 8

# Who owns the message?

By Alex Harris and
Charles Vallance
VCCP

In the 25 years since the first IPA case was written for the COI, there could hardly have been a more dramatic turnaround in the way the public view authority, how they judge it, consume it and construe it.

There are many (including the authors) who believe profound social and technological changes have essentially reversed the rules of authority, particularly in terms of how it is disseminated and transferred. This reversal is neatly summed up in the concept that, in the course of one generation, we have moved from a model of authority based on deference, to one based on reference.

This switch in authority has had an observably profound impact on the way government messages are couched, framed and sourced. Let us consider the implications of the new model for a moment and then look in more detail at what it tells us about the context surrounding government communications. In the course of this assessment one thing will become abundantly apparent: 'Who owns the message?' has become a question that has grown vastly in importance over time (and it certainly matters!).

Figure 1 helps to illustrate how the reversal of authority has turned many of the old hierarchies upside down.

Where once we looked for authority from our leaders and institutions, we are now far more likely to refer to our friends, our family, people like us (often via networked opinion online).

For both COI and government departments, the result has been the gradual development of new models and perhaps it is not surprising that the IPA

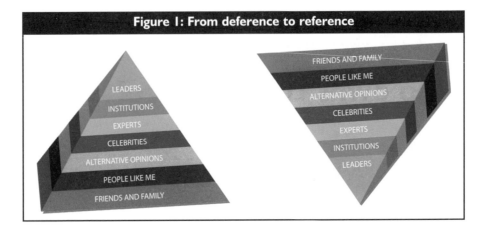

Figure 1: From deference to reference

award-winning cases have shown how understanding in this area has, over the years, displayed growing imagination, innovation and lateral thinking.

The Tobacco Control case shows that anti-smoking advertising has quadrupled in effectiveness to become the most powerful trigger to smokers kicking the habit: more important even than word of mouth or doctor's advice.

The HEA Drugs Education campaign argues compellingly that since the start of the campaign, instead of a continued seemingly inexorable rise, drug use has declined.

Both are examples of advertising's extraordinary success in kick-starting social change.

## How can we consider message ownership?

The consideration of who owns the message can be discussed in relation to the three questions below:

- Most obviously, who is literally presenting the message? Case studies show a range of ownership of message from government agency in the example of the Inland Revenue, a coalition of brands for Tobacco Control to an invented 'brand' in the case of Think!, the Department for Transport campaign. We will discuss the reasons for and the implications of these choices and how they have achieved unsurpassed engagement and results via the acknowledgement of society's evolved model of reference.

- How has the tone and nature of messaging reflected the shift from deference to reference?
- How are different stakeholder groups mobilised to take the message onwards, from peers to partners to press?

## The importance of who presents the message

Clearly the face behind the message is always critical in communications, but nowhere more so than in government messaging. This is for two reasons.

Primarily, because of who the government is, relationships and attitudes to government are complex and fraught. The public have an ingrained suspicion of all but the most straightforward informational government messages, undoubtedly exacerbated by media tales of spin, hidden agendas and the notion of the nanny state. Indeed research shows that, among some groups, government messaging is utterly rejected, particularly by the young. As case studies show, by getting the issue of message ownership wrong, a campaign can be wrong-footed, or worse, from the outset.

Of secondary concern is the nature of the messaging. As previous chapters point out, government communications rarely bring good news and are often asking the recipient to reconsider entrenched (often enjoyable) behaviours.

A key factor in determining appropriate message ownership is: what is the nature of the ask? Are you asking me to do something or stop doing something? How difficult is it for me to do so? And who will benefit from this action – the individual, the community or the state? We will see that the more emotionally intimate the behaviour, the more complex the issue of ownership becomes and the more potentially inappropriate the traditionally imagined heavy hand of government.

### *Brand ownership: how a range of voices provided authority*

Perhaps the gold standard in terms of matching message and messenger is the Tobacco Control IPA paper from 2004, which shows how a range of voices whose authority lay in different fields spoke together to magnify the effectiveness of that campaign.

At the time of writing, smoking was a huge problem, killing 120,000 people a year in the UK – more than five times the number of deaths caused collectively by road accidents, drug or drink abuse, accidents, murders, suicide and AIDS – and, in 1996, smoking rates were rising again for the first time in over 20 years.

While 83% of smokers wished that they had never started, smokers are used to defending their position. As the author of the IPA paper writes:

> ... *smokers had developed barriers and denials to avoid having to give up*
> ... *we needed to fight the power of addiction.*

Research showed that a multiple offensive was required. Health was the key trigger and lessons from international experience uncovered three additional triggers.

1. *Shock – damage you are doing now*. Australia had created a very successful controversial campaign – 'Every cigarette is doing you damage' – a hard-hitting campaign that connected the cigarette to internal organ damage.
2. *Industry – exposing the truth*. California had successfully disabused smokers of some of their beliefs about smoking, which had been fostered by the industry.
3. *Kids – damage your smoking does to your loved ones*. Second-hand or 'passive' smoke messages had had a powerful effect in California and Massachusetts.

However, further qualitative research showed that these messages were hampered by the proposed messengers. For the government to expose the tobacco industry felt hypocritical, and multiple government messaging left smokers feeling victimised. While the NHS undeniably is the authority on health, the shock strand of activity was deemed too hard-hitting.

Put simply, two of the three secondary messages would be more powerful if they came from different brands. Cancer Research UK agreed to reveal the truth about the tobacco industry's 'light and mild' cigarette deception, and the British Heart Foundation (BHF) brought its authority to the link between smoking and the heart in a new and graphic way. In doing this we effectively created a new type of integration: an *integration of advertisers* that would be compelling but not oppressive.

The third piece of 'new news' – damage to loved ones caused by smoking – was felt to be a suitable NHS message, as it focused on protecting children.

For the consumer, different voices meant impartiality, expertise and trust plus a lack of conspicuous agenda. By avoiding the government voice from on high, smokers did not feel bullied or hectored, often a reason for retrenchment into negative behaviours. Rather, the message came from those ground-level organisations that actually provide the support that helps people stay quit and those that deal with the fallout from smoking.

As is so often the case in government campaigns, long-term success hinged on the delivery of a successful 'customer experience'. A key turning point for the tobacco strategy was when the team reframed the challenge as public service as opposed to public information. Indeed some NHS primary care trusts reported up to a 25% increase in referrals to smoking cessation clinics as a direct result of the campaign.

Tracking further proves that message ownership matters: while 67% of smokers agreed that the advertising 'really caught' my attention, among those aware that the message was from Cancer Research UK, endorsement levels rose to 84%.

### *Identifying a source of authority that young people would listen to*

The HEA Drugs Education case (1998) describes how qualitative research (and common sense) suggested that young people involved in or considering drugs would not be receptive to direct government communications.

The adult world, fuelled by the media, was in a state of panic and, in behaving as such, had rendered its point of view utterly irrelevant. Penetrating the youth fortress would mean tough decisions on message and medium, as discussed elsewhere, but also in terms of messenger.

Young people were looking for a voice that was credible, informed and non-judgemental. A resource already existed: the National Drugs Helpline had been operating since April 1995 but in England it had no awareness or brand image.

By including the number on all materials the campaign was able to open a dialogue with young people and offer a trusted and neutral space that they could visit as and when they had questions or concerns. This established a peer-to-peer relationship and was the antithesis of the usual concerned grown-up voice – of parents, teachers and the media – that nagged and threatened.

Of course, the use of National Drugs Helpline branding also gave the campaign the scope to engage with the target and behave in a way that a government brand never could, as discussed later.

### *How an umbrella 'brand' idea succeeded in creating a voice of authority that explained rather than censored*

A key challenge for all public-sector campaigns is to reach a huge variety of stakeholders who have a range (often non-complementary) of issues and motivations. How to achieve integration and build scale while communicating specific targeted messages?

The Department for Transport case used a huge brand idea – Think! – that provided an umbrella under which all road safety communications sat, and in doing so delivered the flexibility to communicate across a mind-boggling range of targets and messages.

Some highlights from the IPA paper include the breadth of target audience that has been successfully reached, from the Hedgehog animated characters who talked to children, to Crash, the drink-driving campaign, as well as niche messaging among hard-to-reach targets such as the drug-drive campaign.

Think! delivers a great tonal stretch – from censoring to supportive:

> *In its early years, Think! continued to use the imperative voice of govern-ment – 'Think! Don't drink and drive'. But as the campaign evolved we adopted new voices: communications that explain rather than assert – Think! It's 30 for a reason.*

By creating a brand by proxy, the Department for Transport presented a pub-lic face in Think! that neatly side-stepped the pitfalls of direct government communications yet benefited from the multiplier effect of a single voice.

### The importance of tone and messaging in encouraging personal responsibility vs nanny state

The Health Education Authority (HEA) AIDS campaign (1994) illustrates the effective use of mass media advertising to meet the challenge of AIDS.

Nowhere do the issues of message ownership and tone dovetail better than by observing the changes in communications of the AIDS message from the mid-1980s to mid-1990s.

In 1986 the arrival of AIDS was announced direct by the Department of Health, with a campaign featuring apocalyptic images of tombstones and ice-bergs, stressing the seriousness of AIDS and that everyone was at risk. While this generated a high level of awareness and anxiety, a 12-month hiatus in advertising led to a public perception of lessened risk.

The next era of the campaign saw a strikingly different tone adopted, guided by behavioural models. The message came from the Health Education Authority, a government agency rather than a department, and with it a more balanced and factual approach that emphasised the threat while promoting the primary means of prevention (condoms), and the removal of the emotional barriers to buying and using condoms.

Despite a lack of obvious shock tactics, the campaign maintained levels of health concern, encouraged a personal identification with the risk of HIV and helped encourage condom use among young heterosexuals.

### Being honest can lead to greater credibility

When drug users were asked what would make them stop using drugs, by far the biggest concern (63% agreement) was 'worries about my health'. However, success hinged not only upon what but how this message was presented.

As the author of the HEA Drugs Education campaign (1998) paper writes:

> We adopted an open, honest tone, that allowed people to make up their own minds, and admitted that, in this untested market, doctors do not yet have all the facts.

> We recommended that the government take the bold unprecedented step of letting us acknowledge the positive effects of drugs, to demonstrate our insider knowledge. This was crucial to the campaign's credibility.

The critical insight here was that young people will not be told what to do by adults, but when presented with the facts in a clear dispassionate way, will draw judgement based on that information.

This insight was informed by Ajzen and Fishbein's Theory of Reasoned Action (see Chapter 2, pp. 59–60):

> Generally speaking, the theory is based on the assumption that human beings are usually quite rational and make systematic use of the information available to them … We argue that people consider the implications of their actions before they decide to engage or not engage in a given behaviour.

Further credence to this approach is provided by the outstanding results that the campaign achieved, with fewer young people trying drugs, fewer planning to take drugs and more drug users quitting.

### A supportive tone from a helpful personality can be more successful than hectoring

Tax Self-Assessment was launched in 1997 with an objective of getting taxpayers to complete their own tax forms – a big behavioural challenge given the low interest of the sector and complexity of message.

Unlike previous case studies discussed, the campaign ran as a piece of communications direct from Inland Revenue as befits a less emotionally complex task in which the government brand owns the relevant expertise.

However, it was only after Hector the tax inspector (and civil service bowler-hatted stereotype) was replaced with the far more supportive tone of the 'Tax needn't be taxing' campaign that the initiative really flew.

Using analogies with other apparently difficult tasks (e.g. learning the piano, abseiling down a building, asking someone out for a date), brand spokesperson Adam Hart-Davis was able to empathise with people's concerns and provide reassurance that help was available.

Post-campaign, not only were record numbers of people filing their tax returns on time, but internet filing rose more than twenty-fold.

As the IPA paper references, perhaps most remarkably, there was a dramatic uplift in the sense that the Inland Revenue (which had now become HM Revenue & Customs) was changing for the better.

> Adam Hart-Davis has become part of the Self Assessment brand, to which he brings positive and appropriate qualities: he is trustworthy, sensible, authoritative … he has gravitas, is official but not establishment. He brings an air of relevant familiarity … in an area towards which taxpayers do not otherwise feel particularly warm.

The approach perfectly straddled the poles of expertise and approachability, positioning the Revenue as an archetypal modern service brand.

All these elements build to create a sense of the type of tone and messaging that best delivers genuine behaviour change.

When the tax pitch was under way, *Marketing* reported that:

> *Some brands are meant to be unpopular and all the better for it … MCBD should be aware that hectoring works … as a nation we respond to nanny-ish unambiguous telling offs.*

However, at the heart of their strategy and those of the other case studies outlined here, was a belief, supported by behavioural psychologists, that the key to changing behaviour is support and reassurance. As the IPA paper states:

> *Almost without exception, outside experts told us that hectoring people typically only entrenches negative behaviour. Many cited the example of smoking: shouting at someone to quit won't work, whereas supporting them and reassuring them about the difficulties might just do the trick.*

## Mobilising stakeholders to take the message onwards

Perhaps one of the defining features of a government brief is the sheer range and scope of shareholders who need to be reached, influenced and persuaded. The nuance of media choice and selection is discussed elsewhere; however, this section focuses on the ways in which key influencers beyond the primary target have been mobilised to take ownership of the message and move it onwards deep into communities, and with a level of authenticity and authority that advertising direct simply can't achieve.

### *Partners on the ground*

Doctors, police, social workers, helpline operators: these are the groups who literally deliver the experience on the ground – the individuals who help switch awareness into behaviour change. Again, across case studies, there are learnings to suggest that the most successful campaigns have provided guidance, inspiration and motivation to those groups working at the coalface.

In the case of the HEA Drugs Education campaign, materials were adopted by teachers to be used in classrooms. The HEA has had requests for approximately 150,000 copies of the ads by 15,000 organisations and was adopted for the training of drugs professionals. As the author of the paper states:

> *As a result, our campaign has indirectly impacted on young people by informing those that deal with them on a day to day basis.*

An additional benefit was the saving of an estimated £3 million in the production of support.

A Road Safety Officer said of the Think! campaign:

> *Think! encourages people to come out of their 'silos' to work together. It has managed to get a lot of professional support behind it across a broad spectrum of organisations.*

The Inland Revenue (now HM Revenue & Customs) is a service organisation keen to position itself as a modern, customer-friendly brand, yet the bowler-hatted bureaucrat was at odds with this vision let alone reflective of the Inland Revenue's diverse workforce. With the retirement of Hector the tax inspector and the launch of the 'Tax needn't be taxing' campaign, the agency was able to reposition itself as a modern service brand.

> *The campaign's messages about help and support were very well received and created a sense that the Inland Revenue may be trying to lighten up.*
> Researchworks, 2002

By influencing the 'customer experience' itself, the message is hugely amplified thanks to the resonance of a human interaction compared with the processing of a piece of communications.

### Creating a 'noise cloud'

At the very start of social change, is the sense that something is happening out there. Broadcast media are key to delivering a statement of intent, as is the deployment of those on the ground. But for an initiative to take wing, people need to be talking about it.

The most successful campaigns contain a hook – be that in message or delivery – that the media pick up and amplify.

In the case of Tobacco Control, only 18 days into the campaign the *Observer* ran a cartoon referencing 'fatty cigarettes', showing just how far and fast the campaign had seeped into the nation's psyche.

Similarly, while pre-1995 pro-drug articles were rife in style magazines, the Drugs Education campaign found that style press editorial was covering drugs in an increasingly balanced or even negative way over the course of the campaign. Analysis of *The Face* and *Mixmag*'s content found that, by 1997, only 18% of their articles on drugs took a pro-drug stance. This is particularly potent given the trust and intimacy of the relationship between this kind of magazine and its readership.

However, as the Deference to Reference model shows (Figure 1), change begins to accelerate when the discussion is taking place on the street and at home.

The author of the Tobacco Control paper talks about how the coalition of brands got people talking:

> *The integration of advertisers appears to fuel the smoking debate. Smokers are more likely to discuss the advertising with their friends and family (a key prompt to quitting).*

> *Smokers are also more likely to think that 'more and more people are giving up smoking these days'.*

Talking about the message among peers makes it real and relevant and creates a sense of momentum – a virtuous circle of awareness, discussion and behaviour (perceived and actual). This builds to a sense of social pressure, very real but crucially an organic and self-perpetuating process rather than a government-down mandate. To quote the Think! IPA paper, 'behaviour is a function of social context'.

So in summary and in answer to the initial question, ownership of the message certainly matters, more so than ever in a world of reference, in which authority brands with traditional modes of address can fail to resonate. However, as the case studies have demonstrated, new approaches to how public messages are voiced, sourced and projected have meant that advertising remains unsurpassed as a tool for driving long-term social and cultural change.

# Part 4

# Does it work?

# Chapter 9

# Budget setting

By Peter Buchanan

COI

When the Editor and I saw the first draft of the following chapter – 'Measuring success' – from Rebecca Morgan and John Poorta, we both thought some additional observations on budget setting would be useful. This is designed to complement Rebecca and John's thoughts concerning the importance of measurement, and its role in forecasting and controlling cost as a campaign develops; all of which comes together in the all-important return on marketing investment.

Budget setting in the public sector is particularly challenging since the subject in question may not have been attempted before. Due to the complexity of many campaign audiences (such as the disabled, under-age smokers, drug users or the elderly poor), robust commercial data may not have been collected via the normal mainstream audience research methodologies.

Of course, on some occasions, historical data will be available, or a 'read across' may be possible from other campaign evaluations or audience data.

One solution is to develop your own checklist against which a budget can be constructed. A single measure will not yield sufficient data, but by selecting a number of relevant factors and testing a notional budget against these measures, a clearer plan of the investment required, with supporting evidence, can be constructed. Individuals may wish to develop their own checklist, but an example menu might be constructed as follows:

- furthering the department's corporate objectives
- a strong ROMI (Return on Marketing Investment) business case
- clear, quantified communications objectives
- performance criteria vs objectives (recall, attitude shift, claimed behavioural change)
- response targets (volume, conversion, response pattern)
- cost per response

- likely campaign decay rate
- adjustment for inflation
- availability of new research (e.g. to assess public comprehension or resistance)
- likely effect of editorial coverage (supportive, neutral, critical)
- campaign timing vs a previous campaign period
- target audience media consumption patterns
- inclusive or specialist nature of the audience
- the media environment prior to campaign launch
- competing or complementary messages
- the influence of stakeholders or opinion formers
- a change in the ambitions for the campaign
- availability of econometric modelling data.

The idea of a 'basket of measures' is also reflected in the IPA monograph – *Marketing in the Era of Accountability* – which observes '… it is not the case that any particular business effects reflect overall performance, but rather the *number* of them.'

One important area that can provide a greater degree of certainty due to the ability to measure volume and quality of the data across communications channels, individual media and audiences, is direct response. Investment in sophisticated reporting, analysis and forecasting should provide a far greater degree of certainty for those campaigns where the main objective is the generation of response and subsequent conversion or take-up of programmes.

One opportunity, often not available to public-sector marketers, is the test market (frequently public service campaigns must be announced to the whole population simultaneously). However, if the opportunity to test creative options, regions, communications channels and media weights is available, then it should be seriously considered.

A further possibility is to fine-tune the budget proposed in accordance with the scale illustrated in Figure 1.

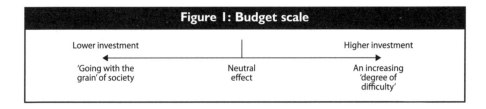

**Figure 1: Budget scale**

Lower investment ← → Higher investment

'Going with the grain' of society | Neutral effect | An increasing 'degree of difficulty'

I think 'going with the grain' is fairly self-explanatory. But the process can be accelerated via new legislation (smoking ban in public places), technological breakthroughs (availability of breathalysers) or the extension of services (JobCentre Plus).

Examples of a 'degree of difficulty' might include the following:

- 'bad news' messages
- complexity of message/difficulty in comprehension
- suspicion of political intent/media spin
- low interest in the subject matter
- misperception/currently entrenched views
- subsequent politicisation of the campaign/message.

At the time of writing, this is a somewhat untested concept, except for some development work by Opinion Leader Research in 2004 as part of another project for the COI. In the future, I would like the opportunity to explore this concept in more detail.

Finally a realistic but somewhat sobering thought from the American Advertising Agency Association:

> *Advertising budgeting appears to be a complex, poorly structured process that encompasses measurement of historical performance, forecasting future performance and negotiations for resources. Simple rules of thumb are often mentioned, but almost never seem to be the sole determinant of budgets. These rules, like models, test markets and tracking data, 'provide one more stake in the ground'. Models are used by many companies, but seem to be more as a reality check than to generate 'optimal' budgets.*
> Professors Farris, Reibstein and Shamers, AAAA (1998)

# Chapter 10

# Measuring success

By Rebecca Morgan and John Poorta

Lowe Worldwide and Leo Burnett

Recent data show that, in aggregate, the UK government is the third largest advertiser behind consolidated P&G and Unilever. Given that the government is spending taxpayers' and not shareholders' money, is so much the greater burden of proof for funds invested efficiently and effectively.

From our analysis, the fact is that advertising has proved a truly efficient form of government investment – more often the most efficient means possible of using a particular fund to address a particular issue.

To put this in context, the evidence cited in the government and COI IPA cases adds up to some staggering proven returns on monies invested in advertising: tens of thousands of lives saved, billions of pounds of value retained in the economy, thousands of policemen, teachers, services and healthcare personnel recruited to keep our society moving.

## A spectrum of effects

This chapter showcases the specific measures used to prove these effects, highlighting best practice examples common across the papers and some of the more imaginative ways authors have found to prove their cases.

When looking at types of measures, there is often a debate about the value of intermediate measures vs the harder commercial ones. Communications teams and agencies have been known to argue that intermediate measures are the most important, given they can't control the consumer experience beyond the advertising. However, the evidence from the cases is that the most successful show full-spectrum effects across intermediate, behavioural and ROMI (Return on Marketing Investment) dimensions. Put simply, the most effective campaigns tend to show a wide range of effects, so the more measures that move the better. Although profit per se is not relevant to government campaigns, the most successful cases do think in terms of the financial value of the effect.

In order to reflect the need to look at full-spectrum effects, we have organised the analysis into a framework of:

1. Intermediate measures – awareness, message communication, attitude shifts
2. Behavioural measures – responses, enquiries, compliance
3. ROMI
4. Other effects – efficiency, human and societal impact.

However, before we dive into this analysis it is worthwhile drawing out one further introductory thought. If effectiveness is essentially defined as 'achieving goals', it is worth noting that proof of effect actually begins with a clear picture of the scale of the task. There is substantial evidence that campaigns with clear objectives tend to be more successful than those without, and perhaps due to the scrutiny they receive, government campaigns tend to emanate from crystal-clear objectives. Some of the papers bring those objectives notably to life, many using a piece of compelling quantitative data to set the scene;

- The 2000 Reading and Literacy case sets in historical context the task of improving reading and literacy levels: 'the average reading ability of children has remained much the same since 1948' (NFER/National Literacy Trust).

- The 1996 Army Recruitment case, 'Be the best', cites that enquiries to Army Careers Information Offices had fallen by more than 50% from over 144,000 in 1986/7 to just 58,000 in 1993/4

- The 2006 TDA Teacher Recruitment case, 'A Class Act', really captured the magnitude of the task by quantitatively describing the looming teacher crisis – six years of straight decline plus '50% of all existing teachers were due to retire by 2010 – some 200,000 teachers who would need to be replaced'.

- The 1998 Army Recruitment case cited the amount of negative column inches impacting the environment within which the advertising had to perform: 'Over a two month period in 1995 there were 120,000 negative column inches of news coverage, equating to an annual equivalent of £42 million of media expenditure at rate card.'

Observations and statistics like these provide the prologue to the drama of evaluation, which then unfolds through the intermediate, behavioural and ROMI measures.

## Intermediate measures

Sometimes called 'the soft measures', here we are talking about how different government campaigns have recorded and analysed whether and how their communications activity has actually been received.

A communications team is asking itself at this point, has my campaign been noticed? If so, has the intended message been taken out and understood by our key audiences? Has it changed perceptions or attitudes, and are people attitudinally more predisposed to act on it?

These measures are the vital precursors to looking at data that record actual behaviour. If the above 'soft' measures are looking good, we are more likely to be convinced that the campaign has contributed to stimulating the recorded behavioural shifts in the 'hard' data.

Based on what we've studied, we have arrived at six principles of best practice in the category of intermediate measures; these are now discussed in turn.

### *1. A suite of measures is best*

In their monograph *Marketing in the Era of Accountability*,[1] Binet and Field posit the view that effectiveness needs to be proven through a balanced scorecard of intermediate measures. This view allows for the complex associations present in people's minds so that the more of the measures that move, the more convincing the case. It's a volume game, and certainly our analysis of cases supports this point.

The most successful cases contain intermediate measures that are (1) plentiful; (2) wide-ranging and discrete in their topics; and (3) a healthy mix of quantitative tracking and qualitative research. Here are some examples:

- The 2002 Police Recruitment paper, 'How thinking negatively ended the negative thinking', uses seven different intermediate tracking measures to validate the activity. These included spontaneous recall of the message, how advertising shaped job perceptions, and ratings of personal respect of the police by those aware and not aware of the advertising.
- The Police Recruitment paper is also one of a select few citing qualitative

creative research to support the strategic approach, and thus help prove ultimately that the psychology of the advertising worked.

- The 1998 Soldier Recruitment case, 'Be the best', uses a plethora of tracking measures very convincingly to show that the advertising worked as intended against a qualitative recruitment strategy – that is, that the ads defined the qualities needed to be a soldier (ambitious, self-confident, with common sense); drove recognition that a particular personality type was best suited to an army career from both the target and parent points of view; and drove recognition of the benefits of a job in the army (professional training, a sense of public service, career opportunities).

- The 2006 Tax Self-Assessment paper used a suite of intermediate measures to indicate that the advertising had worked as intended: high awareness for a low-involvement topic; message comprehension; specific concerns that were addressed; and claimed action taken by the target.

For communications teams and agencies setting up campaign measures, the first job is to balance a breadth of measures with making sure they are still specific enough to be indicative. The examples above fulfil both criteria: they use between five and ten measures, and have ensured that each measure contributes separately and specifically to the picture.

## 2. Simple comparative measures can have value

The value of intermediate measures is not necessarily to show the campaign is working, but rather to illuminate how and why it is working. Often the how and why is a subtle and complex task, but sometimes it can be delightfully simplified using basic comparative measures. By this we mean either pre and post measures or looking at those aware and not aware of the campaign. There is something very satisfying and convincing in the symmetry of contrast. And the most compelling government cases cite clear non-aware to aware shifts in attitude and claimed behaviour;

- The 2004 Tobacco Control case shows that, pre-campaign, only 28% of people saw second-hand smoke as a health risk to children, vs 56% seeing it as the number one danger following the advertising.

- The 1988 Drink-Driving case demonstrates the change in claimed drinking and driving by comparing all the key tracking study measures for the campaign year with those of the year prior. (And to further discount any seasonal effect it also compares January of the campaign year with January of the previous year (see Table 1)).

| Table 1: The change in drinking and driving in one year's campaign | | | |
|---|---|---|---|
| | Pre-campaign Nov 85–86 | During campaign Jan 87–88 | % change |
| Interviews | c.3,000 | c.3,000 | |
| Occasions recorded Drinking | 38,830 | 36,500 | –6 |
| Drinking 6+ units | 15,270 | 14,270 | –7 |
| Driving after any drink | 12,900 | 11,430 | –26 |
| Driving after 6+ units | 2,470 | 1,830 | –26 |

Source: RBL

- The 1988 Drink-Driving case also shows marked positive differences in the claimed behaviour of those who did not recognise the current TV compared with those who did recognise it – one of the simplest measures available (see Table 2).

| Table 2: Behaviour of those who did not recognise ads compared to those who did | | |
|---|---|---|
| All who drank outside the home | Did not recognise current TV (%) | Recognised current TV (%) |
| Drank and drove | 65 | 42 |
| Drank 4+ units and drove | 31 | 22 |
| Drank 6+ units and drove | 11 | 8 |
| Drank over personal limit | 7 | 3 |

Source: RBL

The paper then went one step further to support the results above by ruling out any suggestion that those who recognised the TV were in some way different in car behaviour to those who didn't – in fact they both had the same attitudes towards seatbelt usage and leaving a gap to the car in front.

It is probably the case that if you do not have a pre to post story then you don't have an effectiveness story.

### 3. *Measure against a category norm*

Most marketers are obsessed with benchmarking. It makes us feel safe and it is tremendously useful in assessing whether our campaign is really moving things on and genuinely impacting the status quo. Of course, benchmarking in fmcg is long established and relatively straightforward, but for government advertising where new policies or behaviour changes are the order of the day, it is much less obvious. Here are just a couple of examples where the authors have found a benchmark where one might not have been readily available:

- The 2006 Tax Self-Assessment case compares advertising awareness for HM Revenue & Customs against other financial service brands data, garnered from other IPA papers. It is entirely appropriate that tax should be considered in the context of financial service brands – and, indeed, scored higher awareness than NatWest, Barclays, Lloyds or HSBC.

- The 2006 TDA Teacher Recruitment case showed superior cut-through for the advertising versus some other police recruitment campaigns.

### 4. *Measure effect among specific target groups*

If the point of communication is to strengthen brand franchises and customer bases then it stands to reason that you must measure effects among particular groups of customers. In seeking to get people to either start doing something, stop doing something or do something differently, much government communications activity is concerned with reaching specific sub-groups and hard-to-reach audiences.

Communications teams and agencies need to be able to show results against those key groups. Here are some good examples where effects among particular target groups are clearly identified:

- The 2000 Reading and Literacy case shows that literacy levels were of most concern among C2DE families and, within that, dads were particular influencers. It shows that motivating these groups had a disproportionate effect on reading and literacy levels and measures within these groups specifically.

- The 1988 Drink-Driving case uses intermediate measures of claimed behaviour to show marked improvement among the prime target of men aged 20–34 and hard-core offenders aged 20–24. The paper shows that the claimed occasions on which men aged 20–34 drank 6+ units and drove fell from 13.7% to 9%.

## 5. Use intermediate measures to prove shifts in attitude

One particularly useful learning when it comes to intermediate measures, is when they are used to prove that a particular messaging psychology has had a telling effect on attitude shifts. This means communications teams and agencies must be specific at the outset about precisely what attitudes need to be changed, so the attitudinal measures line up accordingly. Most typically, successful cases look at attitude change by region, or more commonly over time and between individuals:

- The 2006 Vehicle Crime case uses attitudinal measures to prove the advertising delivered key tenets of the strategy: the messages that 'vehicle crime is opportunistic' and that 'you could avoid it happening to you'; shift in attitude towards 'not being a victim of vehicle crime' and it 'being possible to avoid'; and also that it is a 'shared responsibility' to tackle vehicle crime.

- In the 2006 TDA Teacher Recruitment case, given one of the major issues that the advertising needed to overcome was the negative perceptions of teaching, attitudinal measures are used very well to show significant improvements in positive perceptions of teaching and give the profession a sense of momentum (see Figure 1).

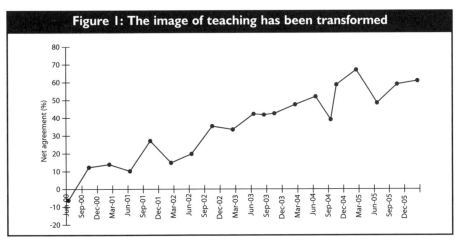

**Figure 1: The image of teaching has been transformed**

Source: TDA advertising tracking studies, 2000–06.
Base: all respondents

- The 2006 TDA Teacher Recruitment case also showed the correlation between advertising message and attitudes towards teaching. The authors showed that at the point when the messaging was concerned with raising

169

the status of teaching, the numbers believing 'teaching was not a career for high fliers' halved. And when the advertising focused on day-to-day enjoyment then the belief in enjoyability rose also.

- The 1988 Drink-Driving case shows changes in terms of 'drinking and driving becoming more socially unacceptable' and *'not* drinking and driving becoming more socially acceptable' – two sides of a very important coin.

- The 2004 Tobacco Control case shows how, over the course of the campaign, attitudes such as 'made me feel guilty about smoking', 'made me think of the impact on loved ones' and 'made me realise not only old people suffer from smoking-related diseases' all shifted significantly (see Figure 2).

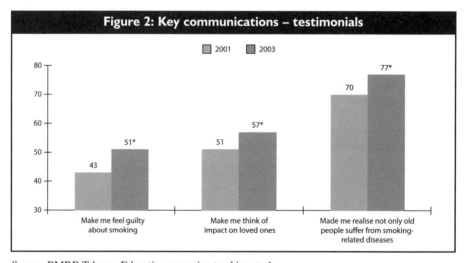

**Figure 2: Key communications – testimonials**

Source: BMRB Tobacco Education campaign tracking study
Base: smokers 2001 ($n=480$); 2003 ($n=1275$)

One additional point we'd make is that asking questions pre and post campaign isn't enough. Ideally you need to monitor continuously to see if the attitude change is enduring.

### 6. Look out for 'halo' effects

Measuring the effects of a campaign requires focus and specificity – econometric modelling being the epitome of this. However, government advertising topics can be universal and matters for broader public concern – for example, road safety, recruitment of policemen or soldiers – so it is notable when cases show effects beyond the immediate objective at hand.

- The 2002 Police Recruitment case shows that despite the fact that the activity was specifically about attracting the right sort of applicants, two significant secondary effects occurred: (1) people's *personal* perceptions of the police became more positive (as can be seen from Figure 3); and (2) perceptions *generally* became more positive.

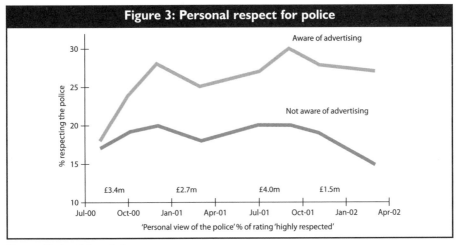

Figure 3: Personal respect for police

Source: Taylor Nelson Sofres
Base: 18–34s, split by aware/not aware of police advertising

An intended broader effect the Inland Revenue campaign was designed to create was to improve the Inland Revenue's reputation. In addition to having to get the majority of people filing their returns by the end of January each year and in addition to migrating more people from paper to online filing, the campaign was charged with making taxpayers believe the Inland Revenue was a more helpful service. This was not however about using taxpayers' money to enhance the government's image. The public purse cannot be used to do that. This was about encouraging people to think of the service as being less 'out to get them' and more 'out to help them'.

In turn, this would affect behaviour such that more people would feel less inclined to hide income but would seek tax-saving advice from the Inland Revenue instead. In other words, a more helpful image would contribute to a more successful collection of taxes. Figure 4 shows how the 'Adam Hart-Davis' campaign improved perceptions of the Inland Revenue service.

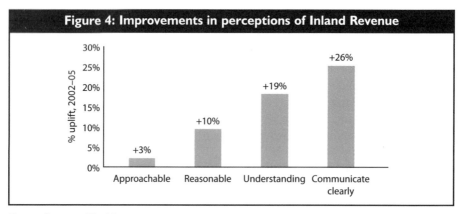

Figure 4: Improvements in perceptions of Inland Revenue

Source: Synovate Tracking
Base: SA taxpayers
Note: This question was not asked in the 2006 study

So, in summary, a suite of intermediate measures showing awareness and attitude shifts, preferably among specific target groups and measured pre and
post, are very much part of proving effectiveness. But remember they are
more useful in showing why and how a campaign has worked rather than the
indisputable fact that it has. That is the topic for the next two sections.

## Behavioural measures

The previous section in this chapter outlines some of the ways it is possible to
measure and assess whether a communications campaign has been noticed,
whether it has got the right message or information across effectively, and
whether it has changed attitudes and prompted a *claimed* change in behaviour.

This section looks at various ways in which it is possible to record, measure
and analyse the effect of a communications campaign on actual behaviour.

Before we look at some of the techniques for doing this, let's just consider why
this part of assessing effectiveness is so crucial. Of all the IPA papers analysed for
this book, not one campaign fails to have a behavioural outcome required of it.

Some may require an attitude change to occur as part of stimulating a new
behaviour, or as a necessary precursor to it. However, new behaviour outcomes are the ultimate goal. Private-sector companies want customers, as a
response to marketing investment, to take action, to choose their brand (or
buy it more frequently or pay more for it than another brand). This is equally
true of government. The government invests money in communications

campaigns because it believes it is an efficient way of prompting action: stimulating people to comply with new law changes or apply for a public-sector job or pay their taxes more quickly, etc.

Recording awareness or attitude shifts is an important part of the story but not enough to assess the true effectiveness of government communications. Measuring the action taken by audiences is crucial to the vast majority of government campaigns.

There is a contrary argument worth considering here. Communications directors and advertising agencies may sometimes argue that their role is to create a positive attitudinal predisposition, or an environmental context in society, from which various government policy implementation agencies can then follow through and operate more effectively in changing behaviour directly. Therefore, it could be argued that just measuring the awareness and attitude shift would be a fair judgement of the contribution of the advertising. After all, meeting the ultimate behavioural objectives we hope a campaign will stimulate (e.g. the recruitment of more teachers or, say, the reduction in road tax evasion) may rely heavily on the quality of the recruitment or detection processes that exists at the policy implementation level.

An audience, inspired by advertising – for example, to want to improve their qualifications – may not act on this improved attitude if they feel that the research process they then have to undertake (to understand which course or qualification they need) is confusing or too time-consuming. Or perhaps they find the college experience too intimidating or the learning process itself impractical.

This is a valid argument. But although a minister may be reassured that a communications campaign has been both noticed and has shifted attitudes in society, he or she is normally looking for more. Ultimately the marketing team is expected to help get more of the population actually doing the right things to create the society the minister has given the mandate to help create, or to reduce the number of people who are doing the wrong things.

Additionally, it is vital that either the communications team within a government department, or at the COI, or indeed the advertising agency, base the communications strategy on the reality of the policy delivery system in the first place. If the policy delivery system is flawed, or has not been improved or changed in some way to overcome barriers, it may be sensible to discuss whether communications investment should be postponed until an improved policy delivery system is in place, or perhaps have a discussion that adjusts expectations on what can and can't be achieved in the circumstances.

Alternatively, it may be possible to build into the communications strategy itself a response mechanism that helps the respondent through the next phase of the intended action we hope for. Perhaps offering people an easy first step, in what might be an otherwise difficult process to go through, would make an unlikely outcome more achievable.

Certainly, in a modern world, where there are many different communications channels and disciplines to be leveraged, understanding the interplay between the channels and how each may be used to fulfil a specific role (some changing attitudes, others stimulating specific action) could be key to helping audiences adopt an new attitude and, in parallel, prompt people to act.

All in all, if you want to truly measure whether your campaign is effective, you need to have measures in place that are recording behaviour and doing so in such a way that links the behaviour back to the communications, thus being able to identify the cause and effect.

Based on studying a wide selection of IPA public-sector papers, it seems to us that beyond just asking 'Have we met the targets the Home Office have set us?', the IPA papers throw up a number of interesting ways of measuring or assessing changed behaviour.

We've grouped them into five areas, which are outlined below.

## 1. Easy wins

As with intermediate measures, there is rarely a single silver bullet of measurement in assessing behavioural response. It often pays to have a number of proof points, a number of ways that make up a complete picture. Some approaches or techniques are complex and technically sophisticated, but others are just simple, common-sense ways of looking at things, which almost, due to their very lack of complexity, create a sense of being robust, straightforward and direct; there's no black box jiggery-pokery going on here.

Here are three examples:

- The paper that describes the Home Office's Police Recruitment 'Could you?' campaign that ran between 2000 and 2002 cites one very simple technique to prove a direct behavioural response. At the time of the paper being written, the campaign had generated 101,795 telephone enquiries and significantly more web hits, from which 66,346 application requests were yielded and from which, in turn, 5,998 officers were recruited: a 52% increase on the ongoing recruitment level.

The link between the advertising and the ultimate recruitment level achieved was simple. The campaign team ensured that the advertising response channels were unique to the campaign (i.e. completely different from the myriad local police force recruitment enquiry lines already in existence), with the enquiry contact details being made available only from the 'Could you?' advertising. Advertising was the only way to find out where to enquire. As the paper states, 'Enquirers ringing or clicking on these channels must have been prompted directly by this advertising.'

Second, the campaign managers captured the details of the applicants and then tracked them separately from the applicants provided by other on-going local recruitment channels. With the campaign 'isolated' in this way, they were able to ensure there was no 'contamination' of the response data from other potential campaign influences.

So if you want to avoid the expense and difficulty of isolating the effect of advertising after the event (via, say, an econometric analysis), design an isolating principle into the structure of the campaign upfront instead. This entails building in a unique response mechanism to your campaign, creating, if you can, unique enquiry or response channels, and tracking the respondent journey from your unique response channel right through to the ultimate action the campaign was intended to create.

For some campaigns that involve multi-stakeholders and multi-response channels, this isolation idea may be easier said than done. However, if it is possible to do, it is worthwhile, as it will provide cleaner direct data to help you assess how the campaign is faring.

- A second relatively simple technique to identify behavioural response is something a number of the government IPA papers utilise, including the police campaign above (see Figure 3). It is a basic but still powerful technique. And that is, to simply plot the communications activity along a time axis (by day, week, month or year), overlaying it with the telephone response/enquiry and website visit numbers (Figures 5 and 6).

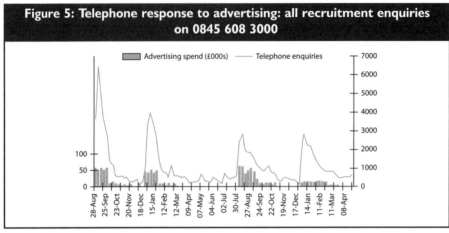

Figure 5: Telephone response to advertising: all recruitment enquiries on 0845 608 3000

Source: Broadsystems

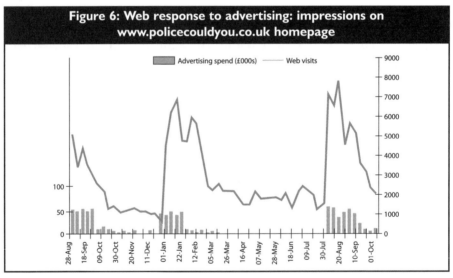

Figure 6: Web response to advertising: impressions on www.policecouldyou.co.uk homepage

Source: Home Office

This provides a quick and impressive visual correlation between campaign activity and behavioural response. Although it may be necessary to interrogate the response curve more rigorously, having a look at a graph like those in Figures 5 and 6 can provide a good initial indication of the scale of the response to the campaign. It's simply a question of monitoring the data and plotting them (Figure 7).

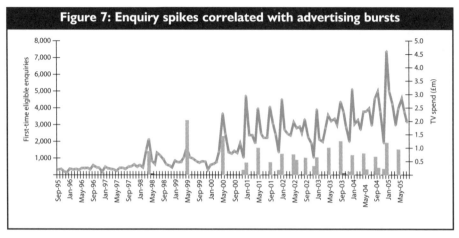

Figure 7: Enquiry spikes correlated with advertising bursts

Sources: TDA, Nielsen Media Research

- A third example of a simple way of looking at behavioural response is taken from the Inland Revenue 'Adam Hart-Davis' Tax Self-Assessment campaign, which broke in July 2002. In this case, one of the campaign tasks was to halt a four-year decline in the number of people filing their tax returns on time by January each year. The campaign met its target, holding the filing-on-time level at just over 90.5% across three years. The significance of this achievement however is more vividly appreciated by comparing the annual 90.5% figure achieved with the projected figure if the decay rate of the previous four years (0.44%) had continued instead (Figure 8).

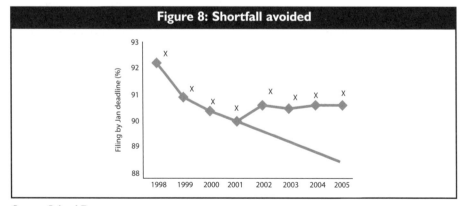

Figure 8: Shortfall avoided

Source: Inland Revenue

The chart not only shows the point at which the downward trend was halted by the campaign, but also illustrates what would have happened had the campaign not taken place. The technique of using past trend data to project what might happen in the future, helps to identify the scale and significance of the behaviour actually achieved by the campaign.

## 2. Comparisons

The IPA papers also illustrate that while sometimes the straight reporting of a behavioural effect is enough, there are times when drawing on evidence from further afield, or making a comparison to other similar or relevant campaigns, can illuminate the success of a campaign even more.

The 1994 Smoke Alarms paper, for instance, makes a strong case for how the sales of smoke alarms went up whenever the Home Office advertised the importance of smoke alarms in saving lives. However, it was also a very clever idea to look at the sales of batteries because it discovered that when it advertised the importance of smoke alarm maintenance, the sales of 9-volt batteries went up, creating an entirely new seasonal peak hitherto not seen in the battery market.

The 2004 'Could you?' police paper also utilised a comparison to demonstrate not just how successful the campaign had been in changing behaviour: by looking at the logs of the campaign website visits, the team was able to analyse which web pages had been viewed the most and for the longest. From this they were able to ascertain that the site's simulation pages were playing a key part in helping visitors understand the realities of policing and, in so doing, filtering out people who might not have what it takes to do the job. The importance of the campaign website was illustrated by comparing the amount of pages visited and the amount of time spent with similar data from eight other Home Office campaign websites; www.policecouldyou.co.uk was significantly higher.

These examples may provide some ideas for comparing your results with the results of other similar campaigns. But is it fair or appropriate to do so? After all, each brief has its own targets to achieve, different audiences to persuade, different budgets to work with, different attitudinal barriers to overcome and different levels of difficulty-of-task to cope with. Is it fair, for example, to compare the performance of the 'Gremlins' campaign (designed to persuade adults with very low basic skills) with another education campaign but designed to recruit people to higher education (people with better skills and higher expectations)?

Setting norms for education briefs, recruitment briefs or compliance briefs is probably unhelpful because it can lead to false expectations. Setting hard targets, however (for example, the numbers of applicants needed to achieve a particular ratio of recruitees), is essential in order to estimate a desired media weight and an effective communications strategy. Nevertheless, the above uses of comparison do serve to illustrate that, occasionally, it might be useful to look outside your immediate project to prompt discussion on whether a campaign is as effective as it might be.

### 3. Feel the quality

Hitting the numbers is one aspect of measuring behavioural change. However, an increasingly important aspect of government advertising has been the need to reach quite specific, harder-to-reach or more resistant-minded audiences. So sometimes demonstrating the 'quality' of the response is another indicator of success. Here are a few examples.

Perhaps the best example within the IPA government papers for showing a quality and not just a quantity of behavioural change is the Reading and Literacy paper in 2001. The authors demonstrated that 'the uplift in performance (in Key Stage 2 Level 4 Literacy Tests) of the children from the schools in socially deprived areas was four times higher as a direct result of our campaign'. To get to this evidence and to quantify and isolate the impact of a campaign (consisting of TV commercials and a 'reading tips' booklet response mechanic) required a systematic Russian doll narrowing-down of data, pursuing it right into the heart of the targeted communities.

First, they proved the telephone requests for the 'reading tips' booklet had been driven by the national TV advertising, that 79% of the requests had come from parents and, of these, 91% were parents of the targeted school age. They also identified that, in particular, parents of boys (who struggle more than girls with literacy) had responded.

Then, using PRIZM area profiling, they were able to locate that the response was biased towards hard-to-reach lower socio-economic and least affluent households. The paper then proved that, as a result of the advertising, schools from the least affluent PRIZM areas had also requested the booklets to hand out to parents. Then the paper explains how they tracked parents of children in those schools, one month and 15 months after receiving the leaflet, measuring that the majority of parents were still using the reading techniques suggested in the booklet.

Finally, they compared the Key Stage 2 Level 4 Literacy Test results attained in those schools with those attained by similar schools in the same socially deprived catchment areas but that had not requested and distributed leaflets (see Table 3).

| Table 3: Comparison of literacy test results among state primary schools from socially deprived areas | | | | | |
|---|---|---|---|---|---|
| | 1997–1998 | | | 1998–1999 | |
| | 1997 | 1998 | Change | 1999 | Change |
| % of primary schools from socially deprived areas who responded to the advertising | 55 | 56 | +1 | 64 | +8 |
| % of primary schools from the same socially deprived areas who did not respond to the advertising | 60 | 61 | +1 | 63 | +2 |

Base: 200 state primary schools that responded to the advertising and 200 that did not
Source: DfEE/PRIZM profiling

In essence, it was a simple control technique but it took a fantastically dedicated and rigorous pursuit of attaining the right data and using it scrupulously fairly to provide a real reading of behavioural change among hard-to-reach audiences. The lesson it teaches us is, think about the step-by-step effect that you will create, measure it every step of the way and find a control to compare the results.

Social inclusion is another issue close to the government's heart. Unlike the Reading and Literacy campaign, which needed to focus on reaching a specific hard-to-reach audience, the 2002 Police campaign needed to ensure it didn't exclude from its broader targeted campaign, potential female and ethnic minority recruits, both under-represented in their workforce profile. The team created ads and cast personalities in the campaign that were known to be admired and respected by these audiences, and put in place analysis to see whether the campaign was proving successful. Applications from and enrolment of both these audiences improved as illustrated in Figure 9, which shows an increase in female officers.

Quality of response comes in many guises. This example looks at quality from the perspective of cost. Since 2000 the Inland Revenue had been trying to persuade taxpayers to file their returns online. It was estimated this would save £3 for every return received via the internet. However, the previous campaigns had fallen short and the Department was way behind the target originally set (39,000 actual online filings vs 315,000 targeted).

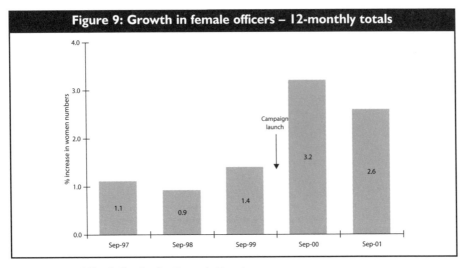

**Figure 9: Growth in female officers – 12-monthly totals**

Source: Home Office Police Service Strength. Broadsystems

The paper demonstrates that, in addition to fulfilling the larger overall task of halting the decline in timely return filing (resulting in a record-breaking response of 8.91 million returns being filed by January 2005), the campaign was able to stimulate a significant increase in online filing.

This increase amounted to receiving 30,000 online returns every day, almost as many as had previously been generated in a whole year. Migrating people to a new, more cost-efficient filing channel generated a further £7.9 million in savings for the Inland Revenue.

### 4. Halo effects

Although most campaigns have a set of direct targets to achieve (often meeting short- to mid-term numbers relating to a specific audience and policy objectives), it is possible to measure and observe broader behavioural effects beyond the immediate objectives of the campaign. These kinds of measures are often useful in analysing how the campaign is changing behaviour because often they underscore the fact that something really is happening.

We turn again to the Police Recruitment paper to give us a number of examples of a halo effect created by the 'Could you?' campaign. One halo effect it created was to improve the application levels of all the local police campaigns running at the time (Figure 10). Figure 10 shows that recruits coming via local campaigns ('extra recruits') immediately started to rise as the national

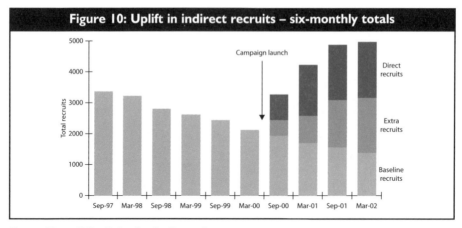

Figure 10: Uplift in indirect recruits – six-monthly totals

Source: Home Office Police Service Strength

campaign broke, and then continued as the national campaign progressed. It was estimated that the national campaign improved local recruitment by 72%.

A second halo effect created by the campaign was how it helped curtail resignations in the Force and how it created more positive media reporting of the police. The paper illustrates how the power of a communications campaign can reach beyond the focused job in hand, and that it's a good idea to think about and monitor broader behavioural effects.

### 5. Splendid isolation

An important principle in judging effectiveness is both acknowledging and then considering the possible effect that other factors, apart from the campaign being assessed, may have had on the behavioural results being observed. To prove beyond reasonable doubt that the campaign did all that the evidence suggests it did also requires the systematic elimination of other factors.

Econometrics is frequently used in private-sector companies (and indeed in private-sector IPA Effectiveness papers) to isolate the effect of communications from other factors such as price, distribution and competitive activity, any or all of which could have changed at the time the communications were running.

Although econometrics is a very valuable tool in untangling the impact of each of the possible influencing factors, there are many examples in good private-sector papers where econometrics is not used.

And this is also true of government papers. Therefore, let's look at some examples of papers that have not used econometrics and then we'll look at a couple that have.

- The 1994 Smoke Alarms paper recognised that they would need to consider other market forces such as price and distribution as possible influences in prompting greater ownership of fire alarms. However, it discovered, via Nielsen data, that in fact the minimum retail selling price had remained unchanged at £3.99 over the previous three years (the campaign duration) and that the distribution level in DIY multiples (where the vast majority of sales occur) had already been at 100%. In fact, they discovered that, far from retail distribution driving sales, it was the government's advertising that had prompted greater merchandising of fire alarms in these stores. In other words, the retail contribution to the increased sales was partly an advertising-led effect too.

- The 2004 Army Recruitment paper had to deal with a strange quirk in the data, which showed a falling away of applications into the second year of the campaign. If the campaign was performing inconsistently, how could the first year's impressive figures be trusted? It must have been something else all along that had caused the applications. However, the plausible answer lay in the fact that at the beginning of the second year, the RAF and the Navy had undertaken vigorous recruitment activity themselves and it was simply a competitive effect – an effect that would be expected in such circumstances.

- HM Revenue & Customs' Tax Self-Assessment case needed to consider whether its apparent success in improving on-time filing was not in fact simply a function of a changing profile in taxpayers. Indeed, there were some significant shifts in the self-assessment profile during the duration of the campaign. However, these were due to an influx of construction workers and new taxpayers (each group 9% less likely to file on time) and a reduction of people with simpler tax affairs (7% more likely to file on time) and, if anything therefore, made the task harder, not easier.

- In seeking to compare the Literacy Test results of one set of schools vs another set, the authors of the Reading and Literacy 2000 paper needed to ensure that the only discernible difference between the schools was that one set had participated in the campaign and the other had not. It eliminated other factors by reasoning that both sets of schools were running at the same low rate of literacy improvement up until the campaign, that both had a similar profile of children claiming free school dinners, that both had been exposed to the local National Year of Reading and the Books for Schools promotions, that both would have received government grants to buy more books and that both had introduced the Literacy Hour. By doing this, it was able to ascertain that the only difference between the two sets of schools was the Reading and Literacy Campaign.

- The 2004 Northern Ireland Road Safety paper is another example of an effectiveness story where it was crucial to isolate the effect of advertising. To make the case that it was the nine-year campaign that had resulted in 2,774 fewer people being killed or seriously injured (KSIs), the paper isolated a list of potential variables. It was able to show that there had been a steady level of detection, ticket issuing and prosecution for speeding and drink-driving, indicating that police activity had not significantly increased.

This paper also looks at road engineering and, while recognising that there had been a significant increase, it was coming from such a low base (investment per head of population in Northern Ireland being significantly lower than in the rest of the UK) that it was very unlikely to have had such a drastic effect. Most powerfully, the paper demonstrates that, because historical data had shown a correlation between the growth of road vehicles and the growth of casualties, the stark reality is that the 33% growth in licensed vehicles for 1995–2003, compared to 1986–1994, could have produced a 33% increase in the killing and maiming of people. However, over the campaign period KSIs had in fact reduced by 42.32%.

Now let's look at a couple of examples where econometrics has been used to isolate the effect of government campaigns.

- The TDA Teacher Recruitment campaign of 1998–2005 needed to consider a number of non-communications factors that might have influenced people to become teachers. Some of these were: the introduction of financial incentives for new people who undertake teacher training; the introduction in 2000 of more flexible and financially attractive ways into teaching; changes in eligibility, making it easier to enter. The paper is able to dismiss many of these potential factors by simple logical argument alone, but it turns to econometric analysis to isolate and quantify precisely what contribution this communications campaign made vs other primarily locally driven communications campaigns. The analysis proves the campaign was responsible for driving 50% of all enquiry traffic (Figure 11).

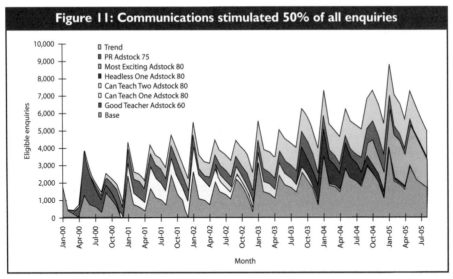

Figure 11: Communications stimulated 50% of all enquiries

Source: OMD Metrics

- Having started this section of the chapter with the simple things that can be done to measure behavioural change, it is appropriate to end it with one of the most sophisticated analyses ever recorded in IPA Effectiveness papers: Vehicle Crime Reduction. Econometricians Holmes and Cook, who undertook the analysis on behalf of the Home Office, described the task as 'the most complex and challenging project we have ever worked on'. The basic objective was not just to isolate the overall effect of the Vehicle Crime Reduction campaign but also the specific contribution that each media channel made. This would also help determine an optimum media mix.

Due to the fact that each region in the country was receiving support, the only way of measuring the impact was by comparing the response from areas with high media investment with the response from areas with lower media spend. This in turn meant that it was essential that each media mix/weight configuration was tested against a control area that was very similar in characteristics, such as the vehicle crime level, the age profile of the population, the age profile (and inherent built-in car security therefore) of the vehicle population. It resulted in a total of 37 pairs of regions being analysed across four different media.

The analysis, which was described as 'exemplary' by the National Consumer Council, concluded, among other things, that '100 TVRs led to an initial reduction in theft from vehicles of 1–2% and a 0.5–1.5% reduction in theft of vehicles'. If you think that doesn't sound like much, it meant that the 1000 TVR campaign that ran would reduce the incidence of car crime by 180,000 in one year alone. It was also concluded that ambient media played a vital role, every £380,000 spent resulting in an initial 3.5–5.7% reduction in vehicle crime.

All the above examples of ways of recording and measuring behavioural change illustrate that public service communications campaigns are assessed with utmost rigour. They illustrate that communicators and government departments seek to understand how their campaigns work, and seek to ensure they have a positive impact on issues or needs in society.

## Return on marketing investment

The previous sections of this chapter demonstrate that there are many government campaigns that are assessed by how well they get noticed and change attitudes (the so-called 'soft' measures) and how well they affect actual behaviour (the so-called 'hard' measures). In the end, however, even though it can be argued that the campaign has been worthwhile, the numbers have been hit, objectives have been met, etc., how can we judge whether the campaign has been a good investment of taxpayers' money?

How can the Director of Communications or Head of Marketing inside a government department make a financial case to senior policy people, or to the Secretary of State and ultimately to the Treasury that investing money in a communications campaign will yield a good return on investment. After all, there are many calls on government budgets; why should communications expenditure be a better investment than, say, the building of new schools or the increase in nurses' salaries?

Most people would accept that a government of any nation has an undeniable duty to inform the population of many things. In fact, it would be a dereliction of duty not to inform the population of, for instance, changes in the law of the land (e.g. the requirements, under law, of businesses to ensure their services are accessible to disabled people), or newly discovered risks (e.g. AIDS, global warming) or newly created entitlements (e.g. adult learning grants). In a sense, communication campaigns and advertising campaigns are just modern-day town criers distributing and sharing information. In a free society, the government cannot rely on the free press to inform people of such information. Newspaper and programme editors and media channel owners are all free to print and broadcast what they choose, not what the government chooses. With paid-for communications, however, the government can ensure that the information it has a duty to impart, gets out there.

However, just as tax payers need to be reassured that the government spends its budgets wisely on the other duties we expect it to undertake (e.g. the revamping of the National Health Service or commissioning new defence systems), we are entitled to ask whether the government spends our money wisely in communications terms too.

So, here is a collection of various ways in which IPA papers have calculated the return on investment of government communications campaigns.

### *Cost efficiency at generating responses*

Many government campaigns these days seek to stimulate people to visit a website or call a phone line to find out more information or to access, say, an application form. The thinking is that, for instance, a PR campaign in the press may create heightened awareness about a topic, which in turn stimulates some people to visit the campaign website featured in the newspaper article. The website provides more information and further heightens the interest of the visitor, who then decides to call the phone line to apply for the subject in question.

This is a typical responder journey. Not only is this a typical way of interesting an audience and stimulating them to take some initial action, it is a great way of collecting data: the number of web visitors, the number of callers, who they are, how many go on to follow up or become candidates or enlistees. Hence, it is possible, by just being methodical and creating databases, to calculate how efficient a campaign has been at generating an interested and action-taking audience.

There have been a number of Army Recruitment campaigns over the years that have looked at this kind of measurement to demonstrate investment efficiency. The example of the 1998 'Putting the Army back in business' paper considers 'the financial value of better quality applicants', specifically the cost savings achieved in the applicant-to-enlistee ratio. The major cost associated with recruitment is not in processing the initial enquiries but in processing actual applications. This cost at the time was approximately £800 per applicant.

Prior to the campaign, there were 3.9 applications for every successful enlistment, so the cost for each enlistment was £3,120. Over the course of the campaign, as it generated responses from more appropriate candidates, there were 2.9 applications per enlistment, creating a saving of £800. If, however, this extra efficiency had not been attained and instead the original ratio of 3.9 applications per enlistment had continued, the government would have had to spend an additional £31.3 million in application costs – an average of £7.8 million per annum – to gain the enlistments achieved. Measuring the ratio of enlistment to enquirer, improving it from 3.9:1 to 2.9:1, was, in this case, the currency of payback (see Table 4).

| Table 4: Measuring ratio of enlistment to enquirer gives savings gained | | | | |
|---|---|---|---|---|
| Year | Actual applications | Application at 3.9:1 | Difference | Saving (£m) |
| 1994/5 | 29,286 | 36,227 | 6,941 | 5.6 |
| 1995/6 | 41,132 | 43,458 | 2,326 | 1.9 |
| 1996/7 | 38,102 | 53,438 | 15,336 | 12.3 |
| 1997/8 | 39,998 | 54,311 | 14,313 | 11.5 |
| Total savings = £31.3m | | | | |

Source: Army Recruitment – 'Be the Best' campaign

If we calculate the total additional sum invested in 'Be the best' soldier advertising over this period (assuming investment behind the old campaign had remained at £1.6 million/year), this is £14.9 million.

We can then deduct this from the savings of this approach, to reach a net saving overall of £16.4 million.

A similar measure is used to demonstrate good value for money in the 2002 Police Recruitment paper. Not only does it show that the campaign improved the recruitment application ratio from 1:7 to 1:5, creating 13% greater efficiency in the recruitment process, it also compares the actual cost per recruit with those of other recruitment campaigns recorded in IPA papers (Table 5).

Although the Reading and Literacy paper calculates the value of its achievements in larger societal and human terms (see later) it also demonstrates cost efficiencies in meeting its targets by looking at the response levels it achieved via the phone line. It does this by comparing the average advertising cost per response of all government response campaigns over the previous three years,

| Table 5: Recruitment campaigns | | |
|---|---|---|
| | Cost per application | Cost per recruit |
| Police recruitment | 151 | 583 |
| Army recruitment | 208 | 652 |
| Metropolitan Police | 156 | 819 |
| Nursing recruitment | 234 | 846 |
| RAF recruitment | 309 | 965 |
| RAF officer recruitment | 494 | n/a |
| Navy recruitment | 634 | n/a |

Source: Police recruitment campaign – how thinking negatively ended negative thinking

as recorded by the COI, and compares it with the cost per response of its own campaign. It demonstrates that the cost per response it achieved, namely £63.41, was reduced threefold.

### *Payback time*

While analysing the cost of response is a rigorous way of assessing the efficiency of every pound spent, ROMI ultimately needs to be judged in the context of meeting the objectives originally set. And, having met them or perhaps exceeded them, asking ourselves, has the investment paid off, has it paid for itself? Of course, at one level the value of payback in human terms (e.g. lives saved by road safety campaigns) cannot be truly captured by figures of financial return. However, there are financial costs associated with accidents and death and crime etc., so putting a figure on the human benefit does provide compelling evidence of the valuable contribution communications makes to our society, both in the short and long term.

In the case of Vehicle Crime, the Home Office had set the target of reducing car theft and theft from cars by 30% within five years. Over the four-year campaign period, it actually fell by 37%. The 2006 Vehicle Crime IPA paper uses an econometric model to show that just over half the total reduction in vehicle crime was attributable to the advertising. Using Home Office figures that estimate the cost of individual car crimes (including policing, insurance costs, Criminal Justice System time, etc.), it is possible to calculate that just in the four years the campaign actually ran, the £21.4 million spent on advertising saved 28 times that figure in the cost of crime – just over £590 million. The econometric model used to isolate the immediate effect of advertising over the four years the campaign actually ran, between 1999 and 2002, also showed that a longer-term effect in behavioural change could be expected. This was calculated by observing that for every 1% initial reduction, crime levels were still 0.77% lower 18 months later.

The paper argued reasonably that these figures were evidence of people, having initially been prompted by the advertising, now developing long-lasting crime prevention habits (e.g. not leaving keys and valuables in cars). Using this recorded statistical decline, the mathematical model predicted that the impact of the advertising would still be evident up to 20 years after airing! Indeed the econometricians themselves, Holmes and Cook, calculated that, over a ten-year period, the campaign would have influenced £1.5 billion worth of crime reduction, an ROMI of 71:1.

The value of reading and literacy is unarguable in our society. So how did the Reading and Literacy IPA paper calculate the ROMI of this campaign? The authors of the paper were able to show that the campaign had encouraged over 300,000 parents to become actively involved in helping with their children's reading, affecting over half a million children, 38% of whom were children from lower socio-economic classes. Based on these data, the paper calculates both the 'social value' and the 'financial value' of the campaign.

The social value was calculated by citing the Haringey Reading Project, a highly respected three-year study that demonstrated 27% more children reached the reading standard when parents were involved. Using this figure, it was possible to calculate that 27% more of the 545,566 children now receiving help from their parents as a result of using the campaign booklet, would achieve pass marks. Furthermore, the anticipated improvement was proven through the actual attainment figures achieved by the schools from socially deprived areas. These human effects, as recorded by improved reading and literacy exam results, were then converted into financial terms. This was done by calculating the impact of the improved literacy achieved by the campaign on the likely savings to future benefit payouts and the likely increases in future tax payments. The paper concludes that, even if only 1.3% of the total children activated had been affected, the campaign would have paid for itself in just one tax year.

The Tax Self-Assessment IPA paper of 2006 demonstrates the ROMI for this campaign in another way. Having proven, through analysis of intermediate and behavioural measures that show how the 'Tax doesn't have to be taxing' campaign had stemmed the previously downward trend of on-time filing, the paper uses National Audit Office estimates to extrapolate the financial savings that would follow. The National Audit Office had estimated that each late filer owes an average net amount of £1,000. Then it is possible to calculate the incremental savings generated by stemming the natural downward trend, at £521 million.

In addition, based on HM Revenue & Customs' own estimate, every tax filing completed online saves an additional £3 per filing. Having stimulated just over 2.6 million online tax returns between 2003 and 2005 it was possible to estimate that the campaign had saved HM Revenue & Customs a further annual saving of £7.9 million. However, the real value of the online filing savings can be seen in the 'lifetime' value of people who, having been converted to online filing by the advertising, carry on with it over a sustained period.

By making a fairly conservative assumption that each online filer would remain in self-assessment and file online for just a further five years, the long-term saving would become even more apparent – estimated at £26.1 million. The following extract, taken directly from the paper, illustrates just how fairly the calculation was made. It demonstrates how, in arriving at each year's contribution to the total saving, it was scrupulously ensured that double-counting was avoided:

> *We have taken care to avoid double-counting in our calculation. For any five-year period, the first four years will contain taxpayers who have already been counted in the previous five-year calculation and so need to be stripped out. To achieve this, we have used the formula of: (4 years × incremental online filers × £3 saving) + (1 year × total online filers × £3 saving) = 5 year total. For example, in 2005 the incremental total of online filers is 909k (2005's total of 1600k – 2004's total of 691k). So the five year saving is (4 years × 909k × £3) + (1 year × 1600k × £3) = £15.7 million.*

By factoring in all the on-time and online savings, the campaign cost of £22.5 million created a return of £24.31 million in savings for every £1 spent.

With the 2004 Northern Ireland Road Safety campaign, the authors were able to show that, over a nine-year period, there were 279 fewer deaths and 2,540 fewer serious injuries on the roads. Basing the resulting economic payback on accident and death costs supplied by the Department of Transport, it was possible to value the ROMI of an £8.68 million campaign spend, at £704.35 million.

The 2006 TDA paper also translates its achievement of recruiting 67,000 trainee teachers, at a campaign cost of £57 million, into an ROMI calculation. Had the trainee teachers not been recruited, enormous amounts of money would have needed to be spent on supply teachers to cover the classes. The calculation below (Table 6) shows that, by taking into account the high attrition rate during teacher training and the fact that the average teacher stays in the profession for 15 years, the actual savings flowing from the recruitment

| Table 6: Savings from teacher recruitment campaigns | |
|---|---|
| Extra trainee teachers | 66,829 |
| Attrition rate | 34% |
| Total additional teachers | 44,107 |
| Average length of a career in teaching | 15 years |
| Average salary of a teacher (2002) | £28,580 |
| Total costs of additional teachers | £18.9 billion |
| Daily cost of a supply teacher (2002) | £180 |
| Average length of school year | 200 days |
| Total savings from suppy teachers | £23.8 billion |
| Net savings from additional teachers | £4.9 billion |

Sources: National Association of Headteachers 2002 survey for the costs of supply teachers; DfES Pay Data for starting salaries

campaigns would be £4.9 billion. In other words, the campaign would have paid for itself 86 times over.

## *The value of the secondary, broader effects*

Some of the IPA papers are also able to consider the value of broader effects emanating from government communications campaigns. Although there are not many of these, the few that do this are interesting.

'Added value' is the term the 2002 Police Recruitment paper uses to describe an effect this campaign achieved without really meaning to. Such was the impact of the 'Could you?' campaign, as discussed earlier in this chapter, that it affected people's perception of the level of crime in the country at the time, reducing it by 13%. As a way of putting a value on this effect, the paper calculated that it would have cost the country £940 million in increased police running costs to have actually reduced crime by this amount. On this basis, it was possible to say that, had the campaign just been responsible for 5% of this reduction, its 'added value' would have been £48 million, more than three times its actual cost.

The TDA 2006 paper argues that, beyond successfully recruiting 67,000 trainee teachers with a high ROMI payback, the campaign also helped create some significant and positive ripple effects in society. The paper suggests that the campaign, having created a strong desire among 67,000 people to teach, will have benefited British children in their ability to attain better qualifications, and British society in terms of productivity and prosperity. Specifically, the paper argues that it is hard to imagine how the pupil attainment achieved

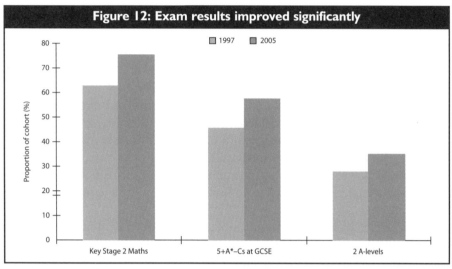

**Figure 12: Exam results improved significantly**

Source: Statistics of Education, Schools in England, 1995 and 2005 Editions

over the last eight years, at all levels, could have been sustained without the influx of this number and quality of new teachers (Figure 12).

It also asks the reader to consider how the campaign, by stimulating the new teachers, and in turn facilitating better academic attainment, will have had an indirect effect on the relatively better productivity figures achieved in Britain vs other OECD countries over the campaign period (see Figure 13).

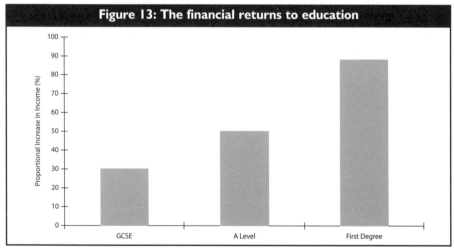

**Figure 13: The financial returns to education**

Source: S. Mackintish, 'Further analysis of the returns to academic and vocational qualifications', DfES Research

Furthermore, the paper, by referring to academic research, alludes to the relationship between the campaign and its role in boosting overall national income (Figure 13).

### Examining alternative ways of spending the advertising budget

Government advertising often suffers the criticism that the money would be better spent on the relevant problem at source; for example, more books for children, pay increases for nurses, more school facilities, extra police support. However, a number of papers demonstrate that while some of the above investments may very well be desirable, communications activity is not necessarily a bad alternative form of investment. In fact, it may be a more efficient one.

The 2002 Police paper, for instance, needed to contend with initial concerns about the wisdom of spending just over £15 million on the recruitment campaign: 'They should stop wasting money on advertising and just pay the Police more.' The option of paying the police force even a modest £2,000 per head increase to entice new recruits would have cost an extra £428 million over the campaign period alone, plus £260 million per annum thereafter. Realistically, £15 million would not have gone very far in salary terms. In contrast, spending just £15 million to stimulate an increase in the size of the force and to recruit high-quality recruits to supplement existing resources is clearly a much more efficient strategy.

It had also been argued that the £15 million campaign could be avoided if officers themselves stimulated enquiries by 'talking up' the job to the public – a kind of member-get-member scheme. But, as they say, time is money. Assuming just 1% of their time was spent doing this over the campaign period, the equivalent cost of £124 million worth of police officer time would have to have been allocated to this task. By comparing the cost of the campaign with the above (and some alternative ways of achieving the same result), the paper calculates the campaign had to date saved the UK taxpayer at least £30 million.

'How else could you spend £3.8 million if you wanted to focus on education and address the problem of child illiteracy; could the money have been better spent?' is the question the Reading and Literacy paper asks of itself. The answer it gives is essentially that the money gets spread very thin and renders it a pretty paltry amount:

> *The money could have been divided up among 148,000 teachers in England's nursery and state primary school sector, giving them each an*

*extra £20.83 in their annual pay packet. It could have gone toward starting salaries for 239 more primary school teachers across the country (covering only 1.4% of the total number of state schools). It could have been used to buy just 65 books for every primary school. Or it could have covered reno-vation costs for 28 schools in Greater London.*

The two examples above, although valid methods of considering the efficiency of communications investment vs alternative investments of taxpayers' money, might leave us with the impression that things are always an 'either/or' deci-sion. But the truth is that communications investment is more often used as a complementary tool to help boost or support other more directly applied actions. Although these two papers do not describe the role of communica-tions as just one facet of a many-headed government strategy to solve a prob-lem, it is easy to appreciate how the Smoke Alarm and Vehicle Crime Reduction campaigns are part of something bigger.

Reading between the lines, it is fairly obvious that both of these campaigns have a specific role to stimulate 'compliance' and thereby help to free up other resources to focus on issues that are more complex. In the case of Smoke Alarms, it would not have been a question of 'Should we spend money on a campaign or give it to the Fire Brigade to spend on local activity instead?' It is clear that the campaign was there to act as a focusing agent, to get the issue on the agenda of house dwellers nationally so that when local Fire Brigades actioned their own local fire alarm drives, people were more predisposed to listening to the local fire-fighter. The campaign was there to help them do their job.

Equally the police force cannot be everywhere, all the time. They cannot pre-vent every possible vehicle crime. In addition, they have other priorities, rang-ing from murder, terrorism and rape to dangerous driving. The point of the Vehicle Crime Reduction campaign was to help the police by encouraging self-responsibility among potential crime victims, not to catch the crook, of course, but to prevent the theft in the first place. With more vehicle owners complying and doing more to reduce the temptation of theft, the police can focus on crime that is more serious.

The Reading and Literacy paper is a good example of the role of communi-cations as a support, rather than as an alternative, to more direct action. This campaign, right from the start, recognised that teachers and schools were important stakeholders and that it was crucial they did not feel offended or put out by a government campaign talking directly to parents about children's reading ability. Normally, it is the remit of the education authorities to converse with parents on education. However, the campaign was welcomed warmly by teachers because they recognised the benefit it was having. Indeed teachers, rather than feeling the money spent on the campaign should have been spent on their salary or their school more directly, became a significant distribution channel for the booklet. In fact, they ordered (and reordered) the booklet in bulk, resulting in a massive demand for 1,166,849 booklets.

## What we have learned ...

### ... about the use of intermediate measures

- A suite of measures is best: the more measures moving in the same direction, the better for making a convincing case.
- Simple comparative measures can have value and can easily be derived.
- Benchmarking your campaign against a category norm is a no-brainer, so look for category norms.
- Always try to trace the effect on the core target group.
- Shifts in attitude are a powerful indicator of likely behavioural and commercial effect.
- There are many other ways in which our targets process messaging; it's worth looking out for these 'halo' effects to strengthen your case.

### ... about the use of behavioural measures

- There are easy ways of showing behavioural changes by measures that can simply be recorded and monitored over time – such as phone calls and website visits.
- Behavioural changes set in the context of other references, such as comparisons with other similar, relevant campaigns, can be useful.
- Hitting the numbers is only half the story. Demonstrating the quality of responses can be valuable in demonstrating success at reaching resistant-minded audiences.
- Campaigns can be working harder than you realise – by changing behaviour permanently or influencing a wider audience, for example. These halo effects are worth looking out for to strengthen your case.
- There are many other factors that influence our audiences and it is critical to eliminate all other possible sources of influence in order to concentrate on the communications effect.

### ... about the use of return on marketing investment measures

- Cost efficiency at generating responses is a valuable measure of effectiveness, such as assessing the cost per response, or per application in a recruitment campaign.

- Looking at both immediate and longer-term ROMI, can provide powerful evidence of effect.
- Evaluation of government advertising in human terms is a valuable analysis to add to ROMI.
- Secondary, broader effects contribute other paybacks beyond the immediate task at hand.
- Examining alternative ways of spending the ad budget answers the criticism that the same amount of money could be better spent doing something else. Try to demonstrate that communications are the most efficient use of the money.

## Conclusion

When we set out to undertake this analysis and answer the questions does it work? and can we prove it?, we couldn't have foreseen the richness we would find across the IPA cases. The length of this chapter, which originally started out with a 2,000-word limit, is testament to that. Arguably, some of the individual cases and measures truly set the standard in terms of the way they have approached and used measurability: for example, the way the Police paper deconstructs the psychology of the effects; the foresight shown in the Vehicle Crime Reduction case in terms of laying out how they would measure and then building the econometric model to do it; the sheer tenacity and forensic examination of the data to prove that the Reading and Literacy campaign had worked; the way that paper also looked at measures some 12 months after the campaign had run, to show true, enduring behavioural effects.

But if all the papers in this book celebrate the achievement of government campaigns thus far, what of future campaigns? As discussed earlier, the task is increasingly about targeting hard-to-reach audiences, which raises some interesting measurement questions. It's likely that broadcast TV may not be the most efficient way to reach these groups, which will require a more sophisticated use of channels and, in turn, make the task of measuring a potentially intricate campaign increasingly difficult. We are very good at measuring the effects of individual channels looked at individually, but, in a world of polychromic consumer behaviour, we will need to get better at measuring the cumulative effect of integrated multimedia campaigns and then disentangling the contribution of individual channels within an overall effect.

It should be an interesting next ten years.

## Note

1. Binet, L. and Field, P. (2007) *Marketing in the Era of Accountability*. World Advertising Research Center (WARC).

# Part 5

# The creative magic

# Chapter 11

# Where do the ideas come from?

 By Jeremy Bullmore

Why, I wonder, does no one ever challenge the assumption that advertising campaigns need creative ideas? In each of the cases in this book the objective was perfectly clear; so why didn't the COI stop trying to be clever and simply publish a series of straightforward and easily understood public interest instructions: 'Don't leave your car unlocked!', 'Check the batteries in your smoke alarm every month!', 'Join the Army!', 'Stop smoking!' – and so on? After all, one of the world's most successful companies has spent billions over the years exhorting people to 'Drink Coca-Cola'; at election times we're confronted with the simple instruction to 'Vote Conservative'; and when, a great many years ago, the Port Importers Association finally recognised the relative untrendiness of their fine product, they told us confidently, 'It's Smart to Drink Port!' We don't need fancy research to tell us what we want to happen. We want people either to do things or to stop doing things. So why don't we cut out all this creative crap and just tell 'em?

As ever, James Webb Young[1] put it as well as anyone, 60 or 70 years ago. No matter how sensible such instruction might be, 'there is always some loss of response due to the inertia which keeps people from taking even the action they might have been disposed to take'. Consider, for example, personal insurance and car tyres; everybody knows that they could be better insured or that they should check their tyres; but, as Jim Young wrote:

> *There are common causes for the inertia in all such cases: either the reward for action is remote and often intangible; or the penalty for inaction is delayed. What kind of advertising message has a chance to overcome such inertias?* **Only one that will arouse such a fear of the delayed penalty, or such a vivid vision of the remote reward, that the emotional reaction will burn out the block to action.** *[My bold]*

These are words that ought to be in the creative brief for every public service advertising campaign. They not only pin down the essential need for an idea but are also hugely helpful in the search for one. Only an idea can burn through that block, can either bring home the reality of the delayed penalty or paint a vivid vision of the remote reward. And all the ideas in this book do one or the other.

The wonderful thing about a brief is that, for those responsible for meeting it, it instantly transforms every bit of human experience into a hypothetical solution. From the moment that a need has been identified – by far the most valuable part of any brief – everything observed from then on, at whatever level of consciousness, is examined for potential relevance. The old saw says, 'Necessity is the mother of invention.' Having to think of an advertising idea, against an agreed deadline, is a bit like being stranded on a desert island. Suddenly, coconuts are not just coconuts: they're potential cooking vessels, milk bottles, weapons, lamps and providers of fabric. The mental process is that of improvisation: you look at everyday things not for what they are but for what they could be. You invite the collision of two apparently disconnected phenomena: Arthur Koestler called it bi-sociation.

Every time Archimedes took a bath, he would have noticed that the water level rose when he got in and fell again when he got out. But it wasn't until he was faced with a brief from his client, to find a way of measuring the volume of a complicated solid, that the immediate significance of this familiar observation struck him. He would never have discovered the nature of displacement had he not been preoccupied by the urgent need to do so.

And so with the ideas described in the following chapter. Logic and reason have their place – but usually after the initial flash of insight. It may be only milliseconds after, and in the telling of it – and the selling of it – the process may be presented as sequential. But it rarely is.

That's where ideas come from: ideas evocative enough 'to arouse such a fear of the delayed penalty, or such a vivid vision of the remote reward' that bald assertion of an accepted truth, by a sort of alchemy, is transformed into a complicity of persuasion.

## Note

1. James Webb Young joined the J Walter Thompson Company in 1912 as a copywriter in the Cincinatti office. He finally retired from the company in 1964. His book, *How To Become an Advertising Man* (Advertising Publications Inc, 1963), is based on the lectures he gave as Professor of Business History and Advertising, University of Chicago. See also *A Technique for Producing Ideas* (Crain Books 1975, NTC Business Book, 1989). He died in New Mexico in 1973.

# Chapter 12

# Creative directors talk about their work

 By Judie Lannon

Editor

We wanted to give a flavour of just how the actual advertising ideas described in this book emerged. It is one thing to describe the chapter and verse of the (apparently) sequential behaviour required of the case history format. But it is another thing to understand what really happened: gain insights into the, often quite idiosyncratic, sources of ideas that bubble up in the creative director's mind. Where do these ideas come from and why does one particular idea feel 'right' for the problem at hand and how is it given the shape and form that a proper campaign requires? What is the best way of stimulating ideas?

Brief writing is a creative art in itself. It must focus on the key consumer insight yet at the same time give creative people the freedom to invent. The more vivid the brief, the more likely effective advertising will flow from it and the faster the blank sheet of paper on which the idea is to be described has something written or drawn on it.

The ideas themselves will come from anywhere and everywhere: from research, from personal insight, from films and the media, from first hand experience and observation. To illustrate how this happens, we chose to talk to a few creative directors to see how they describe what happened after receiving the brief. Here we present a selection of campaigns described by their creators in answer to the question: 'Where did this idea come from?'

## 1. Vehicle Crime

### *By Mark Roalfe, Founder and Chairman, RKCR/Y&R*

There were several strands to the Vehicle Crime work. Strategically the thing that we were battling with was that a lot of the work they'd done before with the hyenas prowling around the car had just been quite scary. It was intended to worry people into protecting themselves against criminals.

We wanted to take a different tack and our insight was to show that the criminals weren't very bright. We wanted to turn the whole problem on its head and show the criminals as not as clever or as smart as you thought they were. The strategy was to empower the viewer to think it's not hard to outsmart these people.

One of our colleagues went up to Moss Side and spent an evening out with the police and there were some interviews with some criminals as well. It was quite an extensive process and it led to the insight that what we need to do is stop scaring people but make them feel they can fight back against criminals.

What we heard from both the police and the criminals was that there was no great master plan behind any of these crimes. A lot of what they were up to was completely opportunistic, just seeing what could be snatched without getting caught.

**Figure 1: Home Office – Vehicle Crime campaign**

That led on to the other insight, which was that the communications needed to be as near as possible to the point where the crimes might actually take place.

I think we were the first to advertise on parking meters. We did ads in car parks where people leave their cars open stupidly or forget their keys or forget to lock them. Also we put ads around petrol pumps because when people go to pay for their petrol they forget the car's unlocked and somebody just snatches what's there.

We also started doing ads on the back of bank receipts, because cash points are another opportunistic moment. We were targeting the media wherever we thought people were liable to experience these sorts of random acts of crime.

The role of the television was to show what criminals are really like – showing that in truth they're not clever master criminals but just a bit of a plonker who's going to take the opportunity if you give it to him.

## 2. Fire Authority Northern Ireland: 'Writings on the wall'

*By Larry McGarry, Creative Director, Ardmore Advertising*

The brief was to increase the use of smoke alarms throughout Northern Ireland. About 92% of the population had a working smoke alarm, which left us only 8% to work on – a very small group.

When we got the brief we decided that we would do the fire training like a fire-fighter just to see what it was like. So we went and got the breathing apparatus and learned how to get away from a burning building, which, I have to say, was probably one of the hardest things you'll ever do in your life.

Until you put yourself in that situation, until you feel that fear when you're literally crawling along the floor at 200 degrees heat unable to see your hand in front of your face and imagining what it would be like not to have the 20 guys around you and the breathing apparatus, you can't possibly understand how you would feel if a house fire was real. We needed to get into the psyche of someone sitting watching a TV programme and convey some of that terror.

But this experience gave us credibility with the fire-fighters so when we sat down with those guys after that experience they were more willing and open in talking to us. They started talking about when they went to investigate a fire when you would assume the room would have burned down but it hasn't. It literally looks as if nothing's happened. There may be a little darkness on the walls, a little

**Figure 2: Fire Authority Northern Ireland – 'Writings on the wall' campaign**

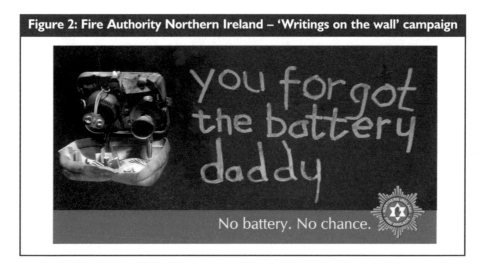

darkness on the ceiling, but really it looks as if nothing happened because smoke kills people and you'd be dead by the time the smoke has burned itself out.

So they made us imagine what it would be like in that room. The room is completely black, you don't know your way around. And how we can tell that is because there are hand marks all over the walls where people were searching for where the door would normally be or searching for a window – just looking for any opening. But in that situation you're completely disorientated.

So I was thinking about what we need to do in order to have the necessary impact. If we could just explain to people what happens in a fire and show them the hand marks on the wall, it's what happens if you don't have a smoke alarm. That's where the 'Writings on the wall' campaign came from.

## 3. Army Recruitment: 'Be the best'

*By Adam Kean, former Creative Director, Saatchi & Saatchi (where the campaign was originally created)*

'When we got the brief the context was to move on from the kind of ads they were running at the time. There was a campaign in the UK that showed a couple of guys sitting in a pub daydreaming about the kind of life they'd like to have rather than the boring civilian life they did lead. There were shots of people windsurfing and climbing mountains and all sorts of things like that. But the Army is different and actually harder work than the expectations created in the ads. So the ads were effectively creating a fantasy world that the real-life Army experience didn't quite live up to.

That was the first thing we noticed about this campaign. The effect of that was that potential recruits wanted to come and talk to them about the Army or even train to join the Army but they were leaving very quickly afterwards because it wasn't quite what they thought.

So we thought that we should tell a bit more of the truth and our idea was that the ads should reflect the kinds of challenges that Army life is full of. But that there are also rewards. So our line when we pitched was 'To be the best, you've got to want to be the best' which was eventually shortened to 'Be the best'.

**Figure 3: Army Recruitment – 'Be the Best' campaign**

We felt that the campaign should be started with some kind of stunt. Our idea was that the first ad would be at 6 o'clock in the morning, and that there should be an ad the night before saying 'set your alarm for 6 and see the Army's new campaign'. In other words, the idea of the whole campaign was going to be a series of challenges. So if you're the kind of person who can respond to challenges, you're the kind of person we want in the Army.

The Brigadier responsible for recruitment went on television at 6.00 am that morning describing the reasoning behind the whole thing. And then we did a series of three ads. One was for the Regular Army, which was about driving. The idea was that it's not just about driving in the normal way when you can see. We switched the lights off on the car and we drove in the dark. So the challenge was not just to be able to drive but to drive in the dark.

The Officer treatment ad showed a kid in a hospital; the kid was ill and there were all sorts of problems that other people in the hospital had. But all of them turned towards the camera and said 'What do we do sir?' and the officer said if you could make this decision you should give us a ring. We were saying it's quite a challenging life in the forces but these challenges can be just as glamorous as windsurfing or mountain climbing – and a lot harder.

## 4. Scotland: Organ Donors

### By Andrew Lindsay, Creative Director, Union Advertising

One of the problems we had with this campaign was that we had very little money for it. So how do we get around that? Essentially the way we got round it was to only run ads when there was a news story in the press so what you got was a double whammy: a news story about somebody's organs failing who then gets a new organ from a donor and beside this story would be the ad.

What we went for was a fairly stark kind of message. The ad said essentially it was really up to you whether a person lives or dies at the end of today. We had these ads, which were just a close-up of somebody's face and the colouring of the face was such that you couldn't really tell if the person was alive or dead.

By making the faces appear lifeless, the reader was forced into a decision: Cure Jill, yes and a line led to an Organ Donor card. If you ticked the box that said Kill Jill, the line went nowhere. It's as though you were saying, I'm not interested. It was a very simple, hard message.

If you've got very little money you've really got to go with something quite powerful, there's no kind of shilly-shallying around with positive messages. You know the stark reality is that if you take an Organ Donor card you can be of some help but if you don't there's a possibility that somebody who needs your help won't get it.

There's been a significant take-up in Organ Donor card carrying so it's been a successful route. I think that although we might not deal with exactly the same route in any future advertising, I think it would still be a pretty hard-hitting kind of ad.

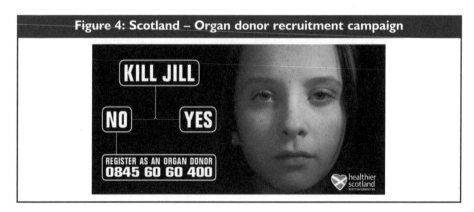

**Figure 4: Scotland – Organ donor recruitment campaign**

## 5. British Heart Foundation: 'I've got you under my skin'

### *By Ed Morris, Executive Creative Director, Lowe*

I remember this campaign because it was a real challenge and quite a forbidding one because it was to follow a very, very successful ad – the one that showed the Fatty Cigarette.

The one weak, missing link of the Fatty Cigarette idea was that it demonised the cigarette – which means that you're able to throw it away and get rid of it for a while. But, in fact, then after the advertising is finished you come back to it. So our challenge was quite a simple one, which was just to internalise the Fatty Cigarette.

That's how I saw it; that was the kind of line I had in my head from the beginning. And do you know, literally, when we came back from taking the brief and discussing that thought – of internalising the cigarette – I got to my pad and just drew an arm holding a cigarette. I drew the fat travelling along the cigarette and into the finger and then down the arm, giving the idea that it's an illness that is caused by the cigarette – through your bloodstream, and into your heart, which is eventually fatal.

And I remember the literal drawing on my pad. I just drew an arm and a little lump under it in one of the veins and I thought yes it's under the skin now and something magical happened. The song 'I've got you under my skin' sprang into my mind. I didn't know the full lyrics to it, I just remembered that being a poignant line. So I went onto the internet immediately, looked at the lyrics and just couldn't believe how well they fitted the subject. It was uncanny, it was like Frank Sinatra had written it for this campaign.

**Figure 5: British Heart Foundation – 'I've got you under my skin' campaign**

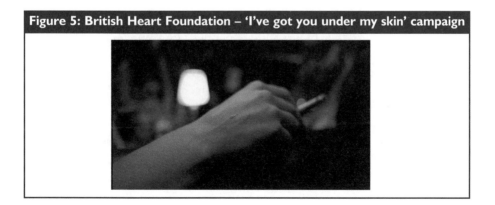

So then of course we had a quick scramble to find out if we could get the track; we could, and we presented it and the client loved the approach because of the way the track fitted so well. The other thing we wanted to do was have a visual device to underline the words of the song. So we had the visual showing the lump, which worked through the body under the skin as the track played. The radio came later by which time people knew what it was for without having to see the visual.

Also this track led to another ad, which contained a bit of a sucker punch. It opens up on a romantic, cool, quite glamorous-looking bar with the track playing. The camera moves around to find a girl and for the first few seconds you think it is a pop promo, it's enjoyable – until we cut to the shock of the lump of fat in her arm.

One of the main findings in this kind of work is that if you start by showing victims, people immediately switch off and say 'that's not me'. So you have to show aspirational kinds of people to hook the viewer in, to get them to identify with the character – and then you deliver the sucker punch.

## 6. Scotland: Blood Donors

### By Frank Stubbs, Deputy Creative Director, The Bridge

We got a brief with a really good insight in it, which was the idea that people didn't give blood because they didn't ever feel they'd been asked. They had the vague belief that blood donors were somebody else. Blood donors were kind of do-gooding 'other' people. That was the thing we had to turn around because there was a shortfall of blood supplies and that shortfall had to be made up from a completely new cohort of donors. So we needed to find ways of turning the tables on people so that they felt it was them being asked.

During this time, my wife had just had a baby so I had spent a bit of time in the hospital and seen the vulnerability of people with young kids and babies – how dependent they are on the system and the people around them. The hospital where both our kids were born had a major sick children's hospital right next door to it so I'd seen at first hand how much people really needed help from other people.

So that felt like a very fruitful emotional area to plumb. The viewer figures for hospital TV dramas like *Holby City* are huge so I knew that people generally are interested in that kind of thing, so we wanted to try to recreate something similar. In all those dramas there's always a story outside the hospital involv-

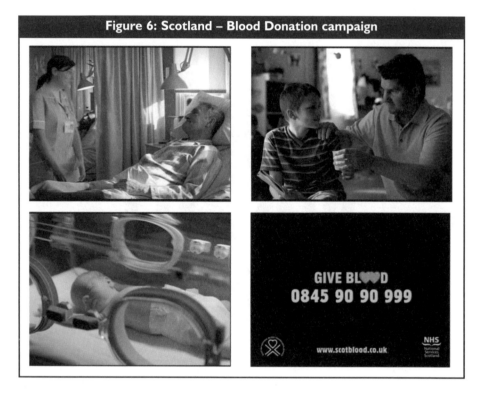

Figure 6: Scotland – Blood Donation campaign

GIVE BL♥♥D
0845 90 90 999

www.scotblood.co.uk

NHS
National Services Scotland

ing somebody else who's not the person who's ill and is somehow making the situation worse by letting the vulnerable person down. So we plugged into that emotion because you feel almost anger towards the people that aren't helping when they should be.

The idea came on us really quickly, because having had that insight, we wanted to draw people into the situation and lead them up the garden path with the idea that there's some nasty person who is not there and who should be there helping, then suddenly turning it round at the end so they realise, oh God, that person's me. That made it personal and really struck home.

## 7. HM Revenue & Customs: Tax doesn't have to be taxing

### By Malcolm Duffy, Creative Director, Miles Calcraft Briginshaw Duffy

There was a lot of discussion about how HMRC wanted to be looked on in a different way. They had always used a stick approach with the advertising like Mrs Doyle from *Father Ted* saying 'go on, go on' and Hector the tax inspector doing a similar thing. We thought there has to be another way to do things rather than this constant nagging. So why not use a carrot approach?

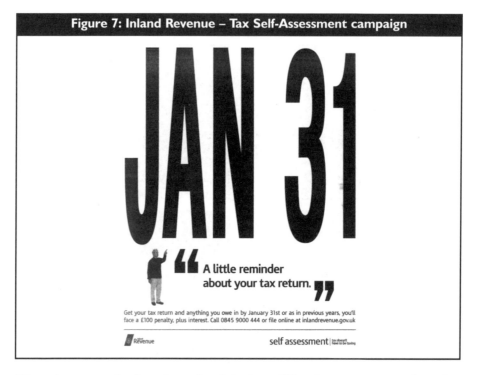

We spoke to people about how they felt about filling in tax returns and we also spoke to some psychologists about how people behave when faced with jobs they don't want to do. So we came up with this idea that 'Tax doesn't have to be taxing', which was a way of saying 'We know there are a lot of jobs we don't want to do but we'll feel a lot better when we've done them.'

We were looking at the whole idea of procrastination and how to get people to stop procrastinating. This really struck a nerve with the audience and confirmed very much that we should be following a carrot rather than a stick approach.

Inland Revenue (now HM Revenue & Customs) had never used this approach before. They felt people needed to be goaded into doing their returns and we felt people needed a bit of sugar on the pill. I think people resist these direct approaches and prefer to be seduced into doing things.

Once we had that breakthrough, it was a case of finding someone to put that across in a very sympathetic way. We had quite a few presenters on our list, then we stumbled across Adam Hart-Davis who'd been on *Tomorrow's World* and presented the programme *What the Romans Did for Us*. He's a very amiable, intelligent guy with a lovely voice, which would obviously work on radio as well as television.

We made an approach to him and he was very up for it. So we did some research and even people who didn't know him felt he was a very warm, intelligent person who summed up what we were trying to do with HMRC. Not just nasty guys trying to take money from us, but actually nice human beings. They wanted to put a more human face on it and Adam really summed that up for us.

He could put dry messages across in an interesting way, which is what the best presenters do, leaving people thinking, well I don't want to do it but I know I have to so why not get it over with?

It's very rare nowadays to find a presenter who will agree to work on TV and radio as well as other media. Adam was very happy to have his face on posters, and he has a lovely distinctive voice, which was great for radio. So he's been perfect for us.

## 8. Northern Ireland: Seat Belts 'Damage'

*By David Lyle, Chief Executive and Managing Director, and Julie Anne Bailie, Executive Creative Director, Lyle Bailie International Limited*

**JAB:** The clear thing that came out of the research was that young people are obviously a key target but what young people were saying repeatedly was that it's my seat belt, it's my choice, it's my life and it doesn't affect anyone else. I will do whatever I want, it's my choice.

That was the psychological barrier that we were up against. People were giving us all sorts of reasons why they didn't like wearing a seat belt – there were all kinds of physical excuses, you know I don't like the feeling of the seat belt, it irritates me, it hurts me, it comes across my shoulder, it comes across my stomach, I don't like it.

But what we realised very quickly despite the fact that none of them actually articulated this in the focus groups, was that the opposite was actually true. This was not just to do with the physical discomfort – there was very little physicality about it – it was actually the psychological discomfort. Wearing a seat belt isn't cool. Wearing a seat belt meant they weren't at the centre of the action, they couldn't control anything, they couldn't put the windows down, they couldn't control their CDs and it was very much an emotional and psychological discomfort.

Figure 8: Northern Ireland – 'Damage' campaign

As a result of that we decided we were really going to take the bull by the horns and address the issue head on. We were going to convince these people that if they're not wearing their seat belts it doesn't just affect them and that it's not just their choice.

It actually means that if you don't wear your seat belt you can become a multiple killer, ruining lives both inside the car and outside the car. So we did something that had never ever been done before. We showed, second by second, what actually happens in a crash when someone in the car is not wearing their seat belt.

**DL:** It was important that the research included all of Ireland because the brief was from two government bodies: the government body responsible for road safety in the Republic of Ireland, in Dublin; and the government body responsible for road safety in Northern Ireland. So we had to have a joint cross-border campaign.

But our research showed that the same psychological resistances existed everywhere. This idea that 'it's my choice' was a common factor even though the incidence of wearing seat belts is much higher in the north than in the Republic of Ireland. Since that campaign, the incidence of people wearing seat belts in Northern Ireland is at the highest level in the UK.

**JAB:** One thing that we know throughout all our work with young people – not just Seat Belts – is that they don't respond well to symbolism or analogies or abstraction. What they do respond to is having someone tell it as it is, which can be very shocking. This doesn't cover every aspect of road safety – for example, our children's campaigns aren't like that, but with the Seat Belts campaign we needed to shock.

## 9. Northern Ireland: Road Safety 'Shame'

*By David Lyle, Chief Executive and Managing Director, and Julie Anne Bailie, Executive Creative Director, Lyle Bailie International Limited*

**DL:** Here, despite similar differences between the north and south, the research led us to the insight that young men, 18–25 (followed by men 25–35), were the target audience because they are the most over-represented in collisions caused by driver alcohol. When they talked about drink they described drinking and driving as related to great times. Occasions that started off as the best times of your life, and a lot of them were sport-related – when you've had a great match and you're enjoying the craic with your mates.

You don't deliberately set out to drink and drive but you get caught up in the heat of the moment. That's what we had to work on.

**JAB:** We were very, very careful to make sure we showed an ordinary decent bloke. We wanted ordinary kids to look at him and think 'that could be me'. So we paid a lot of attention to the casting, right through to the detail of what he'd be wearing and his hair and the type of sports bag he has and everything about his body language. People had to be able to look at him and say 'that is me'.

I think it's wrong to demonise people; it alienates them. When you show their behaviour as very erratic they don't identify. So we took great care in that regard. But we were absolutely categoric in the whole positioning of the theme line. It's *never* drink and drive.

**DL:** The commercial starts off by introducing a family scene in a garden with a little boy playing football and there's this vision of him playing football with a guy in his teens or early twenties playing for his local team. The little boy in the garden scores a goal; the guy playing for his local team scores a goal. You see the little boy celebrating in his garden in this idyllic scene with the family. You see the guy, the 19 year old, 20 year old, celebrating with his mates in the bar afterwards – full of excitement and exhilaration.

Then we see him driving home after the match and we then see a fatal mistake because he's so tired. The shock and horror of the ad is that he loses control

Figure 9: Northern Ireland – 'Shame' campaign

of the car and the car rolls into the garden where the little boy has been play-ing football and you're left with the feeling that the little boy has been crushed by the car. We were dramatising the reality of what happens when the best of times suddenly turn into the worst of times.

# Part 6

## A psychological perspective

# Chapter 13

# What we know about how the human brain works

By Professor Geoffrey Beattie

University of Manchester

The first public advertising campaign that really made a lasting impression on me and succeeded in changing my behaviour was a campaign about drugs. I was a teenager at the time, growing up in the damp grey streets of the Belfast of the Troubles. Life was disjointed and fractured. As a teenager, my social life was restricted to the streets around me, endless hours of hanging about 'the corner', which was in reality the front of a chip shop with a warm air vent blowing out rancid air that stank of chip fat on cold winter nights. It was a dangerous and unpredictable place, even the chip shop itself was dangerous, both inside and out. The press called my streets 'murder triangle'.

But, of course, I realised that there was a life somewhere out there better than this, but it was too far away to glimpse or touch. The world of the *NME*, the *News of the World* with stories about the sordid goings-on of rock stars, images of jeans tucked into green boots, Biba, fast cars. 'Fast cars and girls are easily come by' or 'easy to come by', I can't remember which the pop song said, but not here they weren't. The swings in our local park were chained up on a Sunday lest we enjoy ourselves on the Lord's Day.

It was a Friday in my local youth club that he came to talk to us. We were all boys, I remember that. It was a funny sort of youth club, and we were asked to pull our chairs out into neat rows in front of the speaker. My fingers reeked of Coke and crisps. This was not high-tech public service advertising, but it was an advertising campaign nonetheless, designed to change our behaviour, designed to fit into the evening's youth club activities, designed to warn us of the menace of drugs between table tennis and quarter-size snooker, before the dangerous walk home through the streets filled sometimes equally with drunks and terrorists.

There was an opening introduction then a slide show with images of pills and plants, a glossary of terms, some of which I had heard before, many of which I had not: amphetamine, speed, pep pills, black bombers, dexies, black beauties, black and white minstrels, LSD, purple haze, yellow sunshine, blue heaven, sugar cubes, marijuana, dope ('They call it shit here in Belfast', my friend Colin said helpfully, 'I've never seen it, but I do know that. If you want some, all you have to say is "Can I score some shit?"'), grass, cocaine, coke, Californian cornflakes. Shit was never mentioned; it was all much more exotic than that.

But to this day I can remember the slides, with shiny red and black pills, white powder as pure as the snow we never saw in our damp streets, exotic plants. From the opening slide I was captivated. It was as if the drugs were jumping off the slides, almost three-dimensional in their appearance. I don't think that I once blinked in case I missed something. Things were being revealed to me, to us all; we were all drug virgins, and pop culture virgins. I had a series of agonising shocks of recognition and clarity. 'My friend Jack eats sugar cubes' was no longer a song about a fat teenager with a sugar addiction like fat Albert down the street; 'Purple haze is in my brain' wasn't a song about pollution and traffic jams, and the way that street lights can play odd tricks with your vision when the shipyard was closing and the streets were packed.

I was hooked. Hooked on the glamour and the glitz. Hooked on the terms, with their implicit connotations of something better – 'black beauties', 'yellow sunshine', 'Californian cornflakes'. Hooked on finding the way out from a world where the swings never moved on a Sunday. And when the slides showed close-ups of black bombers, I realised that my rusted bathroom cabinet with the shaky mottled glass door, pinned to the wall in our kitchen (because we didn't have a bathroom or an inside toilet), was full of drugs, full of black bombers, used by my mother as slimming pills. That night my friends and I took drugs for the first time, and gabbled away outside the chip shop for hours, hardly noticing the smell of chip fat. It probably wasn't that much fun, but we all felt different, separate from everyone else, empowered in a curious sort of way. 'We're on the drugs', we said to anyone who would listen. And it felt great.

This, of course, is just an anecdote, a single case study about the disaffected youth of Belfast one rainy Friday night a long time ago, but it reminds me of the challenge that public service advertising faces. Get it wrong and you can get it badly wrong. You can actually make things worse than if you hadn't bothered. The speaker that night with his slides and his spiel didn't have a clear understanding of me and my friends, nor of our social situation. When you communicate you need a clear model of the audience, their mental state, their needs and aspirations. He had no such model. You have to be able to read other minds. He couldn't. You also need the right approach.

He went for a cognitive, rational approach and explained patiently to us that drugs were dangerous. But this meant very little to us. Going for a pint of milk was dangerous where we lived. Telling us that drugs affected the biochemistry of the brain cut no ice either. A night outside the chip shop with the drive-by shootings and then the backfiring cars messed up the biochemistry of your brain. We all knew that. We all had friends who had cracked up after hours spent hanging about the corner doing nothing. None of them needed drugs to help them along. And the presenter underestimated the great emotional pull drugs had for us corner boys, the emotional connotations of London, Biba, long blonde hair in the wind, the Stones, the Who, Led Zeppelin, fashion, rebellion, life in your own hands, not in the hands of others, living dangerously because you wanted to, not because others wanted you to, empowerment, sex, especially sex.

That is why the campaigns featured in this volume are so interesting for a psychologist to consider. This book explicitly poses the question of how public service advertising works. So how does it work? How do you make a large heterogeneous set of individuals with limited attention capacity who are desperately clinging on to their behaviour for comfort and psychological security think about changing their behaviour and then getting them to actually change it?

Richard Storey in Chapter 1 puts the challenge quite well:

> ... the typical public service campaign is often required to produce dramatic social transformations on pressing societal issues. Initiatives featured in this chapter have sought to reduce domestic burglaries, decrease the number of road fatalities, reduce injuries and deaths from domestic fires and cut coronary heart disease. No mean feat, particularly when the weapons to achieve it are basically just words and pictures.

But what words and pictures! The campaigns reviewed in the book universally display high levels of creativity to elicit reactions, evoke powerful images, produce emotional responses and interrupt the flow of life for reflection, hesitation and in many cases striking behavioural change. So how does all this work?

The challenge is much more than that involved in commercial campaigns because again, as Storey points out:

> *As many commercial marketing campaigns operate in a zero sum game, their commercial objectives largely feature switched loyalty and substituted behaviour – for example, getting people to buy one pasta sauce rather than another, incentivising people to try Pepsi rather than Coke, encouraging people to place a brand higher on their mental consideration list. While these are by no means simple challenges, they are focused on modifying existing behaviour, rather than initiating it in the first instance. The public service challenge is often one of creating entirely new behaviour.*

This does put the challenge clearly and starkly, and the question for any psychologist is to explain why this might work in some cases and not others, and to identify how we can make it more effective in the majority of cases. These are no mean challenges and in order to provide even a partial answer I need to review how psychology has changed in the past few years and to outline some of the new exciting developments going on in the subject, which may be relevant here. We now know a little more about how the brain works and about how it deals with words and pictures, and about the role of emotions in mental processing and how emotions connect to rational thought, and about how the brain integrates and interprets all manner of messages before deciding often unconsciously and implicitly to go along with the messages.

This book's explicit challenge is to summarise what has been happening over past years in public service advertising to allow for new developments in the future, and I want to interpret my brief in a similar way. I want to be slightly less constrained than some psychologists in my position and move beyond traditional theories of attitude change (with which most advertisers will be very familiar) to discuss a few developments in the subject that are exciting psychologists at this point in time, and to try to suggest how some of this new research might influence advertising even more in the future.

## The relationship between thinking and emotion

I want to concentrate on just three themes, all concerning the relationship between thinking and emotion, which I think are directly relevant to some of the issues raised in this book.

**Theme 1: Every advertiser knows that emotion is crucial to persuasion, which is why so much of advertising is aimed at the human emotional system. But**

**how do emotions connect to rational thought? Research in neuroscience suggests that one often precedes and directs the other, and that much of so-called rational thought is little more than a post hoc justification for our behaviour. When we target thought we may be targeting no more than a store of rationalisations. We might, therefore, change our approach accordingly and target the justification process explicitly.**

Antonio Damasio is at the centre of much of the exciting new research in neuroscience into how emotion and conscious rational thought connect. We now know a great deal about the relationship between emotions, the brain and behaviour. We know that emotion focuses attention, has a major effect on what we remember and is more closely linked to behaviour than cognitions.[1] But we also now know that, in normal people, activation of the emotional system precedes activation of any conceptual or reasoning system and, perhaps as importantly, that the two systems are quite separate.

Damasio famously showed all of this with a very simple gambling experiment. Sitting in front of the participant are four decks of cards, in their hands they have $2,000 to gamble with. The task is to turn over one card at a time to win the maximum amount of money, and with each card you either win some money or lose some money. In the case of two of the decks, the rewards are great ($100) but so too are the penalties. If you play either of these two decks for any period of time you end up losing money. On the other hand, if you concentrate on selecting cards from the other two decks, you get smaller rewards ($50) but also smaller penalties and you end up winning money in the course of the game. But these 'reward/penalty' factors are unknown to the participant at the start of the game.

What Damasio found with people playing this game was that, after encountering a few losses, normal participants generated skin conductance responses (a sign of autonomic arousal) before selecting a card from the 'bad deck' and they also started to avoid the decks associated with bad losses. In other words, they showed a distinct emotional response to the bad decks even before they had a conceptual understanding of the nature of the decks and long before they could explain what was going on. They started to avoid the bad decks on the basis of their emotional response.

Damasio also found that patients with damage to a particular area of the brain called the ventromedial prefrontal cortex failed to generate a skin conductance response before selecting cards from the bad deck and also did not avoid the decks with large losses. Patients with damage to this part of the brain

223

could not generate the anticipatory skin conductance response and could not avoid the bad decks even though they conceptually understood the difference in the nature of the decks before them. In the words of the authors 'The patients failed to act according to their correct conceptual knowledge.'[2]

In other words Damasio and his colleagues demonstrated that 'in normal individuals, non-conscious biases guide behaviour before conscious knowledge does. Without the help of such biases, overt knowledge may be insufficient to ensure advantageous behavior.' In normal people activation of the emotional system precedes activation of the conceptual system and we now know the neural connection between these two systems is located in the ventromedial prefrontal cortex.

More recently, Damasio demonstrated the powerful role of emotions in the generation of moral judgements in that patients with bilateral damage to the same brain region, the ventromedial prefrontal cortex, were more likely to choose 'heroic' and highly emotional personally aversive responses in a series of moral dilemmas presented to them.[3] Haidt[4] developed a new model of moral judgement (and evaluative judgement generally) in which *moral judgement* (or *evaluative judgement*, which underpins all of the campaigns covered in this book) appears in consciousness automatically and effortlessly, but t'Moral reasoning is an effortful process, engaged in after a moral judgment is made, in which a person searches for arguments that will support an already-made judgment.'

In other words, we make our mind up pretty quickly and the 'arguments' presented to us may play little role in our judgement except in the subsequent justification of our behaviour to ourselves or others.

This research explains why so much of the material covered in this volume works. They have targeted the non-conscious biases head-on. Storey writes that 'Numerous studies have identified that emotional stimuli make far more effective prompts than purely rational arguments when it comes to changing opinions and provoking a response.' The way that the brain is hard-wired suggests that this might well be the most appropriate strategy. These non-conscious biases affect behaviour long before we understand the significance of the thing that we are acting towards.

My non-conscious biases and emotive pull towards drugs as a teenager (driven, I hasten to add, by the situation I found myself in) were not overridden by the talk that wet Friday night. All the rational argument about relative danger did little to dissuade me. But there is one interesting corollary of this that few have considered. If rational argument is very much secondary in producing actual behavioural change, but rather it is something that is 'effortful' and mainly used in the justification process, should we be rethinking the nature of the 'rational arguments' we provide?

Do we need to think more carefully and analytically about the nature of the justification process rather than confusing ourselves that it is the rational arguments that are the basis of the behavioural change? Do some kinds of post hoc justifications work better than others? Is there a taxonomy of justifications and can we analyse their relative effectiveness? Can we help the audience already primed to change their behaviour (because of their emotional response) justify their actions with less effort by providing the right, readily available language to construct their justifications and excuses?

These are questions never really posed before, but the answers could potentially be both theoretically and practically very informative for both advertising and psychology.

**Theme 2: People are bad at estimating risk. We have now started to understand how individuals decide on whether a decision is risky or not. What is called 'the availability heuristic' means that people judge an event as likely or frequent if instances of it are easy to imagine or recall. If we want to emphasise the risks associated with any behaviour we need to make any negative images associated with the behaviour as memorable as possible. We can do this most effectively by stimulating the limbic system and the reticular formation in the brain to produce 'flashbulb memories' by making the images both surprising and consequential simultaneously.**

Many of the campaigns featured in the book aim to change behaviour that is both risky and potentially very dangerous – driving too close to other motorists, making chips in the middle of the night while under the influence of alcohol, and smoking in bed, or indeed smoking anywhere. But the problem, as Alison Hoad points out, in Chapter 2, is that 'People often don't believe the behaviour is risky, or alternatively, don't think the danger will befall them.' Psychologists are now trying to offer new insights into risk and how people perceive risk. What is clear is that the perception of risk is both a cognitive and emotional phenomenon and Damasio's research described above suggests that it is the emotional system that is primary and tends to react first.

But how does the more rational bit of the mind compute risk? Risk, according to the dictionary, is 'the chance or possibility of suffering loss, injury, damage or failure'. The definition alone highlights the cognitive aspect of risk, of the mind needing to compute the chance or probability of the risk going wrong and imagining or trying not to imagine the 'loss, injury, damage or failure'. How good are we at actually doing these computations? Some psychologists argue that we are not very accurate, and they point to the fact that when we are asked to assess the risk of any event occurring we rarely have statistical evidence to hand. Instead we rely on inferences based on what we remember hearing or observing about the risk in question. In other words, we make a judgement and this judgement is affected by a number of distinct biases.

One type of bias is called the 'availability heuristic', which is that people judge an event as likely or frequent if instances of it are easy to imagine or recall. You could argue that this makes perfect sense because frequently occurring events are easier to imagine or recall than infrequent events; but availability is also related to factors unrelated to frequency of occurrence. For example, the release of the film *Jaws* suddenly meant that people thought that shark attack was a much more common occurrence than it actually is, on the basis of the graphic depiction in the film itself. One experimental demonstration of this was carried out by Lichtenstein and his colleagues in 1978,[5] who gave subjects the annual death toll of motor vehicle accidents and asked them to estimate the frequencies of 40 other causes of death. They found that accidents associated with vivid images were judged to cause as many deaths as diseases, whereas diseases actually take about 15 times as many lives.

So the problem in designing public service advertising is how to manipulate the availability heuristic so that people will no longer underestimate the risks associated with behaviours that give rise to diseases such as cancer, stroke, asthma or diabetes (hard to form clear images of, hidden, and therefore 'unlikely' to happen).

One way of doing this is to psychologically manipulate the memorability of images. We now know that the most memorable and enduring of all human memories are 'flashbulb memories', which are hard-wired memories designed for human survival and shaped by evolution. These are the kinds of enduring and stable memories that we have if we've ever been in a near-fatal car accident or any other major trauma[6] – emotional memories, where every single aspect of the scene is encoded, apparently for all time, by the joint action of two of the most primitive parts of the human brain, namely the reticular formation, which responds to surprise, and the limbic system, which responds to consequentiality. If you have once driven too quickly and you have a near-fatal crash you will have a flashbulb memory of the event – a clear, rich, powerful and enduring image – and you will perhaps (for the first time) realise how dangerous fast driving actually is.

The big psychological question is 'Can we produce flashbulb memories for events that are not life threatening?' The answer appears to be 'yes' because many of us have flashbulb memories for major cultural events – like where we were and who we were with the day we learned of Diana Princess of Wales's death, ten years after the event. So flashbulb memories can be elicited by events that are not life threatening for the individual.

Emotion seems to be a primary determinant of behaviour, influencing behaviour before our conceptual understanding is in place, as we have already discussed; but it also affects what we remember through the formation of these special primitive memories, designed by evolution for survival. Advertisers could potentially target these qualitatively different indelible memories. One consequence of this would be that it would affect the availability heuristic and lead to a reappraisal of the risks associated with certain behaviours.

The challenge for advertisers is to manipulate the nature of the images they present to an audience, beyond mere originality or shockability to something more meaningful, more personal, and thus more consequential for that individual. This is a considerable challenge but one that could pay dividends with respect to effecting change in risky behaviour. How can we generate flashbulb memories regarding the effects of smoking on coronary heart disease, for example?

**Theme 3: There has been endless speculation in the advertising literature about the possible role of subliminal advertising with 'embeds' dropped into all sorts of messages. But there is a type of subliminal messaging that goes on in everyday communication, and that is the messaging carried out by the hands during talk. Speech and the spontaneous and unconscious images created by the hand of the speaker during the act of talking together create and express propositional meaning. The human brain has evolved to integrate speech and image unconsciously and effortlessly. We can use this new theoretical understanding in designing adverts and advertising campaigns.**

Over the past few years psychologists have started to reconsider the very nature of everyday communication. The traditional view, dating back to Wundt[7] and the foundations of modern psychology, is that there are two primary modes of communication: speech, which is the type of communication used for the expression of ideas and thoughts; and non-verbal communication, which is used for emotional expression and the signalling of relationships such as love and hate, power and authority, dominance and submission.

The traditional view is that these systems of communication are separate and operate in entirely different fashions, with speech operating in a linear and segmented fashion, combinatorial in form, with a syntax, or set of rules, to relate the internal elements (the words) to each other. Speech is a conscious mode unique to human beings but learned over a number of years through the painstaking influence of care-givers. Non-verbal communication (facial expression, posture, gesture, bodily movement) has been understood as quite separate from speech, often displayed with little or no conscious awareness and shared with our animal relatives and non-combinatorial in form, instead working in terms of detailed holistic messages.

This distinction has underpinned much of our cultural reasoning about what it is to be a human being and how one should produce a persuasive message capable of changing attitudes. Speech appeals to reasoning, the higher instincts, the rational side of our being. Non-verbal communication is much more primitive in evolutionary terms and in its functioning, thought to be sent and received largely unconsciously.

Thomas Mann (1924) wrote in *The Magic Mountain* that, '[s]peech is civilization itself. The word, even the most contradictory word preserves contact – it is silence which isolates.'[8] But it is *talk*, in my view, that preserves this contact; it is speech and all the accompanying, intimately timed hand and arm movements that bind the speaker and the listener and draws us together.

If you analyse speakers in action, in sufficient detail, you can see how close the connection really is between what is said in speech and the patterns of the accompanying hand movements. These hand movements often appear to 'illustrate' what is being said through a series of images. But the research of David McNeill[9] changed how we thought about these movements; it gave them a new theoretical import, and it provided them with a central role in human communication. In his view, hand movements were as significant in the communication of thoughts and ideas as the speech itself. He argued that these 'illustrators', which he termed 'iconic' gestures (or 'metaphoric' for the more abstract), do not merely illustrate what is in the speech. Rather they cooperate centrally with the speech to convey propositional or semantic information and 'we should regard the gesture and the spoken utterance as different sides of a single underlying mental process'.[10]

But what evidence is there that 'listeners', watching as well as actually listening, pick up on the information encoded in these iconic gestures and somehow combine this with the information encoded in the speech itself? Research we have carried out at Manchester has produced compelling positive evidence on this critical issue.[11,12]

More recently, I started to explore the implications of this new model for TV advertising.[13] Part of the core function of advertising is to communicate semantic information about the distinct features of a product, and to build brand image and identity. Research in this area seems to me to be guided by the traditional theory of human communication, but does the new model of human communication, which maintains that the brain has evolved to deal with speech and the accompanying gesture simultaneously, have implications for how we should think about the design of effective advertisements?

One of our studies[13] compared the efficacy of two types of TV ads. A London advertising agency created two broadcast-standard TV ads for a (then) non-existent fruit juice drink – one involving speech and image, the other speech and gesture. The agency was advised on what iconic and what (more abstract) metaphoric gestures to use for particular properties of the product in one version of the ad (on the basis of the spontaneous and unconscious gestures generated by people when they talked about the product). Three gestures were selected for use in the speech–gesture advertisement. The agency decided on their own images for the speech-image advertisement.

The study revealed that the iconic and metaphoric gestures were particularly effective at communicating core semantic properties of products compared to other non-gestural images. Complex visual images of the kinds used in TV ads have many properties; gestures, on the other hand, are able to isolate just the core dimensions that one wishes to communicate. This could well be why they are so effective. Plus the fact that the human brain, throughout its long evolutionary history, has evolved to interpret these sorts of images alongside the more fledgling speech (comparatively speaking, a rather late development). New advances in brain imaging may help to reveal the neurophysiological underpinnings of this whole process, of how the brain deals with the natural images encoded in these gestures and speech simultaneously.

## Conclusions

New research in psychology is telling us a little more about how the brain works. Emotion seems to be a primary determinant of our behaviour, influencing behaviour often before our conceptual understanding is in place. The research even suggests that much of what we think of as the reasoning underpinning our actions is no such thing: it is merely the mind catching up and justifying what has already been decided for it through this semi-autonomous emotional system.

If we recognise that the reasoning underpinning possible behavioural change is often nothing more than justification, we may change the focus of our targeted messages. We may try to help people justify rather than decide.

Research also demonstrates that emotion affects what we remember through the formation of special primitive memories, called 'flashbulb memories', designed by evolution for survival. If we can produce flashbulb memories for the negative consequences of risky behaviour, then we can be confident that the rational part of the brain, in the process of doing its computations on the probability of risky behaviour going wrong, will suddenly start to draw the right conclusions, i.e. more conservative conclusions, and we may see much less risky behaviour as a consequence.

Research also tells us that speech and certain types of image in the form of gestures are more closely integrated than we ever realised, and that the mechanism for certain types of subliminal advertising may be there in the actions of ordinary individuals as they talk. The images in the hands are unconsciously and effortlessly combined with the information in the natural speech stream. Since these images are almost certainly never faked by speakers in everyday life (because of the sheer complexity of the process), they may have a special premium in persuasion. But, of course, once we recognise this complexity we can then engineer messages involving these images to maximum effect.

The final point that I wish to make is that psychology is currently an exciting place, and maybe even as exciting a place as the world of advertising itself, but there are many unanswered questions. Answers to some of these questions could change how advertisers go about their routine – and not so routine – business in the future, as well as for psychologists themselves.

## Notes
1. Walsh, D. & Gentile, D. (2007) Slipping under the radar: advertising and the mind. In Riley, L. & Obot, I. (eds) *Drinking it in: Alcohol Marketing and Young People.* Geneva: WHO.

2. Bechara, A., Damasio, H., Tranel, D. & Damasio, A. (1997) Deciding advantageously before knowing the advantageous strategy. *Science*, 5304, pp. 1293–1295.
3. Koenigs, M., Young, L., Adolphs, R., Tranel, D., Cushman, F., Hauser, M. & Damasio, A. (2007) Damage to the prefrontal cortex increases utilitarian moral judgments. *Nature*, 446, pp. 908–911.
4. Haidt, J. (2001) The emotional dog and its rational tail: a social intuitionist approach to moral judgment. *Psychological Review*, 108, pp. 814–834.
5. Lichtenstein, S., Slovic, P., Fischoff, B., Layman, M. & Combs, B. (1978) Judged frequency of lethal events. *Journal of Experimental Psychology: Human Learning and Memory*, 4, pp. 551–578.
6. Beattie, G. (2004) *Protestant Boy*. London: Granta.
7. Wundt, W. (1921/1973). *The Language of Gestures*. The Hague: Mouton & Co.
8. Mann, T. (1924) *The Magic Mountain*. New York: Random House: Vintage
9. McNeill, D. (1985) So you think gestures are nonverbal? *Psychological Review*, 92, pp. 350–371.
10. McNeill, D. (1992) *Hand and Mind. What Gestures Reveal about Thought*. Chicago: University of Chicago Press.
11. Beattie, G. & Shovelton, H. (1999) Do iconic hand gestures really contribute anything to the semantic information conveyed by speech? An experimental investigation. *Semiotica*, 123, pp. 1–30.
12. Beattie, G. (2003) *Visible Thought: The New Psychology of Body Language*. London: Routledge.
13. Beattie, G. & Shovelton, H. (2005) Why the spontaneous images created by the hands during talk can help make TV advertisements more effective. *British Journal of Psychology*, 96, pp. 21–37.

# Chapter 14

# The future of public service advertising

By Judie Lannon

Editor

In his introduction, Peter Buchanan describes how the book came about and what his hopes are for it. In conclusion, it is worth commenting on how well the book succeeds in this and what kinds of challenges the future presents.

First and foremost, the book has truly turned out to be of great educational value, a source of reference for anyone involved in public service advertising. Although the book naturally covers only UK cases, it is clear that the problems and issues covered exist in many countries in the developed world and consequently this vast accumulation of learning has applicability well beyond the borders of the United Kingdom. Alcohol and drug abuse, problems of crime and road safety are near universal, while others are specific to different societies. The insights into the prejudices, inhibitions, fears and desires that the cases describe – the stuff of human nature – make fascinating reading and will be familiar to anyone working in the public service arena.

But if the book is to be of real educational value, readers must gain some knowledge of how to apply the lessons to their own experience. In this respect, the book's real value lies in how the authors have analysed particular public service problems in order to set objectives, define strategy and measure outcome. As a textbook in public service communications planning it is unique. Matthew Parris makes an important point in his opening overview: this is not a doctrinaire book proposing a single approach or solution, but a very pragmatic and practical reflection of how the job is tackled – case by case, situation by situation with many different skills brought to bear – strategic thinking, media planning, creative, research. All of these disciplines have a role to play and the cases illustrate clearly how the many different kinds of problems were analysed and solved. Thus what we have is a framework for analysis rather than all purpose prescriptive solutions.

The two chapters on creativity and psychology could be seen as two sides of the same coin. On the one hand we have verbatim reports of just how particular advertising ideas emerged from the individuals who created them: typically, powerful emotional ideas gleaned from any number of different sources. This is followed by a description of just how far psychological research has advanced in its understanding of how people make choices and how important emotions are in influencing behaviour. The two chapters dovetail very neatly despite coming from very different directions.

Finally, it is worth considering what challenges the future presents. A great deal of progress has been made in developing techniques and methodologies for measuring the effects of traditional marketing communications – television, press, poster, and radio. However, the technology revolution of recent years has brought whole new set of media with the potential for people to interact with the sponsors of marketing communications. So the major challenges for the next twenty-five years will include:

### 1. The contribution of different media

The ultimate task is almost always to change behaviour. And the ways of measuring this changed behaviour currently in use have been comprehensively described in the book. But for the communications planner and the sponsor of the communications, it is critical to understand the particular contribution of each medium to the overall effect in order to develop an efficient communications plan. These new media are largely uncharted territory and all marketers, not just government departments need to understand how these new media work.

### 2. Sophisticated techniques and methods

For this task, different techniques and methodologies may need to be applied, and public service planners must stay abreast of the latest developments in the commercial world.

### 3. Close up and personal

Thirdly, we need an even better understanding of human behaviour, not just to arrive at an optimum solution in terms of motivation but also to understand how to get as close as possible to the behaviour under investigation to stand the greatest chance of influencing it.

**4. A focus on outcomes rather than outputs**

Many of the most impressive IPA papers already do this as a matter of course. However, the demands will become even more intense relating to the specific contribution advertising can make to improving the nation's health, reducing bad behaviours or reducing deaths and injuries on the road and in the home, to name just three current examples of key public sector outcomes.

The lessons in this book provide an excellent launch pad for these fresh challenges.

# Appendix

# List of case studies referenced

Full versions of the majority of cases described may be found in the IPA *Advertising Works* volumes listed below. A minority of cases were not published but can be obtained from the IPA dataBANK or WARC online (www.warc.com). When searching for cases at WARC online, use *only* the *words in bold* (as below) as key search terms.

## Advertising Works 16 (published 2008)

- **Organ Donor Recruitment**
  Life after death: the difficult process of signing people up to organ donation, pp 99–118

## Advertising Works 15 (published 2007)

- **British Heart Foundation – Anti-smoking**.
  How advertising helped the British Heart Foundation get 'under the skin' of hardened smokers, pp 243–248
- **TV Licensing**
  50 pints or a TV license? How an integrated campaign made a student TV license 'the norm' over evasion, pp 127–143
- **Vehicle crime prevention**
  Crime doesn't pay but advertising to stop it does. How advertising empowered the nation to protect themselves from vehicle crime, pp 148–168
- **Teacher Recruitment**
  A class act: how communications averted the teacher recruitment crisis, pp 345–368
- **Department for Transport**
  Thinking like a brand: how a brand idea drove down road casualties (IPA dataBANK and warc.com)

## Advertising Works 14 (published 2006)

- **Inland Revenue – Self-Assessment**
  How a change in advertising proved that tax doesn't have to be taxing, pp 45–62
- **Northern Ireland Office – Community Safety Unit**
  Changing behaviour to reduce theft from vehicles, pp 121–130
- **Blood Donation – New strategy, new blood**
  How a new strategy made a difference to levels of blood donation in Scotland, pp 205–218
- **Fire Authority for Northern Ireland – Writings on the wall**, pp 97–110
- **Scottish Children's Hearings – Panel membership**, pp 219–232
- **Lay Magistrates – Reaching those who count – counting those we reached!**
  (IPA dataBANK and warc.com)
- **Department for Transport – 30 for a reason** (APG Award) (IPA dataBANK and warc.com)

## Advertising Works 13 (published 2005)

- **Army Recruitment – Up and over the 'wall of fear'**
  How advertising is helping the Army meet its manning obligations, pp 527–528
- **Central London Congestion Charging Scheme – making sure it worked from day one**, pp 37–68
- **Tobacco Control – WARNING: advertising can seriously improve your health**
  How the integration of advertisers made advertising more powerful than word of mouth, pp 145–176
- **Police Officer Recruitment**
  How thinking locally put Herefordshire Constabulary on the national stage, pp 381–410
- **Safer Travel at Night – 'Know what you're getting into'**
  How advertising was the catalyst for a sharp reduction in rape and sexual assaults by illegal minicab drivers, pp 411-430
- **Northern Ireland Road Safety**
  How a nine year investment of £8.6m in road safety advertising led to a £704 m economic payback, pp 543–546

## Advertising Works 12 (published 2003)

- **Seat belts – 'Damage' campaign: no seatbelt, no excuse**
  Helping to reduce road deaths by 13% a year, pp 639–640

- **Anti-drink driving – 'Shame' campaign**, pp 93–106
- **We don't need no higher education**
  How integrated communications convinced teenagers to aim higher (IPA dataBANK and warc.com)
- **Police recruitment**
  How thinking negatively ended the negative thinking, pp 429–452
- **Northern Ireland Police recruitment** (IPA dataBANK and warc.com)

## Advertising Works 11 (published 2000)

- **Domestic Abuse – Domestic abuse, there's no excuse**, pp 469–484
- **Rear Seatbelts – Sudden Impact**
  How can we measure the cost of a life?   pp 349–382
- **Reading and Literacy**
  How advertising mobilised parents to help improve the reading ability of their children, pp 35–66

## Advertising Works 10 (published 1999)

- **HEA Drugs Education Campaign**
  How advertising turned the tide, pp 3–32
- **The Army**
  How advertising rose to the Army's challenge to 'Be the Best', pp 61–84
- **The Health Education Board for Scotland (HEBS)**
  'Gavin Hastings really does walk on water': How HEBS used advertising to increase physical activity in Scotland, pp 511

## Advertising Works 9 (published 1997)

- **Health Education Authority**
  Accidents will happen: making it possible to be wise after the event (IPA dataBANK and warc.com)

## Advertising Works 8 (published 1995)

- **The Health Education Board for Scotland (HEBS): smoking sticks and carrots**, pp 401–418
- **HEA AIDS Advertising**
  The effective use of mass media to meet the challenge of AIDS, pp 51–79
- **Home Office – Smoke Alarms: every home should have one**, pp 103–126

### Advertising Works 5 (published 1990)

- **DHSS/COI AIDS Public education** (IPA dataBANK and warc.com)
- **Department for Transport: drinking and driving wrecks lives**
  How advertising contributed to social change (IPA dataBANK and warc.com)

### Advertising Works 3 (published 1985)

- **Home Protection Revisited The National Roll-out of a Regional Test** (IPA dataBANK and warc.com)
- **Chip Pan Fire protection**, pp 286–296

### Advertising Works 2 (published 1983)

- **Home protection: how advertising helps fight crime**, pp 197–208

# Index